Machine Learning
Neural Networks, Genetic Algorithms, and Fuzzy Systems

Machine Learning
Neural Networks, Genetic Algorithms, and Fuzzy Systems

Hojjat Adeli

Shih-Lin Hung

John Wiley & Sons, Inc.
New York • Chichester • Brisbane • Toronto • Singapore

Publisher: Katherine Schowalter
Editor: Diane D. Cerra
Managing Editor: Micheline Frederick
Editorial Production and Design: Publishers' Design and Production Services, Inc.

Designations used by companies to distinguish their products are often claimed as trademarks. In all instances where John Wiley & Sons, Inc. is aware of a claim, the product names appear in initial capital or all capital letters. Readers, however, should contact the appropriate companies for more complete information regarding trademarks and registration.

This text is printed on acid-free paper.

Copyright ©1995 by John Wiley & Sons, Inc.

All rights reserved. Published simultaneously in Canada.

This publication is designed to provide accurate and authoritative information in regard to the subject matter covered. It is sold with the understanding that the publisher is not engaged in rendering legal, accounting, or other professional service. If legal advice or other expert assistance is required, the services of a competent professional person should be sought.

Reproduction or translation of any part of this work beyond that permitted by section 107 or 108 of the 1976 United States Copyright Act without the permission of the copyright owner is unlawful. Requests for permission or further information should be addressed to the Permissions Department, John Wiley & Sons, Inc.

Library of Congress Cataloging-in-Publication Data:

ISBN 0 471-01633-0

Printed in the United States of America

10 9 8 7 6 5 4 3 2 1

Dedicated to
Dr. Nahid, Amir, Anahita, Cyrus, and Mona Adeli
and
Dr. Ying-Yueh Chu and Jui-Chih Hung

Contents

PREFACE x
ACKNOWLEDGMENTS xi
ABOUT THE AUTHORS xii

1 INTRODUCTION 1

2 PERCEPTRON LEARNING WITH A HIDDEN LAYER 5

    2.1 Introduction 7
    2.2 A Three-Layer Neural Network Model 8
    2.3 Application to Engineering Design 15
    2.4 Concluding Remarks 23

3 AN OBJECT-ORIENTED BACKPROPAGATION LEARNING MODEL 25

    3.1 Introduction 27
    3.2 An Artificial Neural Network Development Environment—ANNDE 27
    3.3 Generalized Delta Rule with Backpropagation Learning for Multi-Layer Neural Networks 30
    3.4 Implementation 33
    3.5 Application to Engineering Design 33
    3.6 Concluding Remarks 47

4 CONCURRENT BACKPROPAGATION LEARNING ALGORITHMS 51

    4.1 Introduction 53
    4.2 Cray Y-MP8/864 Supercomputer 53

         4.2.1 Vectorization 54
         4.2.2 Multitasking 54
         4.2.3 Monitoring Results and Performance 54
   4.3   Concurrent Backpropagation Learning Algorithms 56
   4.4   Applications 62
   4.5   Computation Results 63
   4.6   Concluding Remarks 74

5 **AN ADAPTIVE CONJUGATE GRADIENT LEARNING ALGORITHM FOR EFFICIENT TRAINING OF NEURAL NETWORKS** **77**
   5.1   Introduction 79
   5.2   Supervised Learning for Feedforward Neural
         Networks 80
   5.3   Effect of Learning and Momentum Ratios on
         Convergence Rate 83
   5.4   Inexact Line Search Algorithm 83
   5.5   An Adaptive Conjugate Gradient Neural Network
         Learning Algorithm 85
   5.6   Applications 90
   5.7   Learning Results 91
   5.8   Concluding Remarks 94

6 **A CONCURRENT ADAPTIVE CONJUGATE GRADIENT LEARNING ALGORITHM ON MIMD SHARED MEMORY MACHINES** **99**
   6.1   Introduction 101
   6.2   Concurrent Conjugate Gradient Neural Network
         Learning Algorithm 101
   6.3   Applications 110
   6.4   Learning Results 114
         6.4.1 Convergence History 114
         6.4.2 Speed-up and the Value of Mflops 120
   6.5   Concluding Remarks 123

7 **A CONCURRENT HYBRID GENETIC/NEURAL NETWORK LEARNING ALGORITHM FOR MIMD SHARED MEMORY MACHINES** **125**
   7.1   Introduction 127
   7.2   Genetic Algorithms 128
         7.2.1 GA Abstraction 128
         7.2.2 Parent Selection 131

        7.2.3 *Crossover Operation* *131*
        7.2.4 *Mutation Operation* *133*
    7.3 A Hybrid Neural Network Learning Algorithm 135
    7.4 Applications 144
    7.5 Computation Results 145
        7.5.1 *Convergence History* *145*
        7.5.2 *Speed-up* *148*
    7.6 Concluding Remarks 152

8 A HYBRID LEARNING ALGORITHM FOR DISTRIBUTED MEMORY MULTICOMPUTERS 155

    8.1 Introduction 157
    8.2 Distributed Memory Multicomputer with Trollius
         Operation System 157
    8.3 A Hybrid Neural Network Learning Algorithm 158
    8.4 A Concurrent Learning Algorithm for Distributed
         Memory Multicomputers 161

9 A FUZZY NEURAL NETWORK LEARNING MODEL 169

    9.1 Introduction 171
    9.2 Supervised and Unsupervised Classification
         Algorithms 171
    9.3 Fuzzy Sets 172
    9.4 An Unsupervised Fuzzy Neural Network Classification
         Algorithm 174
    9.5 A Fuzzy Neural Network Learning Model 183
    9.6 Applications 186
    9.7 Computation Results 189
    9.8 Concluding Remarks 192

APPENDIX A
DERIVATION OF DELTAS FOR OUTPUT AND HIDDEN LAYERS 195

APPENDIX B
AN EXAMPLE OF VECTORIZED AND MICROTASKED MATRIX MULTIPLICATION C=AB 201

REFERENCES 203

INDEX 209

Preface

In the 1980's research on knowledge-based expert systems was actively pursued. research on machine learning is gaining momentum in the 1990's. This book summarizes our research on neural networks and machine learning performed during 1990–1993. We advocate and present a multiparadigm learning approach and show how the learning performance can be improved substantially through adroit combination of various computing paradigms. Thus, our approach is unique in that we attempt to use the best of various computing technologies from mathematical optimization to parallel processing with the objective of maximizing the performance of learning models. A number of algorithms are presented and applied to two different domains: image recognition and engineering design. These are hard-to-learn problems. The learning models presented in this book can be used directly or by extension in other domains.

Hojjat Adeli and *Shih-Lin Hung*

Acknowledgments

Professor Adeli's research in recent years has been sponsored by a number of funding agencies including the National Science Foundation, U.S. Army Corps of Engineers Construction Engineering Research Laboratory, the American Iron and Steel Institute, American Institute of Steel Construction, State of Ohio Department of Development (Thomas Edison Program), Ohio Board of Regents Research Challenge Program, Cray Research Inc., and Bethlehem Steel Corporation. High-performance computing facilities were provided by Ohio Supercomputer Center and National Center for Supercomputing Applications, the University of Illinois at Urbana-Champaign.

Parts of the materials presented in this book are based on the authors' own research articles that have appeared in journals and conference proceedings published by the American Society of Civil Engineers, Elsevier, the Institute of Electrical and Electronics Engineers, John Wiley and Sons, Inc., and North Holland, as included in the references at the end of the book, and are reprinted with their permission.

About the Authors

Hojjat Adeli received his Ph.D. from Stanford University in 1976. He is currently professor and a member of Center for Cognitive Science at The Ohio State University. A contributor to 40 research journals, he has authored over 260 research and scientific publications including four books, and edited 10 books in various fields of computer science and engineering. He is the Founder and Editor-in-Chief of the research journal *Integrated Computer-Aided Engineering*. Professor Adeli has been an organizer or member of advisory boards of 35 national and international conferences and a contributor to 85 conferences held in 24 different countries. He was a *keynote/plenary lecturer* at international computing conferences held in Italy (1989), Mexico (1991), Japan (1991), China (1992), Canada (1992), Portugal (1992), U.S.A. (1993), Germany (1993), and Morocco (1994). He has received numerous academic, research, and leadership awards, honors, and recognitions. His recent awards include the Ohio State University 1990 Lichtenstein Memorial Award for *Faculty Excellence* and 1994 Lumely Research Award *In Recognition of Outstanding Research Accomplishments*.

S.L. Hung received his M.S. and Ph.D. from The Ohio State University in 1990 and 1992, respectively. He is currently an Associate Professor at the National Chiao Tung University, Taiwan, Republic of China. He has authored 13 papers in the areas of expert systems, neural networks, machine learning, and parallel processing.

CHAPTER 1

Introduction

In the decade of the 1980s, artificial intelligence created a lot of excitement. The most significant and widespread outcome of artificial intelligence research was the development of knowledge-based expert systems (Adeli and Balasubramanyam, 1988a, b). But, the knowledge base of expert systems is static, and such systems do not exhibit any automatic learning capability. This book is about machine learning, that is, the development of computing systems with learning capability.

We present a number of fundamentally different approaches to machine learning, including neural networks computing, genetic algorithms, and the theory of fuzzy sets. The focus of the book is neural networks computing, and we will show how the performance of neural networks learning models can be improved by the development of hybrid learning models, where the neurocomputing paradigm is integrated with other problem-solving paradigms in ingenious ways. Thus, our approach is unique in that we attempt to use the best of various technologies, from mathematical optimization to parallel processing, with the objective of maximizing the performance of the learning models.

We have chosen two different domains for application of the learning models: engineering design and image recognition. These are hard-to-learn problems. The learning models presented in this book can be used directly or by extension in other domains.

We start in Chapter 2 with a simple perceptron learning model with a hidden layer. Next, in Chapter 3 we describe development of a backpropagation learning model in an object-oriented programming environment. Concurrent backpropagation learning algorithms are presented in Chapter 4. Chapter 5 presents an adaptive conjugate gradient learning algorithm for the training of multilayer feedforward neural networks. Concurrent implementation of this algorithm is discussed in Chapter 6. Concurrent hybrid genetic/neural network learning algorithms for MIMD shared memory machines (such as Cray Y-MP 8/864 supercomputer) and distributed memory multicomputers (such as transputers) are presented in Chapters 7 and 8, respectively. Finally, Chapter 9 shows how various computing paradigms, including neurocomputing, genetic algorithms, mathematical optimization, and the theory of fuzzy sets, can be integrated in order to create a high-performance learning model.

CHAPTER 2

Perceptron Learning with a Hidden Layer

2.1 INTRODUCTION

Considerable research activity has been reported in the literature on the development of design knowledge-based expert systems using artificial intelligence techniques (Adeli, 1988; Adeli and Al-Rijleh, 1987; Adeli and Balasubramanyam, 1988a, b; Adeli and Chen, 1989; Adeli and Mak, 1988, 1989; Adeli and Paek, 1986; Ohsuga, 1990). True intelligence, however, is often associated with learning. While research on machine learning techniques has been in progress for a number of years, very few papers have reported its application to engineering design. Adeli and Yeh (1990a) report the development of an unguided learning system in the domain of structural design using the approach of explanation-based learning (Kodratoff, 1990). They developed a prototype system, called Structural Design Learning System (SDLS) in a combination of Prolog and Pascal languages.

Adeli and Yeh (1989) presented a model of machine learning for engineering design based on the concept of self-adjustment of internal control parameters and perceptron. They cast the problem of structural design in a form that can be described by a perceptron without hidden units. In this chapter, we present a three-layer neural network, that is,

8 MACHINE LEARNING

a neural network with a hidden layer, and then apply it to the domain of engineering design.

2.2 A THREE-LAYER NEURAL NETWORK MODEL

A neural network with a hidden layer is shown schematically in Figure 2–1. Five components exist in such a network:

1. *Node.* A state variable, s_i, is associated with each node i.
2. *Link.* Links connect the nodes.
3. *Threshold.* A real value (T_i) assigned to a node i in the hidden and output layers.
4. *Weight.* A real value associated to a link. The weight of the link connecting nodes i and j is denoted by w_{ji}.

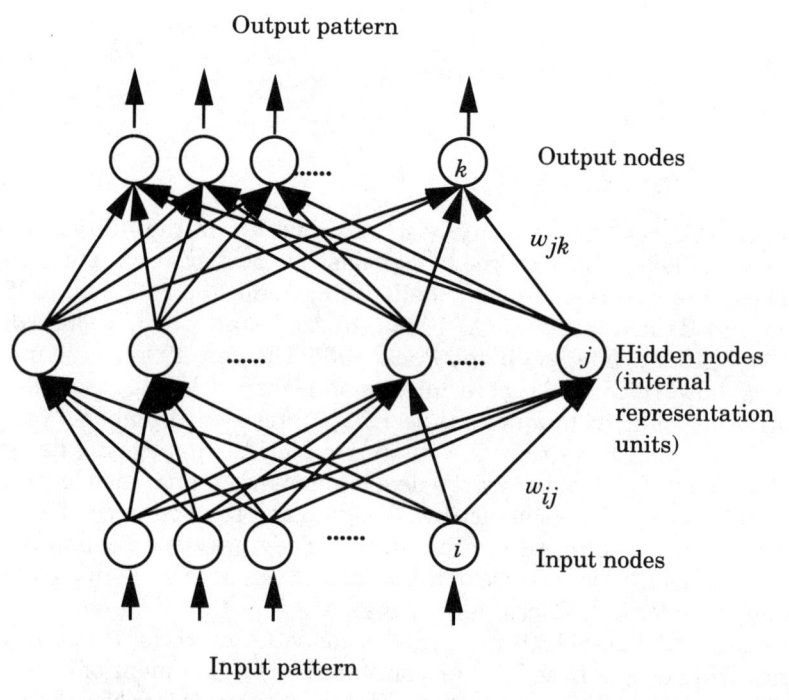

Figure 2–1. A three-layer neural network.

5. *Transfer function.* A transfer function, F_i, describes the state of the node i in terms of its threshold value (T_i), the weights (w_{ij}) of its incoming links, and the state variables (s_i) of the nodes connected to it by the incoming links. This function is usually assumed to be a step or sigmoid function of the linear term $\sum_{j=1}^{n} w_{ji} s_j - T_i$ (Minsky and Papert, 1988). In this chapter, we use the former for the transfer function.

If a given problem domain can be separated into two regions of positive and negative instances such as shown in Figure 2–2, then the two-layer perceptron with no hidden layer can be used for learning about positive and negative instances in the domain, as demonstrated in Adeli and Yeh (1989). In Figure 2–2, the domain I is divided into two regions of positive (I^+) and negative (I^-) instances. The vector **W** represents the boundary between the two regions.

Suppose now a learning domain is described by a division into three regions, as shown in Figure 2–3. In this figure, the domain of learning consists of three regions: region of positive instances, I^+, and two re-

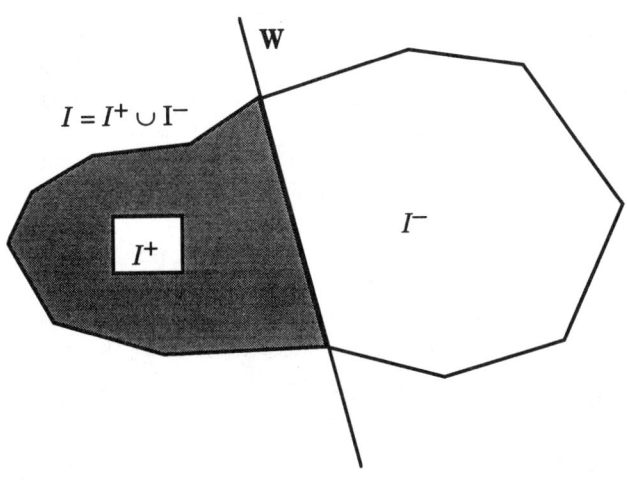

Figure 2–2. The separation of the learning domain by the **W** vector into regions of positive and negative instances.

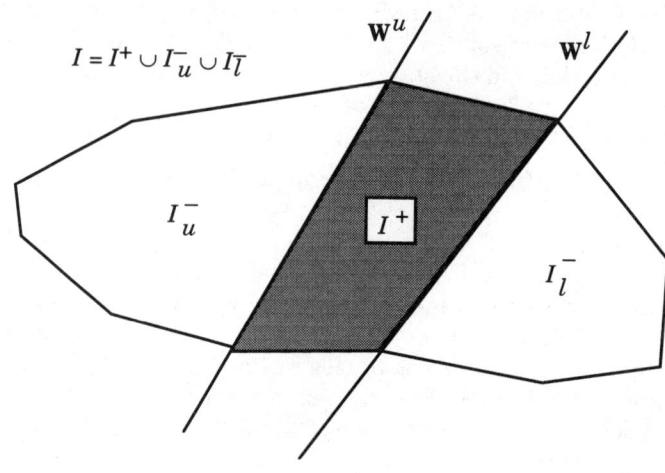

Figure 2-3. The separation of the learning domain by the vectors $\mathbf{W}^u$ and $\mathbf{W}^l$ into regions of positive and negative instances.

gions of negative instances, I_l^- (lower region of negative instances) and I_u^- (upper region of negative instances). In this case, the two-layer perceptron network fails to learn. We can, however, develop a neural network with a hidden layer to learn in the domain represented by Figure 2-3. The vectors $\mathbf{W}^u$ and $\mathbf{W}^l$ in Figure 2-3 represent the boundaries between the region of positive instances and the regions of upper and lower negative instances, respectively.

In our model, called PERHID (for PERceptron learning with a HIDden layer), we combine two two-layer perceptrons in a manner to obtain a neural network with a hidden layer. The first two-layer perceptron consists of the input nodes describing the features of the learning samples (identified by $s_1, s_2, ..., $ and s_n in Figure 2-4) and two output nodes that are the input to the second layer (hidden layer). The hidden layer consists of two input nodes for the upper and lower boundaries of positive instances (identified by $\mathbf{W}^u$ and $\mathbf{W}^l$ in Figure 2-3), and an output node in the form of an AND net.

Now, we apply the perceptron convergence theorem (Minsky and Papert, 1988) twice, once to each single-layer perceptron. Extending

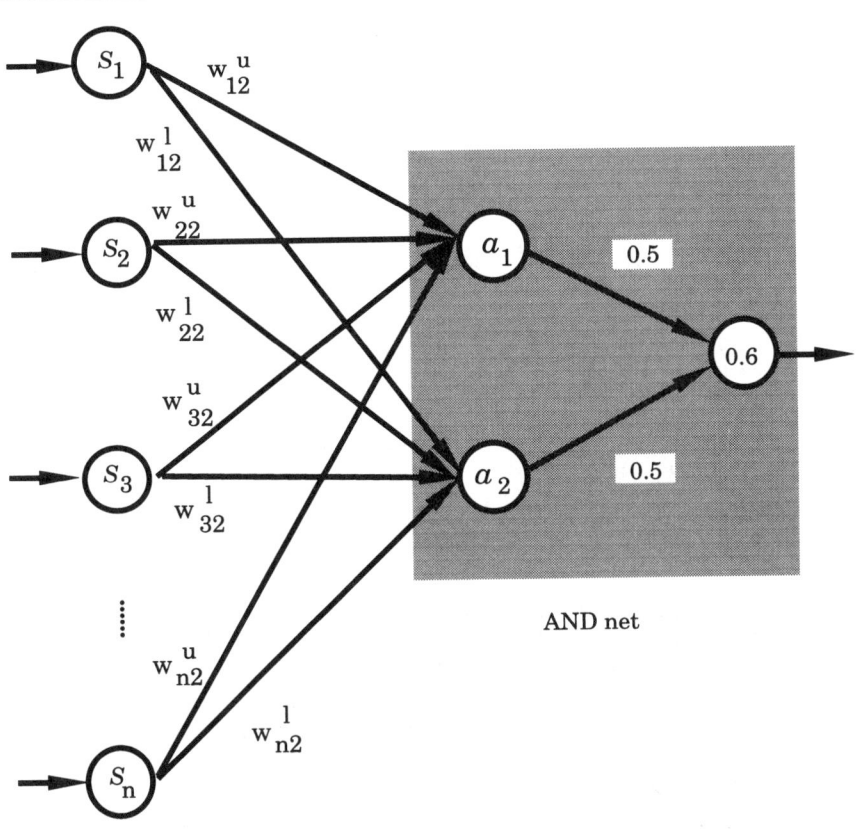

Figure 2–4. A three-layer neural network model—PERHID.

the work of Adeli and Yeh (1989), we define perceptron as a sixtuple entity $(S, \mathbf{W}, F_u, F_l, T_u, T_l)$. As mentioned previously, S and $\mathbf{W}$ represent a set of features of training examples (state variables) and their weights. The quantities T_u and T_l are the upper and lower threshold values corresponding to the upper and lower boundaries of the region of positive instances, respectively (Figure 2–3). Similarly, F_u and F_l are the transfer functions associated with the upper and lower boundaries of the regions of positive and negative instances. Then, the convergence theorem for the first perceptron layer is written as follows: For each positive instance we have

MACHINE LEARNING

$$\begin{cases} F_l = \sum_{j=1}^{n} s_j w_{ji}^{\,l} = s_1 w_{1i}^{\,l} + s_2 w_{2i}^{\,l} + \ldots + s_n w_{ni}^{\,l} \geq T_l \\ \\ \qquad\qquad\qquad\qquad \text{for all instances} \in I^+ \quad (2\text{-}1) \\ \\ F_u = \sum_{j=1}^{n} s_j w_{ji}^{\,u} = s_1 w_{1i}^{\,u} + s_2 w_{2i}^{\,u} + \ldots + s_n w_{ni}^{\,u} \leq T_u \end{cases}$$

Similarly, for each negative instance, we have

$$\begin{cases} F_u = \sum_{j=1}^{n} s_j w_{ji}^{\,u} = s_1 w_{1i}^{\,u} + s_2 w_{2i}^{\,u} + \ldots + s_n w_{ni}^{\,u} > T_u \\ \\ \qquad\qquad\qquad\qquad \text{for all instances} \in I_u^- \quad (2\text{-}2) \\ \\ F_l = \sum_{j=1}^{n} s_j w_{ji}^{\,l} = s_1 w_{1i}^{\,l} + s_2 w_{2i}^{\,l} + \ldots + s_n w_{ni}^{\,l} > T_l \end{cases}$$

or

$$\begin{cases} F_u = \sum_{j=1}^{n} s_j w_{ji}^{\,u} = s_1 w_{1i}^{\,u} + s_2 w_{2i}^{\,u} + \ldots + s_n w_{ni}^{\,u} < T_u \\ \\ \qquad\qquad\qquad\qquad \text{for all instances} \in I_l^- \quad (2\text{-}3) \\ \\ F_l = \sum_{j=1}^{n} s_j w_{ji}^{\,l} = s_1 w_{1i}^{\,l} + s_2 w_{2i}^{\,l} + \ldots + s_n w_{ni}^{\,l} < T_l \end{cases}$$

When one of the following conditions occurs we have to modify the upper and lower weight vectors $\mathbf{W}^u$ and $\mathbf{W}^l$:

- When a positive instance produces an upper bound output greater than T_u or a lower bound output smaller than T_l.
- When an upper-level negative instance produces an upper bound output smaller than T_u or a lower bound output smaller than T_l.
- When a lower-level negative instance produces a lower bound output greater than T_l or an upper bound output greater than T_u.

In these cases, we apply the modification algorithm proposed by Minsky and Papert (1988) to the 3-region learning domain shown in Figure 2–3. For the region of positive instances:

$$\begin{cases} w_{ji}^{u} = w_{ji}^{u} - s_j & \text{if } F_u = \sum_{j=1}^{n} s_j w_{ji}^{u} > T_u \\ & \qquad\qquad\qquad\qquad \textit{for all instances} \in I^+ \quad (2\text{-}4) \\ w_{ji}^{l} = w_{ji}^{l} + s_j & \text{if } F_l = \sum_{j=1}^{n} s_j w_{ji}^{l} < T_l \end{cases}$$

For the upper region of negative instances:

$$\begin{cases} w_{ji}^{u} = w_{ji}^{u} + s_j & \text{if } F_u = \sum_{j=1}^{n} s_j w_{ji}^{u} < T_u \\ & \qquad\qquad\qquad\qquad \textit{for all instances} \in I_u^- \quad (2\text{-}5) \\ w_{ji}^{l} = w_{ji}^{l} + s_j & \text{if } F_l = \sum_{j=1}^{n} s_j w_{ji}^{l} < T_l \end{cases}$$

For the lower region of negative instances:

$$\begin{cases} w_{ji}^{u} = w_{ji}^{u} - s_j & \text{if } F_u = \sum_{j=1}^{n} s_j w_{ji}^{u} > T_u \\ & \qquad\qquad\qquad\qquad \textit{for all instances} \in I_l^- \quad (2\text{-}6) \\ w_{ji}^{l} = w_{ji}^{l} - s_j & \text{if } F_l = \sum_{j=1}^{n} s_j w_{ji}^{l} > T_l \end{cases}$$

We consider the perceptron as a device that can answer either "yes" or "no." Therefore, the outputs of the first layer which are the inputs to the hidden layer are (1, 1), (1, 0), (0, 1), or (0, 0).

The second layer of PERHID is a simple AND net which is connected to the output nodes of the first layer. The inputs of this AND net are thus a pair of binary values (a_1, a_2). The link weights of the AND net are chosen to be 0.5 and 0.5 and the threshold constant is taken as 0.6. Therefore, an AND net performs like an AND gate with a transfer function defined as:

$$F = a_1 \times 0.5 + a_2 \times 0.5 > 0.6 \text{ for all instances} \in I^+, \quad (2\text{-}7)$$

$$F = a_1 \times 0.5 + a_2 \times 0.5 \leq 0.6 \text{ for all instance} \in I^-. \quad (2\text{-}8)$$

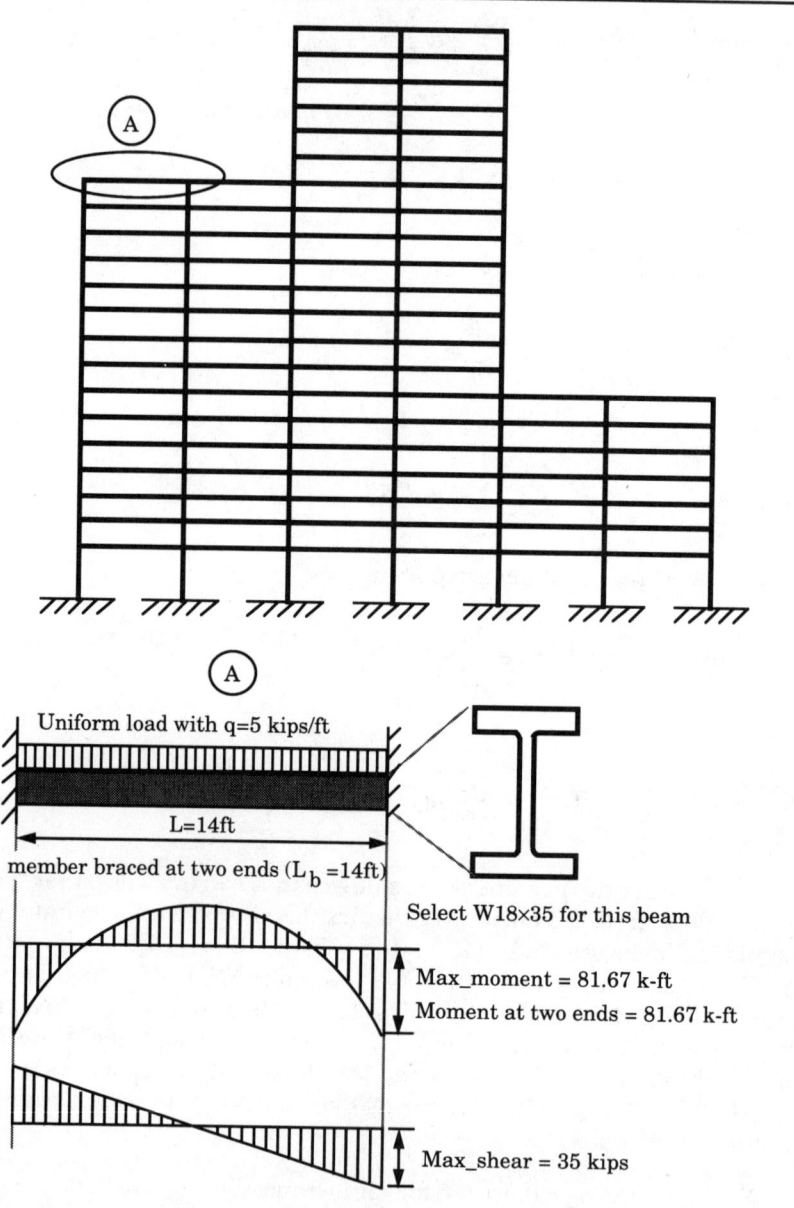

Figure 2–5. An example structure: steel beam.

2.3 APPLICATION TO ENGINEERING DESIGN

PERHID can be applied to classification problems such as pattern recognition or speech recognition. As an example, we apply it to the domain of engineering design. For the sake of comparison with the work of Adeli and Yeh (1989), we apply it to the design of steel beams (Figure 2–5) which are widely used in multistory buildings. We use the same training examples constructed by Adeli and Yeh (1989) as the input to PERHID. These examples are all acceptable, satisfying the design requirements of the American Institute of Steel Construction (AISC) Load and Resistance Factor Design (LRFD) specification. Steel hot-rolled wide-flange (W) shapes from the AISC sections data base (AISC, 1986) are commonly selected for beams. We divide them into t groups: G_1, G_2, G_3, ..., and G_t in a decreasing order of the plastic section modulus Z_x, as summarized in Table 2–1.

Table 2–1. Grouping of the wide-flange shapes in the decreasing order of the plastic section modulus.

	Section designation	Section Modulus (in³)		Number of different sections
		Lower bound	Upper bound	
Group 1	W36×359 — W36×210	833	1510	17
Group 2	W33×201 — W24×176	511	772	17
Group 3	W36×135 — W18×143	322	509	19
Group 4	W30×99 — W18×97	211	312	17
Group 5	W24×76 — W18×71	145	200	18
Group 6	W21×62 — W12×65	96.8	144	18
Group 7	W21×44 — W12×40	57.5	95.4	20
Group 8	W14×34 — W8×28	27.2	54.6	17
Group 9	W10×22 — W6×9	–	26	31
Total number of sections				174

Suppose the acceptable design instances are provided with their corresponding section group numbers, as shown in Figure 2–6, where S_{mn} is defined as the nth instance in the training examples belonging to group G_m. Any selection G_g (g can vary between 1 and t) for the instance S_{mn} satisfies the LRFD design constraints or "safety criterion" if $g \leq m$. In order to select a safe and economical section, the required wide-flange section for S_{mn} is selected from group G_m. Then, according to this safe and economical criterion, the following inputs are constructed to PERHID. For each G_i, the observation domain is $I = I^+ \cup I_u^- \cup I_l^-$, where

$I_l^- = \{S_{11},..,S_{1n},S_{21},..,S_{2m},...,S_{(i-1)1},..,S_{(i-1)m}\}$,

$I^+ = \{S_{i1},S_{i2},....,S_{ik}\}$,

$I_u^- = \{S_{(i+1)1},...,S_{(i+1)p},S_{(i+2)1},...,S_{(i+2)r},....,S_{t1},...,S_{tk}\}$;

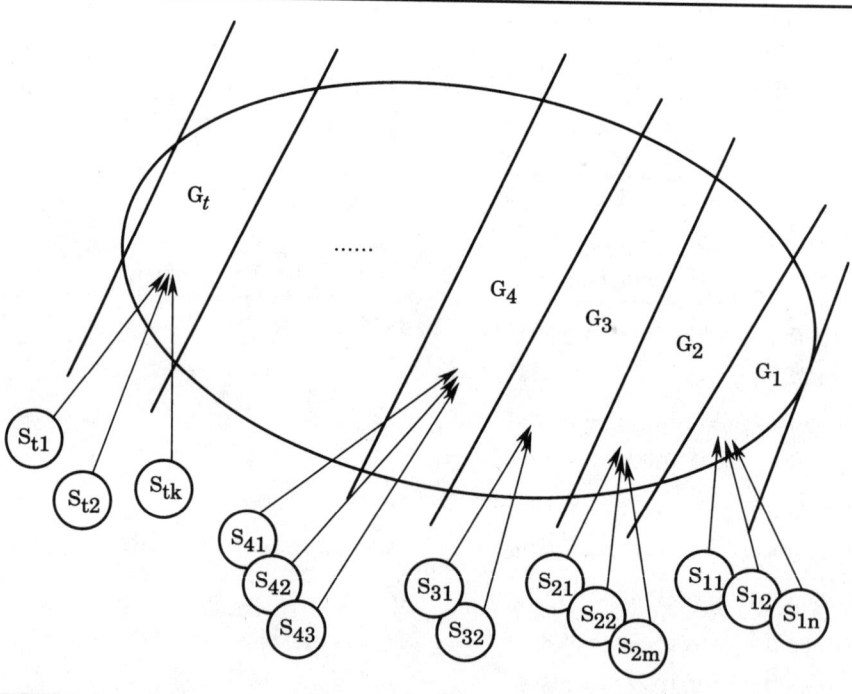

Figure 2–6.

in which S_{ik} represents the kth instance in the ith group. Each instance S_{mn} is a vector consisting of five behavior components: $S_{mn} = (s_1, s_2, s_3, s_4, s_5)$, where s_1 is the member length, s_2 is the unbraced length (less than or equal to s_1), s_3 is the maximum bending moment in the member, s_4 is the maximum shear force, and s_5 is defined as ten times the bending coefficient C_b (This coefficient is intended to take into account the effect of moment gradient on the lateral torsional buckling strength of the beam).

The values of thresholds, T_u^i and T_l^i, corresponding to group i (G_i) are the lower and upper bound values of the section modulus for group i given in Table 2–1, respectively. For example, the threshold values for Group 1 are 1510 (T_u^i) and 833 (T_l^i).

Considering the grouping of the training instances shown in Figure 2–6 and two arbitrary initial weight vectors W_0^l and W_0^u, according to the perceptron convergence theorem, the weight vectors W_0^u and W_0^l will converge to two vectors W_i^u and W_i^l for each G_i, $1 \leq i \leq t$, such that

$W_i^u \cdot S_{nm} \leq T_u^n$ for all $n \geq i$,

$W_i^u \cdot S_{nm} > T_u^n$ for all $n < i$,

$W_i^l \cdot S_{nm} \geq T_u^n$ for all $n \leq i$,

$W_i^l \cdot S_{nm} < T_u^n$ for all $n > i$.

After the weight vectors W_i^u and W_i^l are found, then by knowing the behavior attributes of any structural component (denoted by the vector S), we can obtain the input to the second layer, and consequently the value of the transfer function (F) at the output node of the second layer for each group (Figure 2–7). Any group G with F value equal to one satisfies the safe and economical criterion.

Three sets of examples are used as training instances. The first set of training examples comprises of 16 beam designs. Among the selected sections, two sections belong to Group 1 (S_{11}, S_{12}), three sections belong to Group 2 (S_{21}, S_{22}, S_{23}), one belongs to Group 3 (S_{31}), one belongs to Group 4 (S_{41}), one belongs to Group 5 (S_{51}), two belong to Group 6 (S_{61}, S_{62}), three belong to Group 7 (S_{71}, S_{72}, S_{73}), one belongs to Group 8 (S_{81}), and two belong to Group 9 (S_{91}, S_{92}). The 16 training examples and their attributes are shown in Table 2–2.

Table 2–3 shows the results after learning by indicating all of the W^* vectors for each section group. In order to verify the learning results, a set of verification examples is given in Table 2–4. We presented the behavior parameters for these examples to PERHID. It predicted six

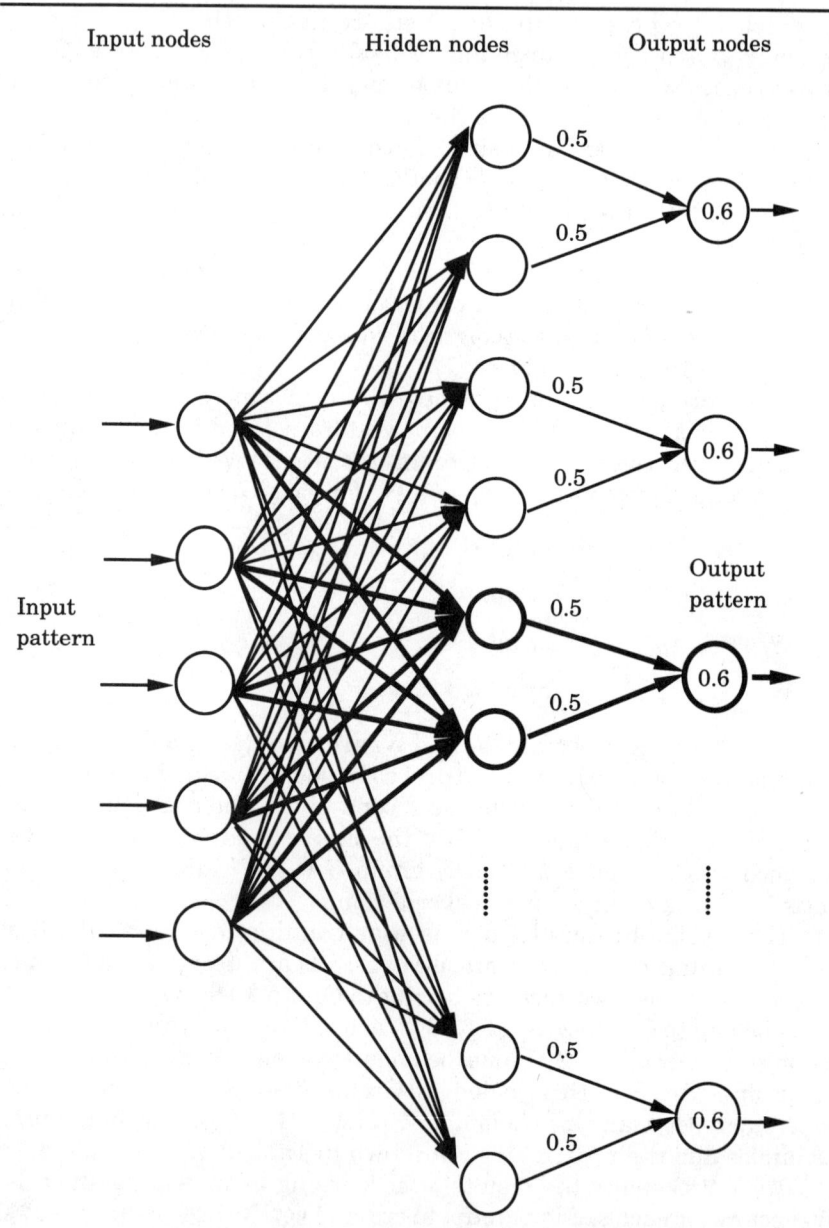

Figure 2–7. PERHID implemented in the structural design domain.

Table 2–2. The initial set of training examples.

	L or s_1 (ft)	L_b or s_2 (ft)	M_{max} or s_3 (K–in)	V_{max} or s_4 (Kips)	C_b or s_5
S_{11}	40	40	1900	190	10
S_{12}	40	40	3700	185	23
S_{21}	35	35	1630	93	23
S_{22}	20	20	1200	240	10
S_{23}	40	20	1200	120	18
S_{31}	40	40	350	35	10
S_{41}	15	15	450	120	10
S_{51}	15	15	350	95	10
S_{61}	20	20	288	29	23
S_{62}	6	6	184	123	10
S_{71}	12	6	184	67	10
S_{72}	16	8	200	75	23
S_{81}	10	10	70	280	10
S_{91}	6	3	36	24	18
S_{92}	6	6	36	24	10

examples correctly (called "successful design" in Table 2–4). It could not predict the first two examples successfully (called "unsuccessful design" in Table 2–4). It should be noted that the single layer perceptron model of learning in the work of Adeli and Yeh (1989) predicted only two examples correctly.

We then added these successful and unsuccessful design examples to the initial training set as extra instances. Therefore, the second training set consists of 24 examples—16 examples from the initial set plus 8 examples from the verification set. The learning results of the second training set are given in Table 2–5.

Again, we added eight examples as the second verification set listed in Table 2–6. The learning results of the third training set (the second verification set) are given in Table 2–7. The double-layer perceptron model of learning presented by Adeli and Yeh (1989) predicted two examples incorrectly. But, in the present work, only one example has been predicted incorrectly (the "unsuccessful design" in Table 2–6). After the learning is performed and the weights are adjusted, a higher degree of accuracy in learning is achieved.

Table 2–3. Learning results for the first training set.

Group No.	Components of the **W*** Vectors					Number of Iterations
	W_1^u / W_1^l	W_2^u / W_2^l	W_3^u / W_3^l	W_4^u / W_4^l	W_5^u / W_5^l	
1	0 / −70784	0 / −32797	0 / 4597	−1 / −18995	−1 / −96337	7853
2	−70508 / −4790	−32702 / −4544	4578 / 1664	−18901 / −7218	−95816 / −4108	7798
3	−4784 / −3321	−4546 / −2989	1664 / 1640	−7217 / −7362	−4109 / −5769	229
4	−3523 / −3122	−3148 / −2064	1751 / 1305	−7591 / −3519	−6518 / −7910	373
5	−3266 / −2447	−2186 / −1110	1345 / 934	−3681 / −2229	−7842 / −5942	354
6	−2451 / −4183	−1056 / 2050	941 / 604	−2233 / −382	−6017 / −4968	853
7	−4115 / −1803	1997 / −1665	609 / 1809	−390 / −2301	−5028 / −2767	830
8	−1803 / −1031	−1665 / −749	1809 / 3719	−2301 / −3968	−2767 / −2911	162
9	−1031 / 325	−749 / 283	3719 / 11855	−3968 / 1456	−2911 / 213	120

Table 2–4. The first set of verification examples.

Group No.	L or s_1 (ft)	L_b or s_2 (ft)	M_{max} or s_3 (K–in)	V_{max} or s_4 (Kips)	C_b or s_5
Unsuccessful design					
G_3	30	15	950	127	18
G_4	25	13	500	80	18
Successful design					
G_2	30	30	950	127	10
G_4	20	10	500	100	18
G_4	20	20	500	100	10
G_5	20	20	300	60	10
G_6	20	10	300	60	18
G_7	15	15	100	27	10

Table 2-5. Learning results for the second training set.

Group No.	W_1^u / W_1^l	W_2^u / W_2^l	W_3^u / W_3^l	W_4^u / W_4^l	W_5^u / W_5^l	Number of Iterations
1	0	0	0	−1	−1	−
	−70784	−32797	4597	−18995	−96337	
2	−70508	−32702	4578	−18901	−95816	1783
	−42557	−15597	4179	−14345	−36234	
3	−42907	−15571	4185	−14311	−36455	2114
	−16720	2511	4676	−19812	−36597	
4	−16770	2586	4663	−19749	−36956	2133
	−3122	−2064	1305	−3519	−7910	
5	−3266	−2186	1345	−3681	−7842	−
	−2447	−1110	934	−2229	−5942	
6	−2451	−1056	941	−2233	−6007	−
	−4183	2050	604	−382	−4968	
7	−4115	1997	609	−390	−5028	−
	−1803	−1665	1809	−2301	−2767	
8	−1803	−1665	1809	−2301	−2767	−
	−1031	−749	3719	−3968	−2911	
9	−1031	−749	3719	−3968	−2911	−
	325	283	11855	1456	213	

Table 2-6. The second set of verification examples.

Group No.	L or s_1 (ft)	L_b or s_2 (ft)	M_{max} or s_3 (K–in)	V_{max} or s_4 (Kips)	C_b or s_5
Unsuccessful design					
G_1	40	40	1200	120	10
Successful design					
G_2	28	14	1200	171	18
G_2	28	28	1200	171	10
G_2	40	20	1200	120	18
G_4	26	13	550	85	18
G_5	26	26	550	85	10
G_6	17	17	200	47	10
G_7	17	8	200	47	18

Table 2–7. Learning results for the third training set.

Group No.	Components of the $\mathbf{W}^*$ Vectors					Number of Iterations
	W_1^u / W_1^l	W_2^u / W_2^l	W_3^u / W_3^l	W_4^u / W_4^l	W_5^u / W_5^l	
1	0 −62031	0 51693	0 5737	−1 −28368	−1 −276918	16586
2	−62184 −42557	51525 −15597	5748 4179	−28393 −14345	−276158 −36234	16499
3	−42905 −16720	−15571 2511	4185 4676	−14311 −19812	−36455 −36597	—
4	−16770 −3122	2586 −2064	4663 1305	−19749 −3519	−36956 −7910	—
5	−3266 −2447	−2186 −1110	1345 934	−3681 −2229	−7842 −5942	—
6	−2415 −4183	−1056 2050	941 604	−2233 −382	−6007 −4968	—
7	−4115 −1803	1997 −1665	609 1809	−390 −2301	−5028 −2767	—
8	−1803 −1031	−1665 −749	1809 3719	−2301 −3968	−2767 −2911	—
9	−1031 325	−749 283	3719 11855	−3968 1456	−2911 213	—

PERHID has been implemented in C language and executed on both a SUN SPARC (with a SPARC CPU and 8 MB of main memory) and an HP9000-340 (with a Motorola 68030 CPU and 8 MB of main memory) workstation. For a given training set, two local weight vectors $\mathbf{W}^u$ and $\mathbf{W}^l$ are obtained separating the positive and negative instances into three regions (Figure 2–3). When the size of the training set increases, these local weight vectors $\mathbf{W}^u$ and $\mathbf{W}^l$ may not be able to predict some of the additional instances correctly. That means the weight vectors $\mathbf{W}^u$ and $\mathbf{W}^l$ have to be improved.

The average number of iterations for the two weight vectors ($\mathbf{W}^u$ and $\mathbf{W}^l$) is 2063 in the first training set, 670 in the second training set, and 3676 in the third training set. However, in the second and third training sets, the weights of only three and two groups, respectively, needed to be recalculated. The CPU times for finding the weight factors for the first, second, and third training sets on an HP9000-340 workstation are about 18, 6, and 7 minutes, respectively (on a SUN SPARC, they are 32, 11, and 40 minutes, respectively). In comparison, for the double-layer learning model of perceptron, Adeli and Yeh (1989) reported CPU times of 800 and 2400 minutes on a SUN3/50 workstation for the first and second training sets, respectively.

2.4 CONCLUDING REMARKS

In this chapter, we presented a three-layer neural network learning model and applied it to the problem of engineering design. The following observations and conclusions can be drawn:

1. In contrast to the symbolic processing machine learning such as explanation-based learning (Kodratoff, 1990; Adeli and Yeh, 1990a), the knowledge of a multi-layer neural network is distributed over the nodes and their connecting links.
2. The multi-layer neural network learning model leads itself to parallel processing effectively. For instance, in the example presented in this chapter, we have nine groups, and the computations associated with each group can be assigned to one processor, without any need for interprocessor communications.
3. In most cases, expert designers rely heavily on experience. The neural network-based learning model for engineering design described in this chapter can be used to capture the design experience. Other works (McClelland and Rumelhart, 1986) also show that a lot of brain behaviors, such as content addressable memory and automatic generalization, can be captured by parallel networks. Therefore, the experience can be represented in some sorts of lower-level pattern associators. Thus, the learning can be regarded as gradually constructing a parallel network capable of accounting for the design experience through the process of reasoning.
4. In PERHID, we implemented multi-layered neural network learning in a banded domain (where the domain of learning can be divided into banded regions, as shown in Figures 2–3 and 2–6). If we can find two instances which are on or close to the two boundaries, then we need only two instances to train PERHID and obtain the global minimum weight vectors $\mathbf{W}^u$ and $\mathbf{W}^l$.

5. Comparing the results of the three-layer neural network presented in this chapter with those of two-layer perceptron (Adeli and Yeh, 1989), we find that the three-layer neural network converges much faster resulting in substantial savings in the CPU time. In the example presented in this chapter, for instance, the two-layer perceptron had to change all the weights in the second and third training sets in order to improve its learning behavior. On the other hand, PERHID changed only the weights of unsuccessful groups in the second and third training sets without a need to change the weights of other groups.

CHAPTER 3

An Object-Oriented Backpropagation Learning Model

3.1 INTRODUCTION

Object-oriented programming (OOP) has received increasing attention in software engineering. A new software development technique associated with OOP, called object-oriented design (OOD), has been proposed and used in software engineering. In the domain of structural engineering, Adeli and Hung (1990) presented an object-oriented model for processing of earthquake engineering knowledge. The model has been implemented in C++ in a prototype system, called OQUAKE. Knowledge representation in OQUAKE is through a combination of frames and scripts.

In this chapter, an artificial neural network development environment (ANNDE) is presented using the OOP paradigm. The generalized delta rule with backpropagation learning strategy associated with a multi-layer artificial neural network has been used in ANNDE.

3.2 AN ARTIFICIAL NEURAL NETWORK DEVELOPMENT ENVIRONMENT—ANNDE

Our objective is to develop an integrated model of machine learning using various learning strategies with n-tuple multi-layer artificial neural networks for engineering design applications. The model consists of five primary components: learning domain, neural nets, learning strategies, learning process, and analysis process. The function of each block is described in the following paragraphs.

A. **Learning Domain.** Includes the input and output patterns for each training instance. For example, in the steel beam design problem of Chapter 2, each steel beam was described by five behavior components: member length, unbraced length, maximum bending moment in the member, maximum shear force, and the bending coefficient. Each steel beam was classified as a member of nine different groups of wide-flange shapes commonly used in steel structures. Therefore, in this case, we have five input and one output patterns.

B. **Neural Nets.** Provide the structure of artificial neural networks depending on the number of hidden layers selected by the user. A complete topology of artificial neural networks is the combination of input layer, hidden layers, and output layer.

C. **Learning Strategies.** Include various learning procedures such as supervised learning, reinforcement learning, and competitive learning. This component is the kernel of the system.

D. **Learning Process.** Performs learning using one of the learning procedures, such as backpropagation learning. The knowledge of artificial neural networks is represented by real values, called weights, assigned to links connecting the nodes. Therefore, learning process in artificial neural networks is the process of changing the values of the weights and reducing the system error to a certain prescribed value.

E. **Analysis Process.** After learning is achieved and the corresponding weights are obtained, the analysis process is used to verify the learning performance and, if necessary, to perform further iterations to improve the learning performance.

Object-oriented languages are a new generation of programming languages. The fundamental concepts of OOP are objects, classes, derived classes, and inheritance. In addition, OOP provides a set of techniques for the development of application programs that are reusable, extensible, and compatible. These properties are essential for development of engineering software (Yu and Adeli, 1991).

OOP provides new ways to structure solutions and a means of directly representing important relationships between objects when dealing with complex problems. Instead of decomposing problems as data and dealing with data, in the OOP approach, problems are analyzed in terms of objects and the relationships among objects.

The OOP paradigm provides a highly modular, flexible, and efficient software development environment. We implement the five aforementioned components of ANNDE as classes, called class LD, NN, LS, LP, and AP, as shown in Figure 3–1. The functions of the five classes

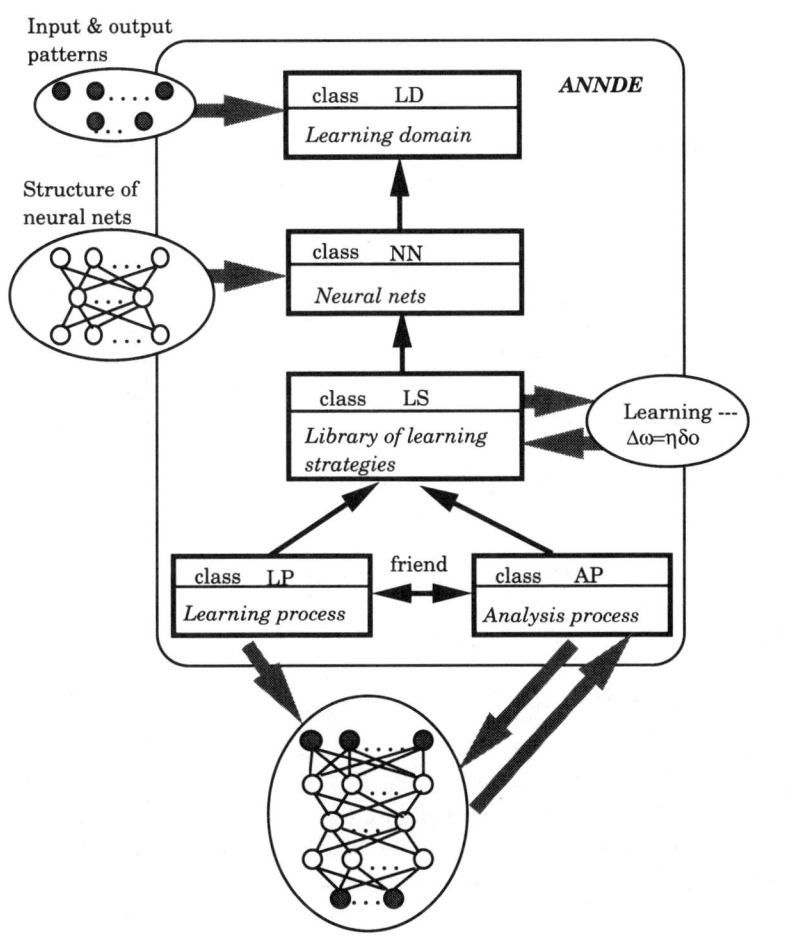

Figure 3–1. The architecture of ANNDE.

are the same as the functions of their corresponding components described previously.

In Figure 3–1, the thin arrow lines between classes indicate the relationship between base classes and derived classes. For instance, class LD is the base class of class NN; classes LP and AP are derived from class LS; and class LP is a friend class of class AP. The thick arrow lines indicate the data flow in the system. Class LD obtains the patterns of input and output, class NN represents the structure of neural networks, class LS provides various learning strategies, class LP performs the learning and stores the knowledge (weight) for each link, and class AP retrieves the learned neural structure and analyzes the given instances.

3.3   GENERALIZED DELTA RULE WITH BACKPROPAGATION LEARNING FOR MULTI-LAYER NEURAL NETWORKS

In the Widrow-Hoff, or delta rule, the amount of learning is represented as the difference (or delta) between the desired and computed outputs. Proposed by Rumelhart, Hinton, and Williams (1986), backpropagation (BP) is an error-correcting learning procedure that generalizes the delta rule to multi-layer feedforward neural networks with hidden units between the input and output units. These multi-layer artificial neural networks can learn in more complicated learning domains than those lacking hidden units (Hung and Adeli, 1991a). The feedforward net with backpropagation of error has been found to be an effective learning procedure for classification problems (Rumelhart et al., 1986).

A neural network with a hidden layer is shown in Figure 1–1. The goal of the learning procedure is to update the weights of the links connecting the nodes, and to minimize the average squared system error between the desired and the computed outputs. For a learning instance p, the error term is defined as

$$E_p = \frac{1}{2}\sum_{k=1}^{K}(d_{pk} - o_{pk})^2 \qquad (3\text{-}1)$$

where d_{pk} and o_{pk} are the desired and the computed outputs for the kth output, respectively, and K is the total number of output patterns (nodes). The average error for the whole system is defined as

$$E = \frac{1}{2P}\sum_{p=1}^{P}\sum_{k=1}^{K}(d_{pk} - o_{pk})^2 \qquad (3\text{-}2)$$

where P is the total number of instances.

A weight w_{ji} is assigned to the link connecting the nodes j and i in two different layers. Except for the nodes of input layer, the input to each node is the sum of the weighted output of the prior layer. Each node is activated depending on the input to a node, the activation function of the node, and the threshold value of the node. Thus, the input to a node in layer j is defined as

$$net_j = \sum_i w_{ji} o_i \qquad (3\text{-}3)$$

The summation is over the nodes in layer i. Note that Eq. (3-3) is written for one instance, say p. But, the subscript p is dropped for the sake of simplicity. The output of node j is represented as

$$o_j = f(net_j) \qquad (3\text{-}4)$$

where f represents the activation function. In order to satisfy the properties of continuity and differentiability, the linear or step activation function employed by Adeli and Yeh (1989) and Hung and Adeli (1991a) cannot be applied in this learning procedure. The following sigmoidal activation functions which satisfy the properties of continuity and differentiability are used:

$$f(net_j) = \frac{1}{1 + e^{-(net_j - \theta_j)/\theta_0}} \qquad (3\text{-}5)$$

$$f(net_j) = \frac{1}{p} \arctan(net_j - \theta_j) + 0.5 \qquad (3\text{-}6)$$

These sigmoidal functions have the general shape shown in Figure 3–2. The parameter θ_j serves as a threshold value for node j. The effect of the threshold value is to shift the activation or transfer function in horizontal axis. The parameter θ_0 is used to modify the shape of the sigmoidal function.

The first step in the learning process is a feedforward operation which calculates the output of nodes from the input layer through the hidden layers to the output layer using Eq. (3-3) and (3-4). Then, the error for each node and the average squared system error are computed using Eq. (3-2). If the error is greater than a certain predefined value, further iterations would be required. In this case, the step of error backpropagation is performed.

We change the weights and threshold value in proportion to $-\partial E / \partial w_{kj}$ in order to reduce the system error:

$$\nabla w_{kj} = -\eta \frac{\partial E}{\partial w_{kj}} \qquad (3\text{-}7)$$

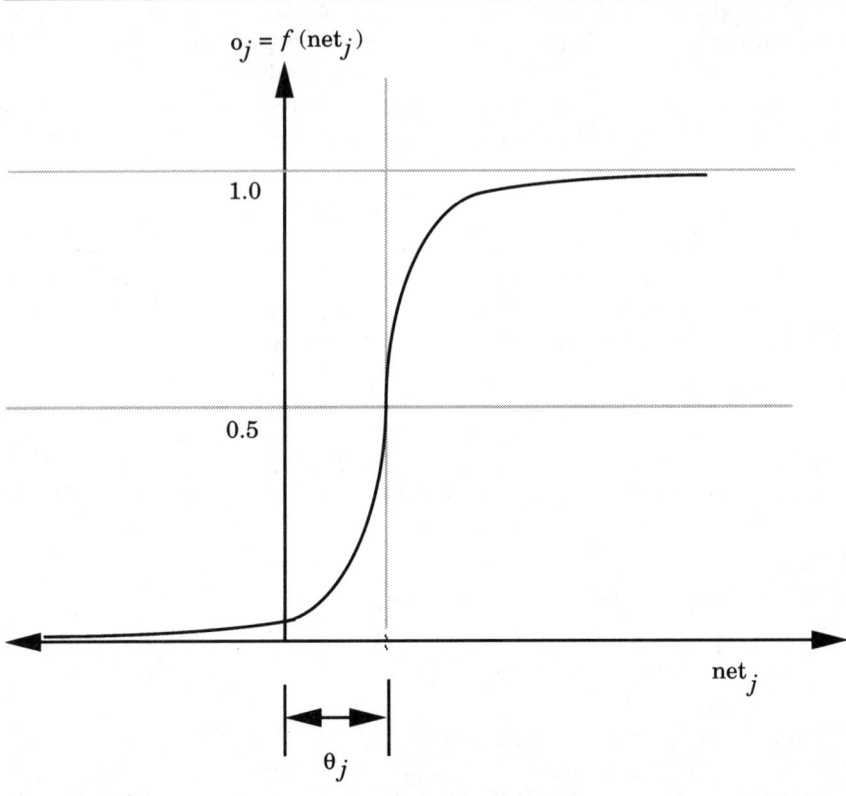

Figure 3-2. General shape of a sigmoidal activation function.

where η is a scale factor called the learning ratio whose significance will be discussed subsequently. We can express Eq. (3-7) similar to the expression for delta rule as follows (see Appendix A for derivation):

$$\nabla w_{kj} = \eta d_k o_j \tag{3-8}$$

where

$$\delta_k = -\frac{\partial E}{\partial net_k} \tag{3-9}$$

It can be shown that the deltas for the nodes in the output and hidden layers can be found from the following formulas (see Appendix A for their derivation).

$$\delta_k = (d_k - o_k)f'(net_k) \qquad \text{for nodes in the output layer} \qquad (3\text{-}10)$$

$$\delta_j = f'(net_k)\sum \delta_k w_{kj} \qquad \text{for nodes in the hidden layer} \qquad (3\text{-}11)$$

As mentioned previously, the term η in Eq. (3-7) is the learning ratio. A large η corresponds to rapid learning but might result in oscillations. On the other hand, some researchers have shown that a small η may result in a failure in learning (Rumelhart et al., 1986; Pao, 1990). Rumelhart et al. (1986) proposed adding a *momentum* term to the delta rule of Eq. (3-8) in the following form:

$$\nabla w_{ji}(n+1) = \eta \delta_j o_i + \alpha \nabla w_{ji}(n) \qquad (3\text{-}12)$$

where α, called momentum ratio, is a constant and the parameters $(n+1)$ and (n) are used to indicate the $(n+1)$st and nth step. The momentum term is used to specify that the change to the $(n+1)$st step should be somewhat similar to the change in the nth step. This modified delta rule is used in this chapter.

3.4 IMPLEMENTATION

ANNDE has been implemented in two different object-oriented programming environments: G++ (GNU C++) on a SUN SPARCstation and in C++ (SUN, 1989) on a SUN-4 workstation.

3.5 APPLICATION TO ENGINEERING DESIGN

ANNDE has been used for learning in the domain of structural engineering. An acceptable design must satisfy the requirements of a design code such as the AISC LRFD specification (AISC, 1986) for design of steel structures and American Concrete Institute (ACI) code (ACI, 1988) for design concrete structures.

Example 1

This example is a load location problem taken from VanLuchene and Sun (1990). A simply-supported beam is subjected to a 4-unit concentrated load (Figure 3–3). The beam is assumed to have a length of one unit. The exact shape of the bending moment diagram for the simply supported beam under the concentrated load is determined by the location of the load. Treating this as a pattern recognition problem, ANNDE is used to learn to recognize the shape of the bending moment diagram for any location of the concentrated load. We know that the maximum

34 MACHINE LEARNING

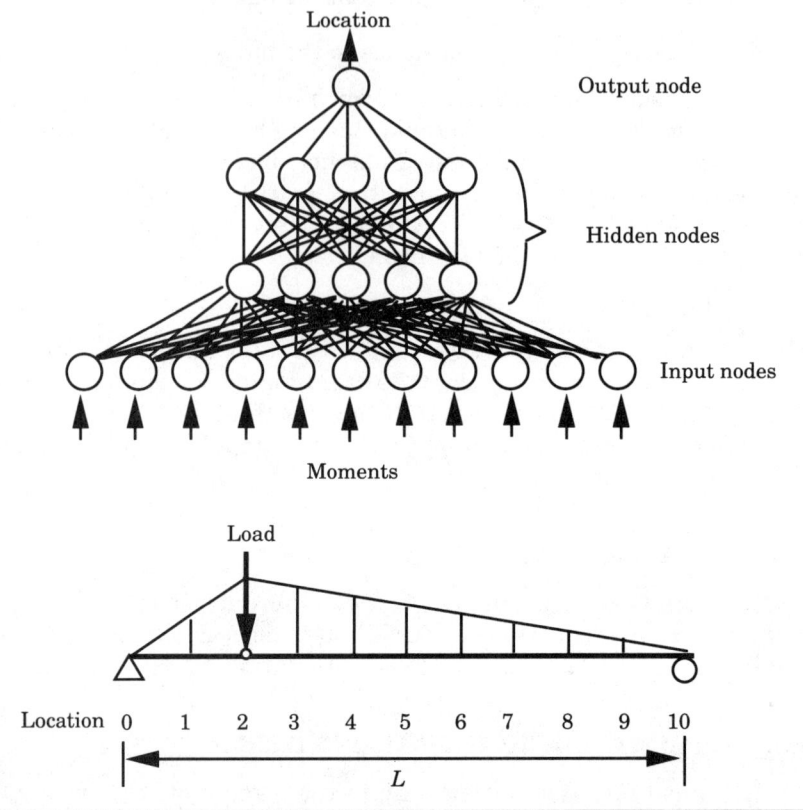

Figure 3–3. Neural network for the load location problem.

bending moment is at the location of the concentrated load. We want to see whether ANNDE can learn this piece of knowledge.

A four-layer neural network (with two hidden layers) was used to learn this problem. The number of nodes in the input layer, the first and second hidden layers, and output layer are 11, 5, 5, and 1, respectively (Figure 3–3). The eleven input nodes represent the values of the bending moment at the locations 0 to 10 (the beam is divided into 10 equal segments for the purpose of bending moment calculation). The output node represents the location of the concentrated load. The training instances used are listed in Table 3–1. The locations of instances are given from the left support as a function of the span length, L.

Table 3–1. Training instances of the load location problem.

Instance	Location											Output (Loading Location)
	0	0.1	0.2	0.3	0.4	0.5	0.6	0.7	0.8	0.9	1	
					Input (Moment)							
Training instances												
1	0	0.36	0.32	0.28	0.24	0.20	0.16	0.12	0.08	0.04	0	0.1
2	0	0.32	0.64	0.56	0.48	0.40	0.32	0.24	0.16	0.08	0	0.2
3	0	0.28	0.56	0.84	0.72	0.60	0.48	0.36	0.24	0.12	0	0.3
4	0	0.24	0.48	0.72	0.96	0.80	0.64	0.48	0.32	0.16	0	0.4
5	0	0.20	0.40	0.60	0.80	1.00	0.80	0.60	0.40	0.20	0	0.5
6	0	0.08	0.16	0.24	0.32	0.40	0.48	0.56	0.64	0.32	0	0.8
Untrained instances for verification:												
7	0	0.16	0.32	0.48	0.64	0.80	0.96	0.72	0.48	0.24	0	0.6
8	0	0.12	0.24	0.36	0.48	0.60	0.72	0.84	0.56	0.28	0	0.7

Training six instances took 145 seconds on a SUN SPARCstation for $\eta = 0.7$ and $\alpha = 0.9$ and using a tolerance value of 10^{-5} for the system error (E). The convergence curve for the learning system error is shown in Figure 3–4. From this figure, we observe that there is no local mini-

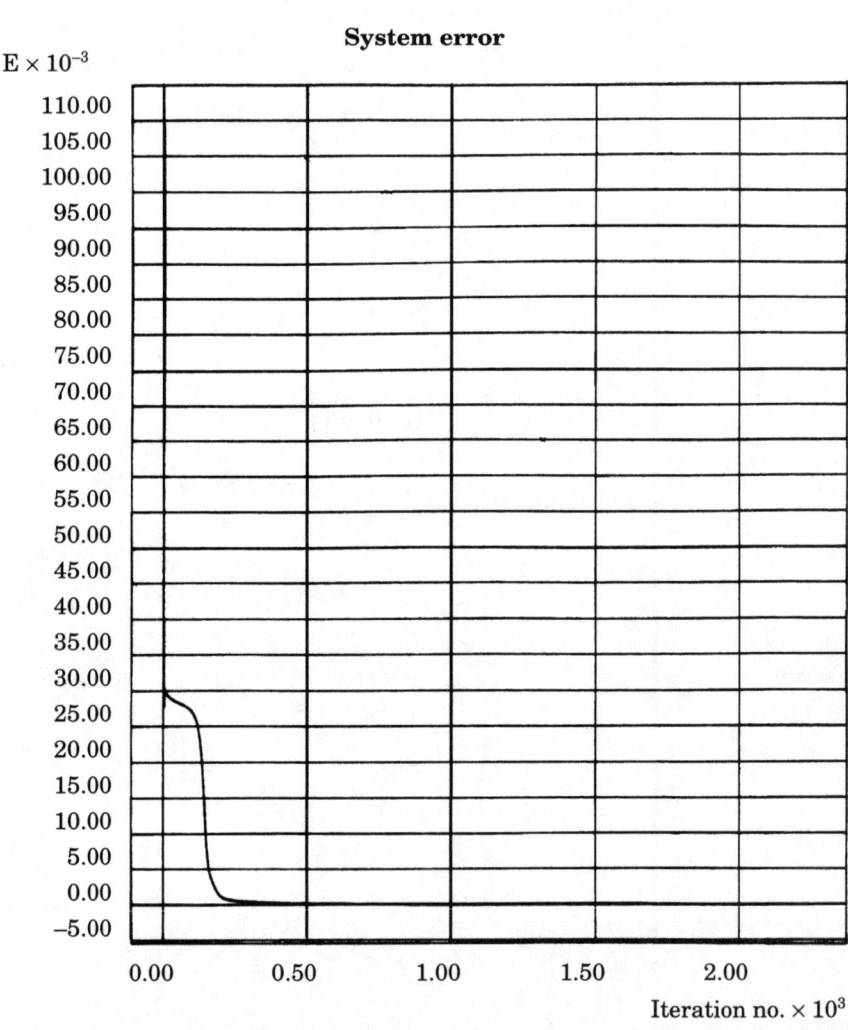

Figure 3–4. System error for the load location problem ($\eta = 0.7$, $\alpha = 0.9$).

Table 3-2. Learning verification results for the load location problem.

Instance	Learned Output	Desired Output	Error (%)
1	1.101471	0.1	1.47
2	0.197748	0.2	1.13
3	0.301645	0.3	0.55
4	0.399293	0.4	0.18
5	0.500180	0.5	0.04
6	0.799798	0.8	0.03
7	0.671955	0.6	11.99
8	0.767665	0.7	9.66

mum or stationary point in the learning process and the learning converges to the prescribed tolerance limit fast.

After training the system, eight instances, including the six trained instances and two new untrained instances, were used to verify the learning performance. The learning verification results are given in Table 3-2. The average learning error for the six trained instances is about 0.6%. The average learning error for the two untrained instances is about 10%, which is much higher than the learning error for the trained instances. However, the learning performance can be improved by additional training.

Example 2

This example is a rectangular concrete beam problem taken from VanLuchene and Sun (1990). A rectangular concrete beam requires five input data: M_u (ultimate bending moment), f_y (yield stress of reinforcing steel), f_c' (concrete compressive strength), ρ (reinforcement ratio), and b/d (width-to-depth ratio of the rectangular section), and one output, d (depth of the rectangular concrete beam).

A three-layer neural network was used to learn this problem (Figure 3-5). This neural network consists of five nodes in the input layer, five nodes in the hidden layer, and one node in the output layer. Twenty-one training instances (see Table 3-3) were provided to the neural network for learning the concrete beam problem. In order to study the

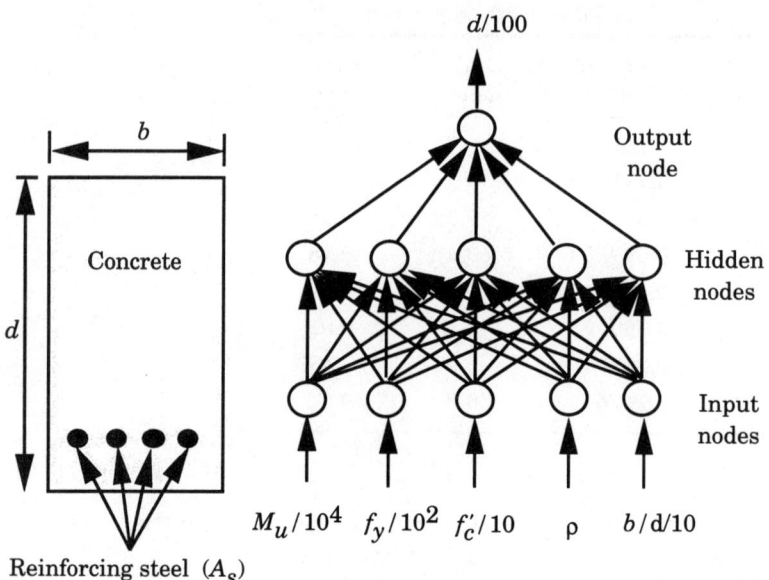

Figure 3-5. Neural network for the concrete beam design problem.

influence of learning and momentum ratios in the learning process, four different pairs of learning and momentum ratios (η, α) were used: (0.7, 0.9), (0.9, 0.9), (0.9, 0.95), and (0.95, 0.95). A tolerance of 10^{-5} was used for the system error.

The system error for the four different sets of learning and momentum ratios are shown in Figures 3-6 through 3-9. The rate of learning increases for the four sets of learning and momentum ratios in the following order: (0.7, 0.9), (0.95, 0.95), (0.9, 0.95), and (0.9, 0.9). The

Table 3-3. Training instances for the concrete beam design problem.

	Instance					Output
Instance	$M_u/10000$ ft–kips	$fy/100$ ksi	$f'_c/10$ ksi	P	$b/d/10$	$d/100$ in.
Training instances						
1	0.0063	0.4	0.300	0.019	0.0750	0.120
2	0.0112	0.4	0.300	0.015	0.0690	0.160
3	0.0183	0.4	0.300	0.012	0.0700	0.200
4	0.0929	0.4	0.375	0.013	0.0560	0.360
5	0.0736	0.4	0.375	0.023	0.0570	0.280
6	0.0185	0.4	0.375	0.027	0.1000	0.140
7	0.0719	0.6	0.300	0.006	0.0875	0.320
8	0.0397	0.6	0.300	0.011	0.0670	0.240
9	0.0572	0.6	0.300	0.013	0.0294	0.340
10	0.0282	0.6	0.375	0.007	0.1200	0.200
11	0.0288	0.6	0.375	0.010	0.0257	0.140
12	0.0476	0.6	0.375	0.014	0.0820	0.220
13	0.0689	0.6	0.400	0.005	0.0500	0.400
14	0.0180	0.6	0.400	0.009	0.0455	0.220
15	0.1016	0.6	0.400	0.016	0.0500	0.320
16	0.0138	0.6	0.500	0.008	0.1200	0.150
17	0.0160	0.6	0.500	0.012	0.0560	0.180
18	0.1753	0.6	0.500	0.017	0.0470	0.380
19	0.0371	0.6	0.600	0.008	0.0400	0.300
20	0.0340	0.6	0.600	0.014	0.2140	0.140
21	0.0640	0.6	0.600	0.020	0.0580	0.240
Untrained instances for verification						
22	0.0172	0.4	0.300	0.017	0.6700	0.180
23	0.0115	0.4	0.375	0.020	0.2200	0.100
24	0.0571	0.6	0.300	0.010	0.0530	0.300
25	0.2373	0.6	0.375	0.015	0.0440	0.450
26	0.0323	0.6	0.400	0.014	0.1730	0.150
27	0.0906	0.6	0.500	0.019	0.0375	0.320
28	0.0083	0.6	0.600	0.011	0.1800	0.100
29	0.0145	0.6	0.400	0.011	0.0560	0.180
30	0.1138	0.6	0.500	0.009	0.0240	0.500
31	0.0904	0.6	0.600	0.018	0.0570	0.280

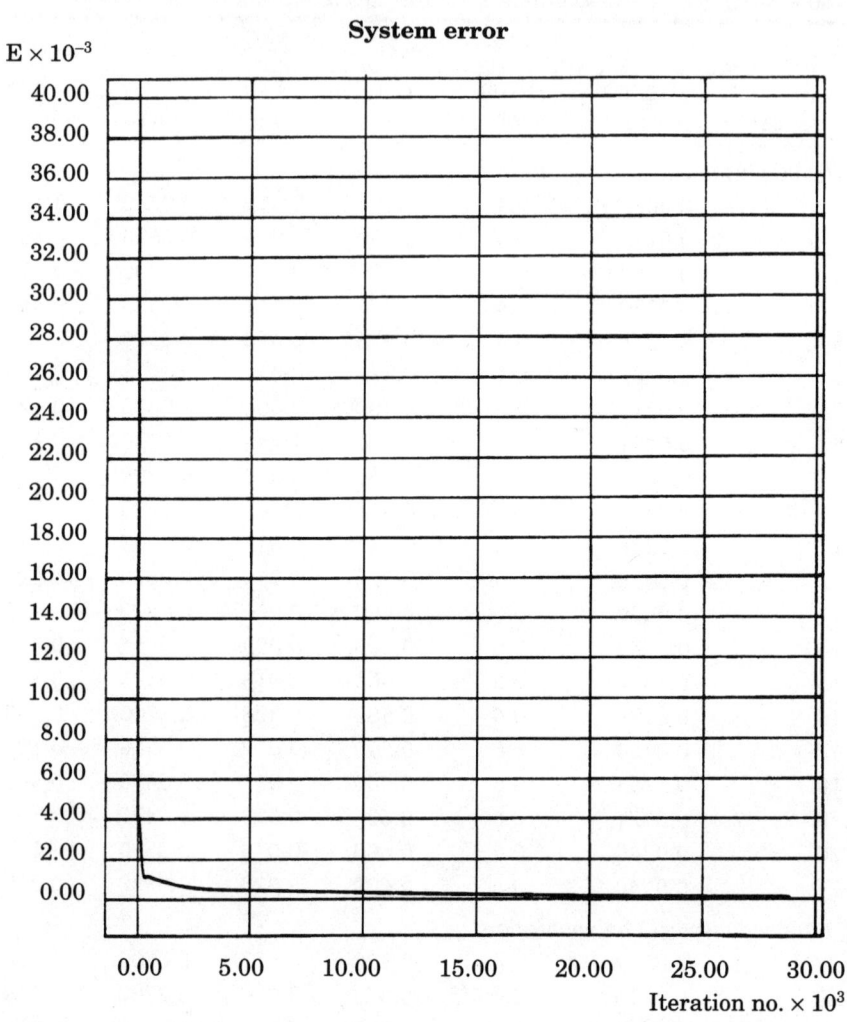

Figure 3–6. System error for the rectangular concrete beam design ($\eta = 0.7$, $\alpha = 0.9$).

average learning time for the four sets is 4.2, 3.8, 3.5, and 3.1 hours on a SUN SPARCstation, respectively. From the figures of system error, we observe the existence of local minima and stationary points in learning this complex problem. For instance, stationary points are observed

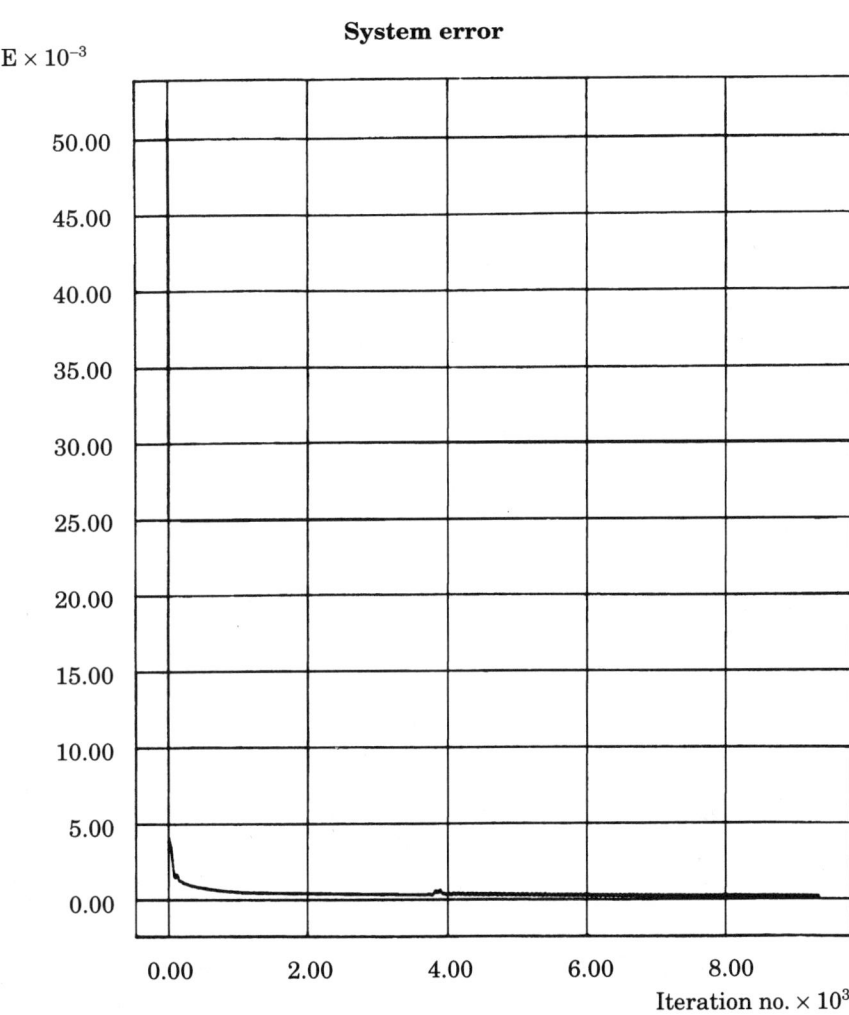

Figure 3–7. System error for the rectangular concrete beam design ($\eta = 0.9$, $\alpha = 0.9$).

in Figure 3–6, as the system error for the smallest pair of α and η shows slow convergence or remains constant over a number of iterations. On the other hand, the problem of local minima (jumps) is observed in Figures 3–7 through 3–9, with the larger values of pair of α and η.

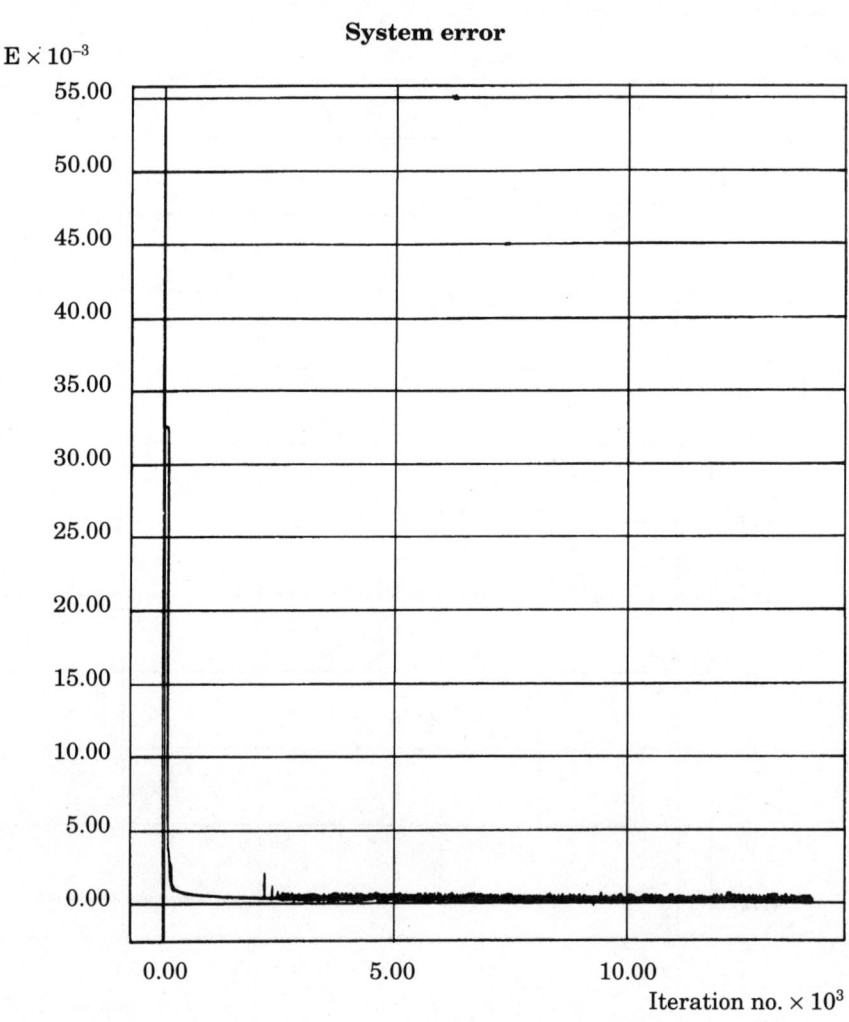

Figure 3–8. System error for the rectangular concrete beam design ($\eta = 0.9$, $\alpha = 0.95$).

After the neural network was trained, 31 instances, including 21 trained and ten untrained instances, were used to verify the learning performance (Table 3–3). The outputs and error percentages of the 31 instances are listed in Table 3–4. The average learning error percent-

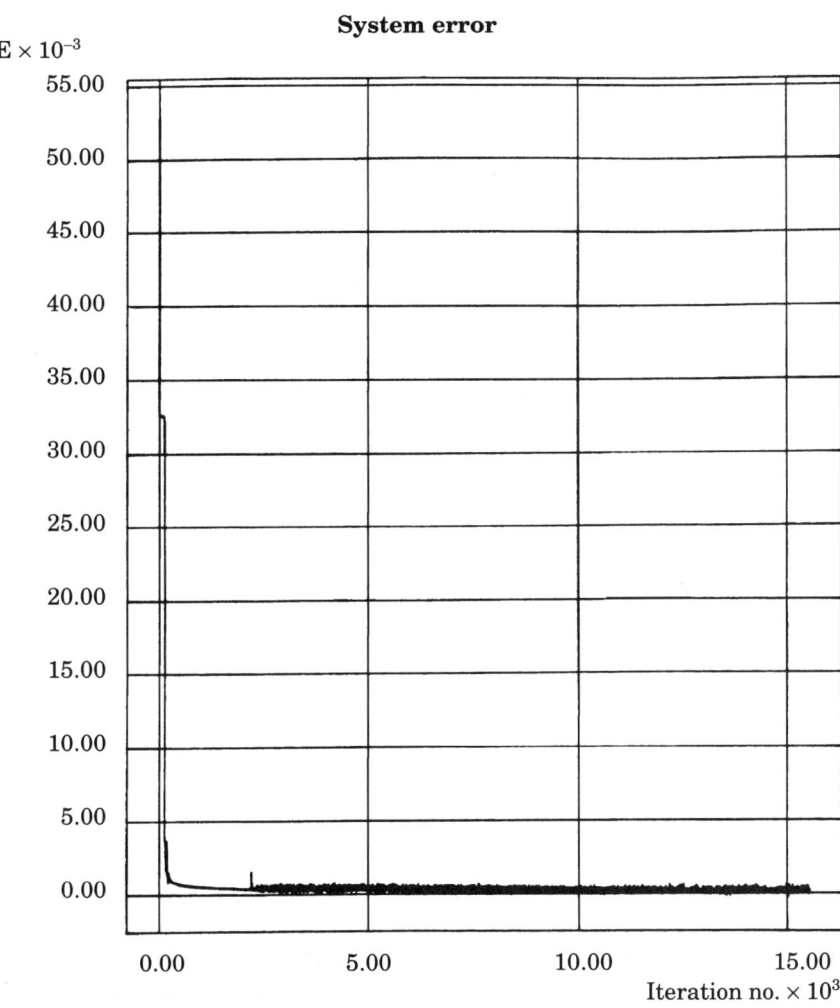

Figure 3–9. System error for the rectangular concrete beam design ($\eta = 0.95$, $\alpha = 0.95$).

ages of the 21 trained instances and the ten untrained instances are about 0.26 and 0.24, respectively. Since the learning performance is acceptable in this example, no more additional training is required to train the neural network.

MACHINE LEARNING

Table 3–4. Learning results for the concrete beam design problem.

Desired output $d/100$ (in.)		Learned output (% error) $d/100$ (in.) (η, α)			
Instance		(0.7, 0.9)	(0.9, 0.9)	(0.9, 0.95)	(0.95, 0.95)
1	0.120	0.134 (11.6)	0.126 (4.87)	0.117 (2.30)	0.113 (6.00)
2	0.160	0.170 (6.34)	0.158 (1.50)	0.154 (3.48)	0.150 (6.51)
3	0.200	0.207 (3.43)	0.197 (1.35)	0.193 (3.26)	0.189 (5.65)
4	0.360	0.373 (3.51)	0.362 (0.66)	0.348 (3.31)	0.341 (5.34)
5	0.280	0.279 (0.42)	0.278 (0.60)	0.269 (4.00)	0.260 (7.27)
6	0.140	0.122 (13.0)	0.140 (0.05)	0.113 (19.4)	0.109 (22.1)
7	0.320	0.323 (1.08)	0.320 (0.01)	0.307 (4.17)	0.301 (5.88)
8	0.240	0.250 (3.96)	0.250 (4.12)	0.243 (1.15)	0.238 (1.02)
9	0.340	0.332 (2.39)	0.336 (1.11)	0.337 (0.94)	0.329 (3.12)
10	0.200	0.190 (5.10)	0.193 (3.59)	0.183 (8.41)	0.179 (10.5)
11	0.140	0.122 (12.5)	0.141 (0.50)	0.132 (5.17)	0.130 (6.88)
12	0.220	0.224 (1.73)	0.219 (0.44)	0.244 (1.90)	0.207 (5.88)
13	0.400	0.371 (7.06)	0.396 (1.04)	0.376 (6.07)	0.333 (4.08)
14	0.220	0.213 (3.04)	0.220 (0.10)	0.214 (2.54)	0.207 (5.88)
15	0.320	0.340 (6.14)	0.325 (1.47)	0.342 (7.10)	0.333 (4.08)
16	0.150	0.155 (3.38)	0.153 (1.83)	0.147 (2.32)	0.146 (2.98)
17	0.180	0.177 (1.77)	0.174 (3.35)	0.179 (0.61)	0.175 (2.96)
18	0.380	0.372 (2.14)	0.376 (0.95)	0.366 (3.77)	0.360 (5.28)
19	0.300	0.286 (4.59)	0.302 (0.58)	0.293 (2.37)	0.287 (4.33)
20	0.140	0.148 (6.00)	0.142 (1.13)	0.123 (12.3)	0.127 (9.76)
21	0.240	0.253 (5.50)	0.237 (1.31)	0.241 (0.51)	0.236 (1.48)
22	0.180	0.176 (2.28)	0.168 (6.82)	0.163 (9.34)	0.158 (12.1)
23	0.100	0.108 (8.09)	0.096 (4.00)	0.114 (13.6)	0.111 (11.3)
24	0.300	0.319 (6.34)	0.321 (7.04)	0.316 (5.20)	0.310 (3.19)
25	0.450	0.376 (16.5)	0.423 (5.61)	0.404 (10.1)	0.414 (8.01)
26	0.150	0.140 (6.51)	0.143 (4.51)	0.140 (6.48)	0.137 (8.53)
27	0.320	0.320 (0.07)	0.309 (3.36)	0.329 (2.71)	0.318 (0.67)
28	0.100	0.124 (24.5)	0.118 (17.5)	0.105 (5.18)	0.110 (10.3)
29	0.180	0.180 (0.27)	0.180 (0.03)	0.177 (1.62)	0.171 (4.83)
30	0.500	0.441 (11.7)	0.477 (4.67)	0.451 (9.77)	0.440 (12.1)
31	0.280	0.311 (11.0)	0.292 (4.15)	0.287 (2.50)	0.279 (0.20)

Example 3

The final example created in this chapter is the selection of a minimum weight steel beam from the AISC LRFD wide-flange (W) shape database (AISC, 1986) for a given loading condition (Figure 2–5). Referring to section 2.3, we divide the W shapes available into t groups in decreasing order of the plastic section modulus Z_x. PERHID, presented in Chapter 2, could learn a satisfactory design and identify its group number only. In contrast, ANNDE is used to learn to select the lightest W shape among all the available shapes, instead of selecting a satisfactory group only. Each instance consists of the same five input patterns described in section 2.3: the member length (L), the unbraced length (L_b), the maximum bending moment in the member (M_{max}), the maximum shear force (V_{max}), and the bending coefficient (C_b). The output pattern is the plastic modulus (Z_x) of the corresponding least weight member.

A four-layer neural network with two hidden layers was used to learn this problem (Figure 3–10). The numbers of nodes in the input

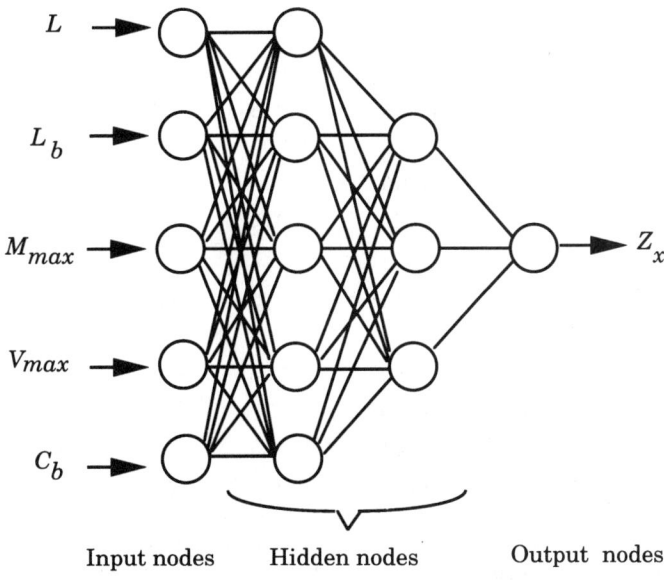

Figure 3–10. Four-layer neural network for the minimum weight steel beam problem (see Figure 2–5).

layer, the first and second hidden layers, and the output layer are 5, 5, 3, and 1, respectively. The learning and momentum ratios are chosen as 0.7 and 0.9, respectively. The system error is limited to 10^{-5}.

Ten instances were used to train this neural network. After the learning process was completed, six verification instances were used to verify the learning performance (Table 3–5). The learning results are given in Table 3–6. The system error is shown in Figure 3–11. Since this

Table 3–5.   Training instances for the steel beam design problem.

	Inputs					Output
Instance	L (ft)	L_b (ft)	M_{max} (K–in.)	V_{max} Kips	C_b	Z_x (in.^{3})
Training instances						
1	0.40	0.40	0.190	0.190	1	0.6313
2	0.20	0.20	0.120	0.240	1	0.3630
3	0.35	0.35	0.035	0.035	1	0.1000
4	0.15	0.15	0.045	0.120	1	0.1400
5	0.15	0.15	0.035	0.095	1	0.1000
6	0.06	0.06	0.018	0.123	1	0.0490
7	0.12	0.06	0.018	0.067	1	0.1000
8	0.10	0.10	0.007	0.028	1	0.0233
9	0.06	0.06	0.004	0.024	1	0.0110
10	0.20	0.20	0.050	0.100	1	0.1590
Verification instances						
11	0.20	0.20	0.030	0.060	1	0.1000
12	0.30	0.30	0.095	0.127	1	0.3900
13	0.15	0.15	0.010	0.027	1	0.0415
14	0.40	0.40	0.120	0.120	1	0.4830
15	0.28	0.28	0.120	0.171	1	0.3900
16	0.17	0.17	0.020	0.047	1	0.0700

Note: In Tables 3–5 and 3–6, the value of plastic modulus for a selected W shape has been divided by a constant 1590 so that the largest value of plastic modulus, 1540 for W36 × 359 is mapped to 0.95. This is necessary because the output for a neural network with a sigmoid activation function is a real number between 0 and 1 (but not equal to 1).

Table 3–6. Learning results for the steel beam design problem.

Instance	Desired output Z_x (in.^{3})	Verified output Z_x (in.^{3})	Error (%)
1	0.6313	0.6307	0.09
2	0.3630	0.3655	0.67
3	0.1000	0.1027	2.71
4	0.1000	0.0992	0.82
5	0.1000	0.0992	0.82
6	0.0490	0.0566	15.5
7	0.1000	0.0965	3.50
8	0.0233	0.0241	3.48
9	0.0110	0.0189	71.6
10	0.1590	0.1590	0.17
11	0.1000	0.0817	18.3
12	0.3900	0.3743	4.04
13	0.0415	0.0296	28.7
14	0.4830	0.5033	4.21
15	0.3900	0.4353	11.6
16	0.0700	0.0514	26.5

is a complex learning domain, the learning process took a long time (8.5 hours on the average on a SUN SPARCstation) to converge, and the problem of local minima and stationary points were observed (see Figure 3–11).

3.6 CONCLUDING REMARKS

An artificial neural network development environment (ANNDE) was presented in this chapter using the object-oriented programming paradigm. It has been implemented in C++ and G++ programming languages. The generalized delta rule with backpropagation learning strategy has been implemented in ANNDE. The following observations and conclusions can be drawn:

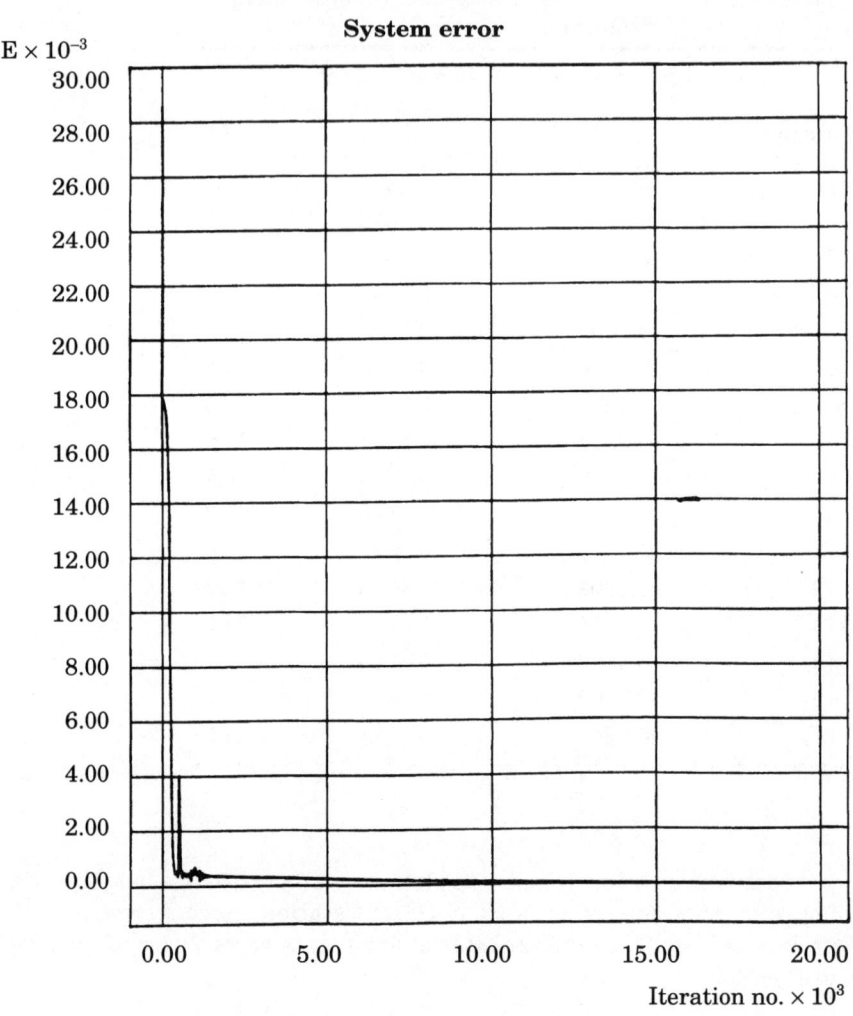

Figure 3–11. System error for the minimum weight steel beam problem ($\eta = 0.7$, $\alpha = 0.9$).

1. Backpropagation learning strategy can be applied to both simple and complex problem domains. However, for complex problem domains, it needs a long training time.
2. Integrating ANNDE with a knowledge-based expert system for structural design (Adeli, 1988) can provide the capacity for creating an intelligent integrated structural design system with automatic learning capability.
3. Backpropagation learning process is a gradient descent method. The learning system may get trapped in some local minimum and stationary point, or may oscillate between such points. In the following chapters, we will present other learning models with the objective of accelerating the learning process.

CHAPTER 4

Concurrent Backpropagation Learning Algorithms

4.1 INTRODUCTION

In this chapter, concurrent learning algorithms are presented for vector shared memory machines and implemented on a Cray Y-MP8/864 supercomputer under the UNICOS operating system. The concurrent neural network learning algorithms have been applied to two different domains: engineering design and image recognition. Two examples are used to investigate and compare the performance of the concurrent learning algorithms.

4.2 CRAY Y-MP8/864 SUPERCOMPUTER

Configured with eight 6 ns (6.0×10^{-9} second) clock cycle processors, the Cray Y-MP8/864 is capable of up to 2667 Mflops with 8 processors (a *flop* is a floating-point operation, such as add, multiply, or reciprocal; *Mflops* means millions of floating-point operations per second of CPU time). The Cray UNICOS operating system supports C and FORTRAN compilers. The learning algorithms have been implemented in C.

4.2.1 Vectorization

As a vector machine, the Cray Y-MP provides the utility of vectorization, thus reducing program execution time by as much as a factor of ten or more in innermost loops. A small amount of overhead, or start-up time, is associated with each vectorized loop. This start-up time involves initializing the vector registers for vector processing. For long loops, the start-up time is only a small portion of the total execution time and is negligible. However, for small loops, the start-up time becomes a rather large portion of the total execution time. In this case, the directive *#pragma _CRI nonvector* can be used to inhibit vectorization of the loop immediately following the directive.

4.2.2 Multitasking

The Cray C compiler provides loop-level multitasking, called microtasking, and function-level multitasking, called macrotasking. It also provides autotasking, which is microtasking performed automatically by the compiler. Autotasking works best when most of the code consists of nested loops (Saleh and Adeli, 1993).

C programs are microtasked by inserting directives at the loop level. The problem of synchronization is handled by inserting directives *guard* and *endguard* between the code segment, called the guarded region. The pair of *case/endcase* directives can be used to force only one processor to execute a code block in a parallel region.

We can maximize the performance by combining vectorization with multitasking in a program. An example of vectorized and microtasked matrix multiplication, **C** = **AB**, implemented in C, is given in Appendix B. In this problem, the directive *#pragma _CRI taskloop* is used to indicate the microtasked loop and a pair of directives *#pragma _CRI guard* and *#pragma _CRI endguard* are used to handle synchronization problems.

4.2.3 Monitoring Results and Performance

Three different methods can be used to measure the speed-up of a multitasked program on the Cray Y-MP8/864. The first method is to run the multitasked program on a dedicated number of processors, through the use of the command *dedcpu*. But, in a multi-user environment, dedicating all the processors to one program is not a readily available option. The second method is through the use of an expert system

CONCURRENT BACKPROPAGATION LEARNING ALGORITHMS

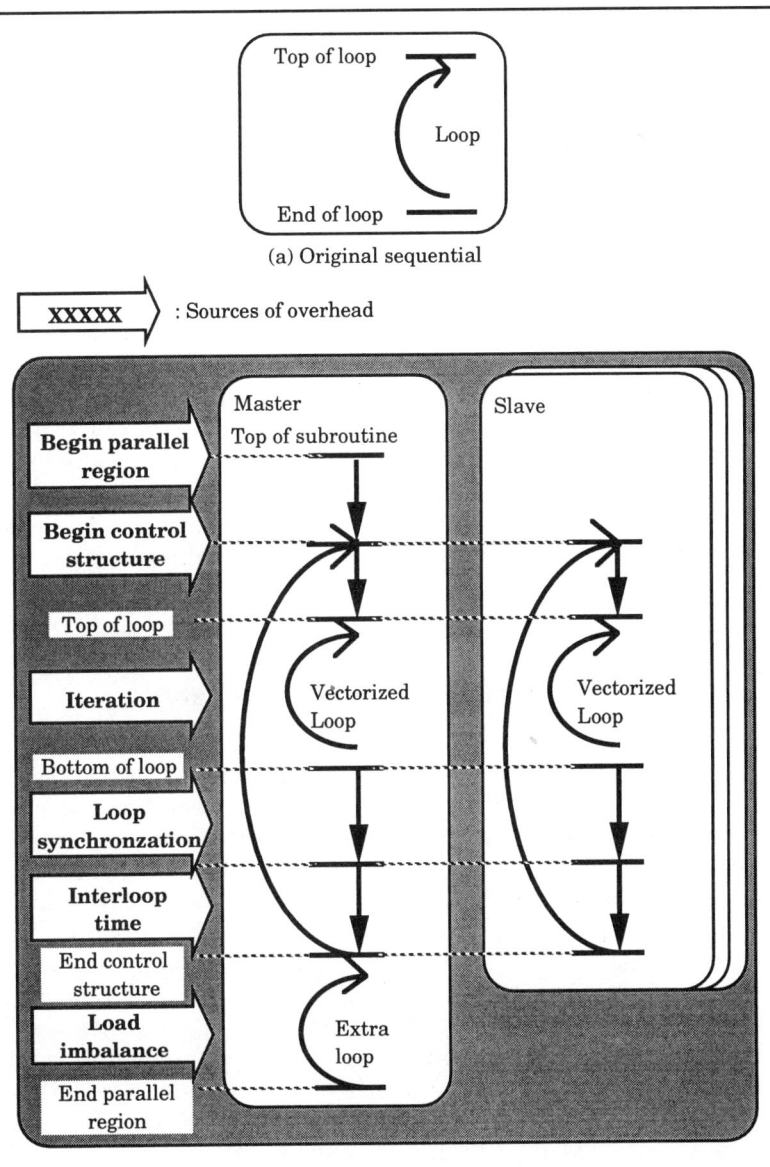

Figure 4–1. Sources of overhead in a microtasked code on Cray Y-MP8/864 supercomputer.

tool, called *atexpert*. This tool determines the execution time of each parallel region, the overhead time, and the maximum speed-up for the whole program. Six different overhead sources can be identified in developing parallel regions (Cray, 1990). They are summarized in Figure 4–1. *atexpert* can estimate the speed-up of the code due to vectorization and microtasking on a single processor without running the code in a dedicated multiprocessor environment. Furthermore, it computes the total overhead time due to various overhead sources.

The third method for monitoring the performance of a multitasked program on the Cray Y-MP8/864 supercomputer is to measure the Mflops. Using the command *hpm* (Hardware Performance Monitor), machine performance can be measured in Mflops during the execution of a program under UNICOS operating system. As a 6.0 ns system, the maximum theoretical performance on the Cray Y-MP8/864 system is 333 Mflops for one processor. For a task executed by only one processor, the value of Mflops due to vectorization falls between 20 Mflops and 300 Mflops (Cray, 1990). Lower values indicate mostly a scalar code or short loops, while maximum values indicate a high degree of vectorization.

4.3 CONCURRENT BACKPROPAGATION LEARNING ALGORITHMS

In general, a neural network learning model consists of two primary components: the topological structure of neural networks and an associated learning rule. The backpropagation (BP) learning is one of the supervised learning methods (Rumelhart et al., 1986). Using the steepest descent method, the BP algorithm tries to find a set of weights, **W**, that minimizes the system error given by Eq. (3-2). The learning procedure is to update the weights between nodes. The change of weight is given by Eq. (3-12). The BP learning algorithm is shown schematically in Figure 4–2. We modify and parallelize the serial learning algorithm presented in Figure 4–2 and implement it on the aforementioned multiprocessor machine. In order to present the concurrent algorithms, consider the topology of the m-layer neural network shown in Figure 4–3. The number of nodes in layer i is $N[i]$. The learning problem is mapped from $N[0]$ input nodes to $N[m]$ output nodes and N_s instances are given as training samples. The total numbers of weights and nodes are denoted by N_w and N_n, respectively.

There are two possible approaches to parallelize the aforementioned

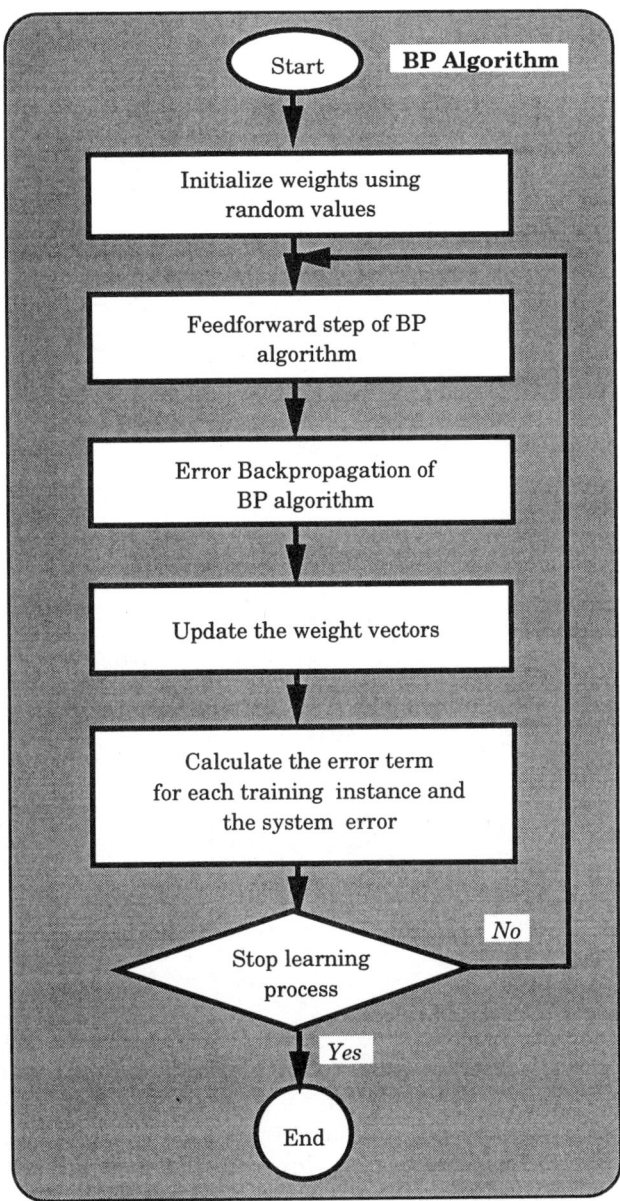

Figure 4–2. Error backpropagation neural network learning algorithm.

58 MACHINE LEARNING

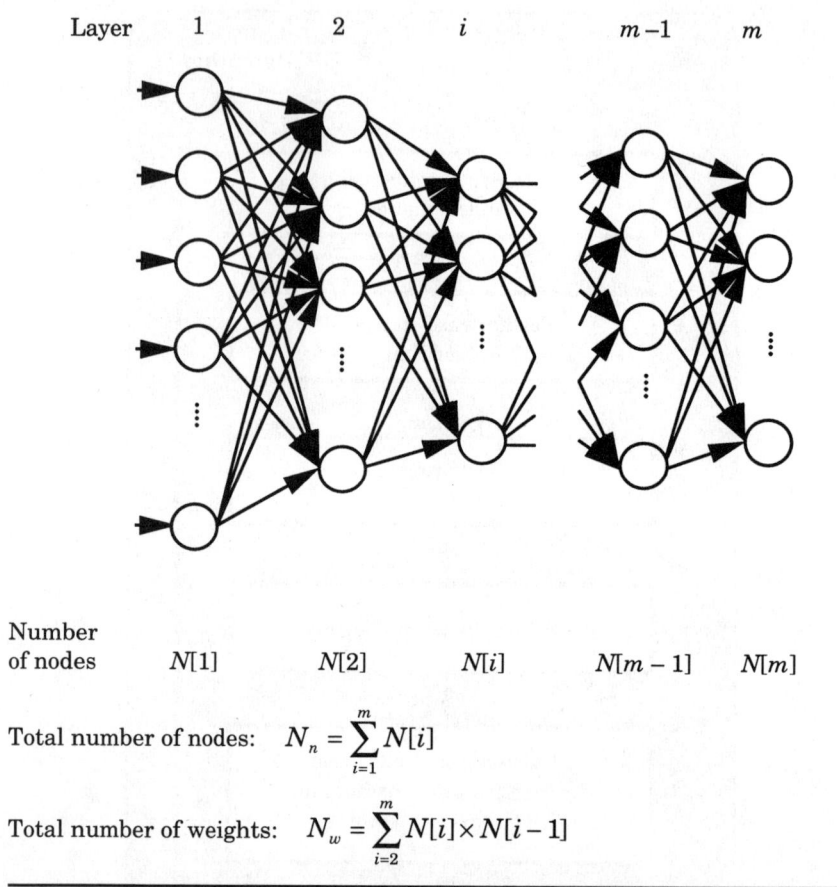

Figure 4-3. Topology of a multi-layer neural network.

serial learning algorithm. One approach is to perform all the computations between the nodes concurrently. The training instances are processed sequentially. In this approach, we can maximize the concurrent processing in the neural network. However, the synchronization problem between nodes is taxing in this approach, because the feedforward and error backpropagation steps must be performed layer by layer.

Moreover, the output of each node is equal to the summation of the product of the weights of its connecting nodes (Rumelhart et al., 1986). Also, vectorization is inhibited in this case.

The other approach is to perform training of instances concurrently. In this case, N_p (number of available processors) copies of the neural network perform the learning process concurrently, and the synchronization problem is reduced to only the computation of summation of deltas of error. Also, the computation in each layer can be vectorized. Thus, this approach is more efficient for vector/parallel machines and thus is employed in this work.

For balancing the load among the processors, the directive *guided* is used to divide the outer loop iteration into chunks of varying size. The size of each chunk is computed at run time using the *Guided Self-Scheduling Algorithm* that attempts to balance the load on each processor so that all processors complete their work at nearly the same time (Cray, 1991). In the algorithms developed in this work, the N_s instances are divided into the same number of groups as the number of available processors (N_p). Each processor executes approximately the same number of tasks concurrently. Vectorization is always applied in the innermost loop. The performance of the concurrent learning algorithms is optimized on the Cray Y-MP by combining vectorization and microtasking. For instance, the feedforward process of the BP learning algorithm in each layer is done as an inner product computation. Therefore, this process is vectorized and carried out by vector registers.

There are four steps in each iteration of the modified concurrent BP learning algorithms (Figure 4–4). They are the feedforward process and calculating the error term for each training instance, calculating the delta for each training instance, accumulating the total system error term and the deltas of weights, and updating the weight vector. In the following, two different algorithms, A and B, are presented, and their relative efficiency is investigated.

Algorithm A

The first three steps have been vectorized and microtasked in this algorithm (see Table 4–1). The last step of updating the weight vector is only a *for* loop containing four floating-point operations: one add and three reciprocals. It has been vectorized only.

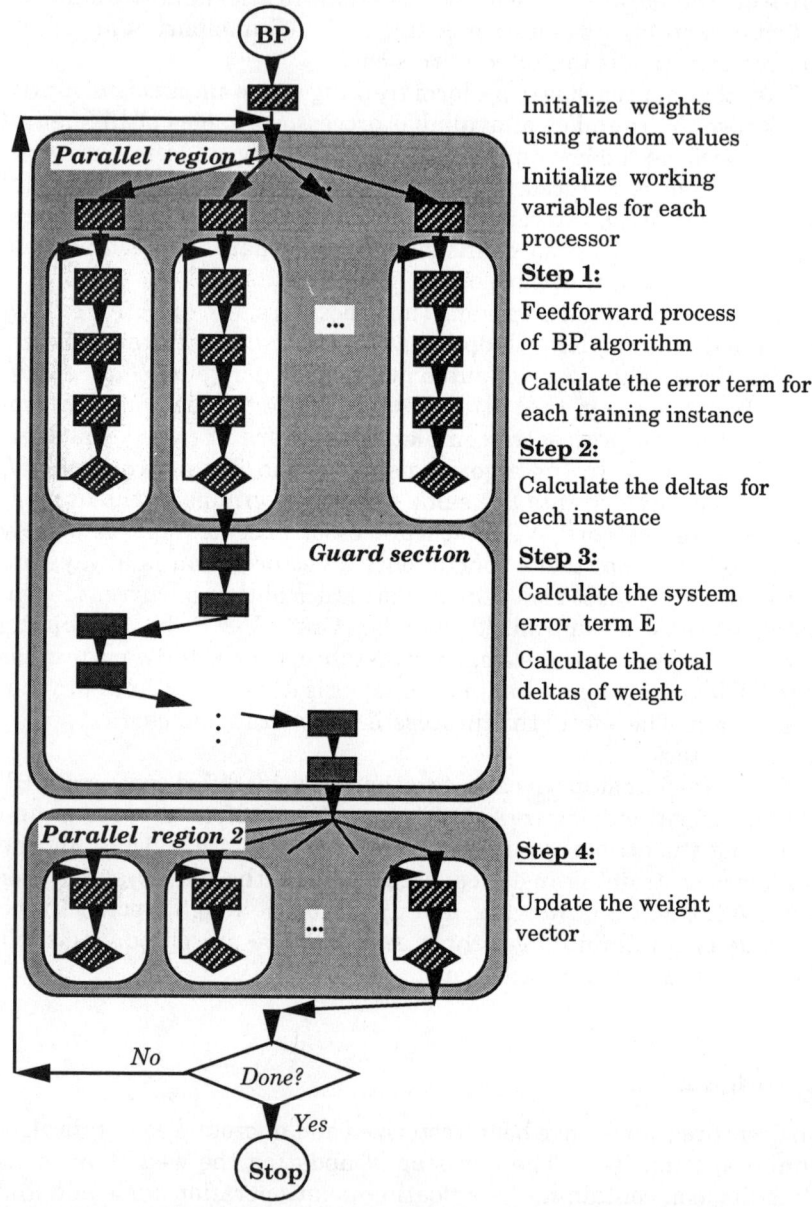

Figure 4-4. Concurrent error backpropagation neural network learning algorithm B.

CONCURRENT BACKPROPAGATION LEARNING ALGORITHMS 61

Table 4–1. Concurrent BP learning algorithms A and B on Cray Y-MP8/864 supercomputer

---

1. Initialize weights using random values and set up the topological structure of neural network.
2. DO
   { Parallel region 1—entry }
   A. For $i=1$ to N_p, do <u>concurrently</u>
      a. Initialize *sub_system_error* and *sub_delta_weights* to zero.
      b. For $j=1$ to *chunksize1*, do <u>sequentially</u>
         b1. Perform feedforward procedure of the BP learning algorithm.   /* V */

         $$o_j = \frac{1}{1+e^{-\left(\sum_{1}^{n} w_{ji}o_i + \theta_j\right)}}$$

         b2. Calculate *sub_system_error*.   /* V */

         $$E_j = \frac{1}{2}\sum_{k}\left(t_{jk} - o_{jk}\right)^2$$

         b3. Calculate the deltas in output layer.   /* V */

         $$\delta_{pk} = (t_{pk} - o_{pk})o_{pk}(1 - o_{pk})$$

         b4. Calculate the deltas in hidden layers (from layer $m-1$ to layer 1).   /* V */

         $$\delta_{pj} = o_{pj}(1 - o_{pj})\sum_{k}\left(\delta_{pk}w_{kj}\right)$$

         b5. Calculate the *sub_delta_weights* in hidden layers (from layer $m-1$ to layer 1).   /* V */

         $$\Delta w_j\mathrel{+}= \eta(\delta_j o_i) + \alpha \Delta w_j$$

      Next j.
   { Guarded section—entry }
   c. Calculate the system error, E, by accumulating *sub_system_error*.   /* V */

   $$E = \frac{1}{2N_s}\sum_{i} E_i$$

   d. Calculate deltas of weights by accumulating the *sub_delta_weights*.   /* V */

   $$\Delta w\mathrel{+}= \Delta w_j$$

   { Guarded section—end}

Table 4–1.   *(Continued)*

Next *i*.
{ Parallel region 1—end}

Algorithm A
B. For *i*=1 to *total_links* , do <u>serially</u>
    a. Update the weight vectors.   /* V */
        $w_j(k + 1) = w_j(k) + \Delta w_j$
Next *i*.

Algorithm B
{ Parallel region 2—entry}
B. For *i*=1 to N_p, do <u>concurrently</u>
    a. For *j*=1 to *chunksize2* , do <u>serially</u>
        a1. Update the weight vectors.   /* V */
            $w_j(k + 1) = w_j(k) + \Delta w_j$
    Next *j*.
Next *i*.
{ Parallel region 2—end}
WHILE (~ stop criterion).

Note: /* V */: Vectorized.

Algorithm B

In order to maximize the concurrent processing, the last step of updating the weight vector is also microtasked in this algorithm. The concurrent learning algorithm is presented in Figure 4–4 and Table 4–1.

4.4 APPLICATIONS

The concurrent BP learning algorithms have been used for learning in two different domains: engineering design and image recognition. We use two examples to investigate and compare the performance of the concurrent learning algorithms implemented on Cray Y-MP8/864 supercomputer.

Example 1—Engineering Design

This example is the same as Example 3 in Chapter 3, that is, selection of a minimum weight steel beam from the AISC LRFD wide-flange (W) shape database for a given loading condition. A four-layer neural network with two hidden layers was used to learn this problem (Figure 3-10). The learning and momentum ratios are chosen as 0.7 and 0.9, respectively (the same values used in Chapter 3). The total number of iterations for learning process is limited to 10,000.

Example 2—Image Recognition

This example is an image recognition problem—recognizing numbers 0 to 9. Shown in Figure 4-5 are the seven by seven (7×7) binary images of the numerals 0 to 9. The upper ten are noiseless binary images, and the other 20 are noisy images. The background value of the binary image is zero and the object pixels have a value of one. This is a hard-to-learn problem, because the patterns in the training set share similar features. For instance, the noisy images of the numerals 2, 5, 6, and 9 are often similar to each other (see Figure 4-5). Thirty training instances were used in this example: ten noiseless image instances and twenty image instances with about 10 percent random noise (5 out of 49 pixels) as shown in Figure 4-5.

A three-layer neural network with one hidden layer was used to learn this problem (Figure 4-6). The numbers of nodes in the input, the hidden, and the output layers are 49, 99, and 10, respectively. The total number of links (weights) in the three-layer neural network is 5950. In this example, the learning and momentum ratios are chosen as 0.2 and 0.3, respectively. The total number of iterations for learning process is limited to 2000. The desired output in this training example is one of the 10 integers 0 to 9. For the simplicity of encoding, we use 10 output nodes to represent the 10 integers. Thus, the desired output vector, say for the integer 4, is {0.1, 0.1, 0.1, 0.1, 0.9, 0.1, 0.1, 0.1, 0.1, 0.1} (Figure 4-6).

4.5   COMPUTATION RESULTS

Example 1

The pie chart in Figure 4-7 shows the time spent in the four steps of the vectorized BP learning algorithm using one processor only. The synchronization section in this example has been reduced to only 0.4 percent. The speed-ups achieved for this example using algorithms A and

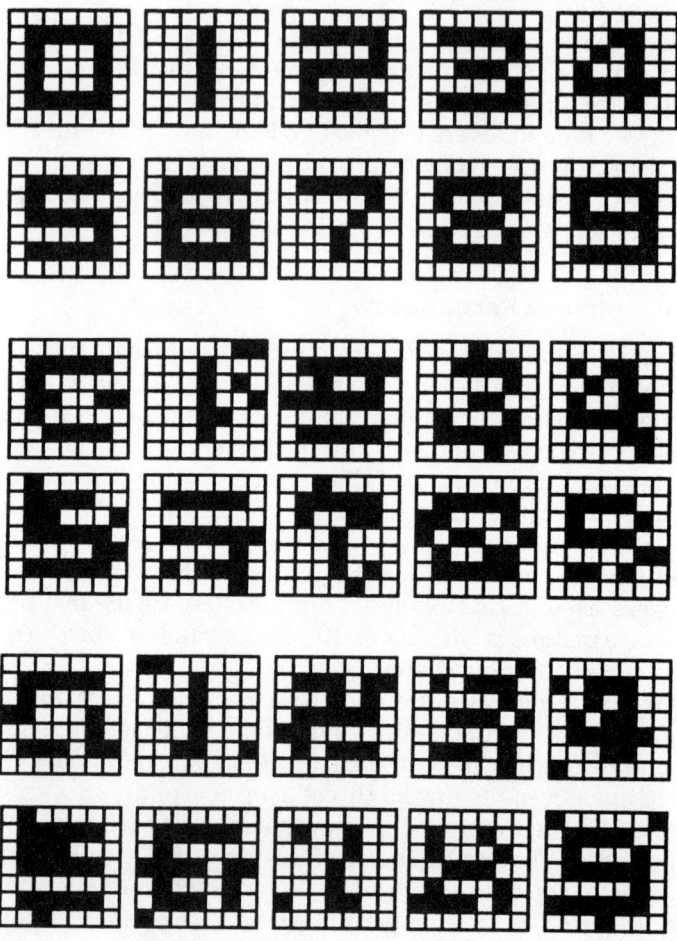

Figure 4–5. Ten noiseless and twenty noisy 7×7 binary images of numerals 0–9).

B, due to microtasking only, are shown in Figure 4–8 (the speed-up is measured with respect to the vectorized code). Algorithm B performs better for this example. Figure 4–9 shows the effect of vectorization on the speed-up for algorithm B (the speed-up of the upper curve is due to vectorization and microtasking). The maximum speed-ups achieved in

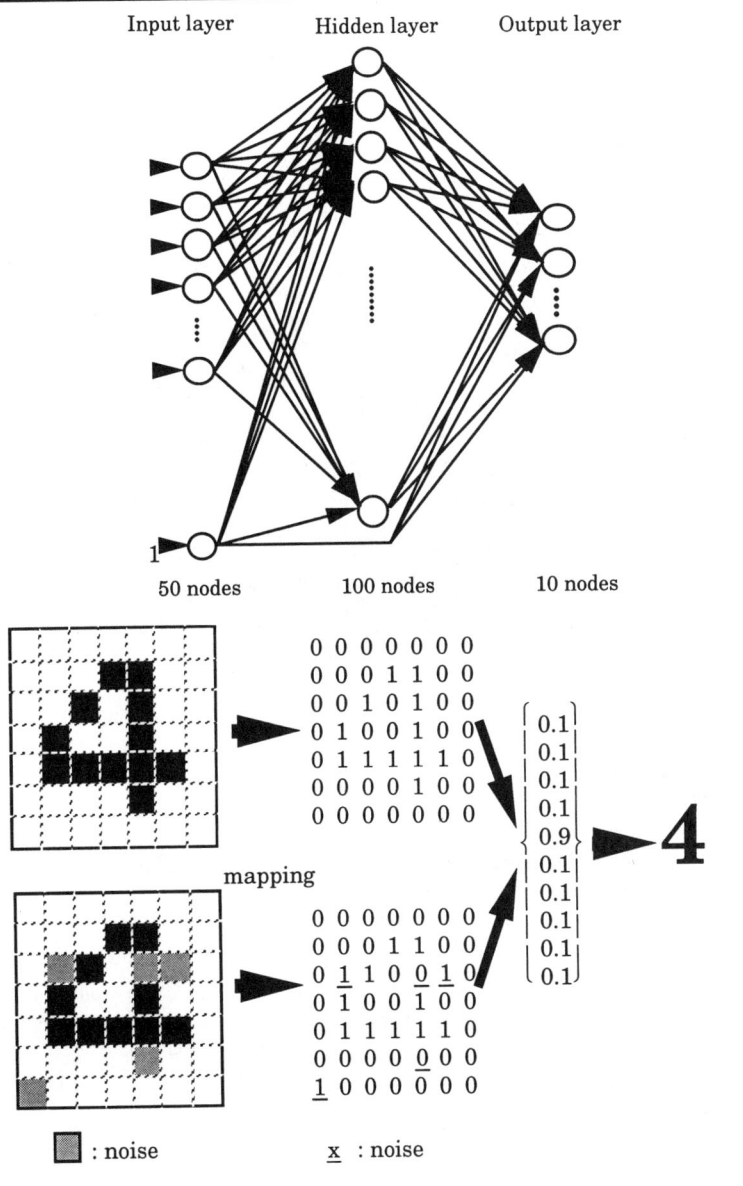

Figure 4-6. Three-layer neural network for the 7×7 binary image of the numerals 0–9.

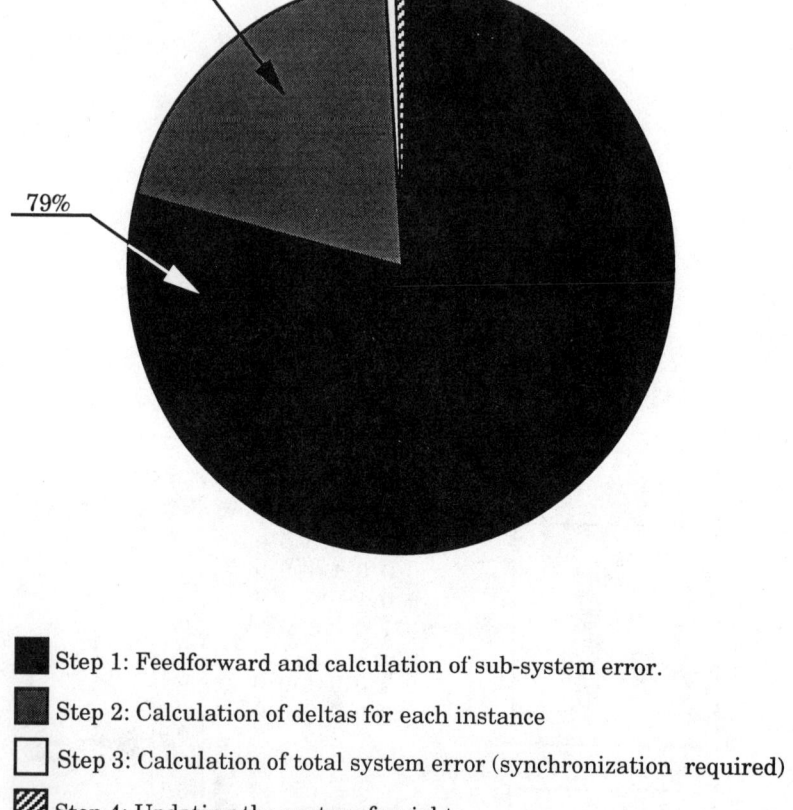

■ Step 1: Feedforward and calculation of sub-system error.
■ Step 2: Calculation of deltas for each instance
□ Step 3: Calculation of total system error (synchronization required)
▨ Step 4: Updating the vector of weights

Figure 4–7.   The CPU time spent in the four steps of the modified BP algorithm for the minimum weight steel beam problem.

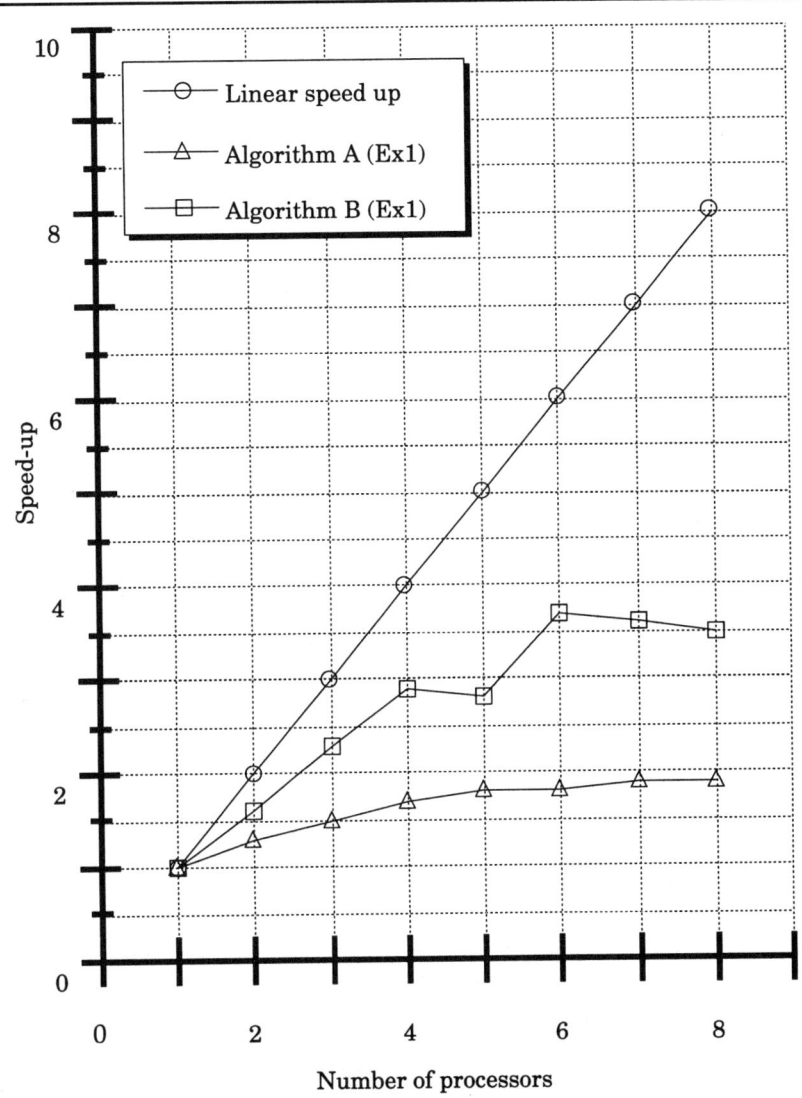

Figure 4-8. The speed-ups for the minimum weight steel beam problem using algorithms A and B.

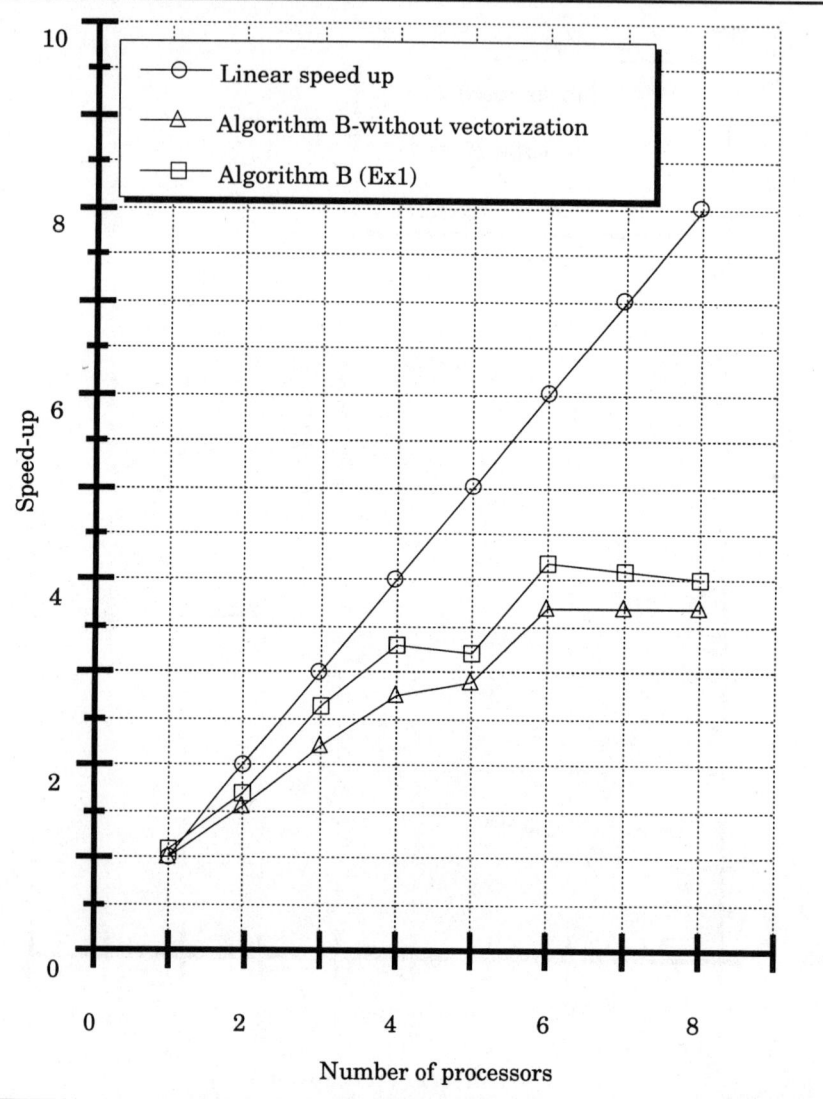

Figure 4–9. The effect of vectorization on the speed-up for algorithm B for the minimum weight steel beam problem.

this example, using eight processors with and without vectorization, are 4.2 and 3.8, respectively.

The speed-up achieved in Example 1 is not high for two reasons. First, the vector length in the vectorized loops is very short (with a maximum of 6). Thus, vectorization is not effective. Second, the overhead in microtasking is very large (on the average, 42 percent of the total execution time). This is due to the fact that there are only 10 iterations (instances) in the outer loop.

The average execution time for this example on a SUN SPARCstation is about 1350 seconds (23 minutes). On Cray Y-MP8/864 supercomputer, using one processor, the average execution time is 6.7 and 8.2 seconds with and without vectorization, respectively.

Example 2

Similar to Example 1, the pie chart in Figure 4–10 shows the time spent in the four steps of the vectorized BP learning algorithm using one processor only. The synchronization section in this example is reduced to 1 percent. The synchronization section in this example is more than Example 1, because the number of links in this example is 5950 compared with only 52 in Example 1. The speed-ups achieved in this example using microtasking only are presented in Figure 4–11 (the speed-up is measured with respect to the vectorized code). Contrary to Example 1, algorithm A performs much better than algorithm B for this example. The speed-up achieved for this example using algorithm B is not high, because the second parallel (microtasking) region (see Figure 4–4) constitutes a very small portion of the code, resulting in a large amount of overhead time for creating parallel microtasks. The speed-ups achieved in each one of the two microtasking regions using algorithm B (due to microtasking only) are shown in Figure 4–12.

Figure 4–13 shows the effect of vectorization on the speed-up using algorithm A (the speed-up of the upper curve is due to both vectorization and microtasking). The maximum speed-up due to microtasking is 6.7 using eight processors. A maximum speed-up of about 33 is achieved when microtasking is combined with vectorization.

Table 4–2 summarizes the performance achieved in vectorizing the code using a single processor in terms of Mflops. We achieved a performance of about 93 Mflops for Example 2, which is a large-scale neural network with 5950 links.

We have used 30 training instances in this example. That means

70 MACHINE LEARNING

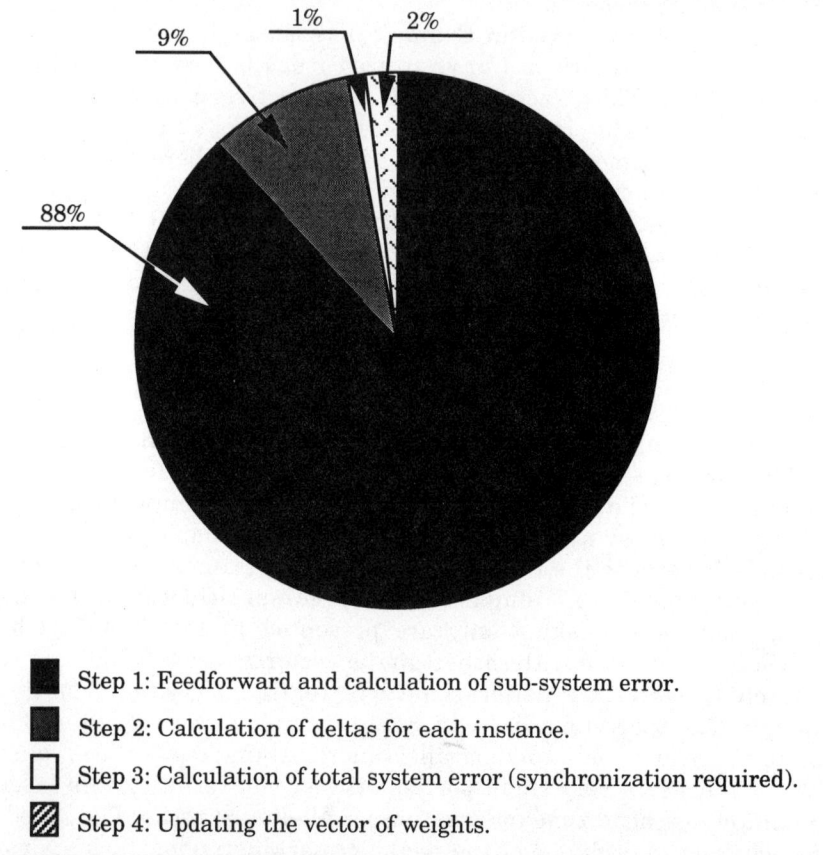

■ Step 1: Feedforward and calculation of sub-system error.
■ Step 2: Calculation of deltas for each instance.
☐ Step 3: Calculation of total system error (synchronization required).
▨ Step 4: Updating the vector of weights.

Figure 4–10. The CPU time spent in the four steps of the modified BP algorithm for the 7×7 binary image of the numerals 0–9.

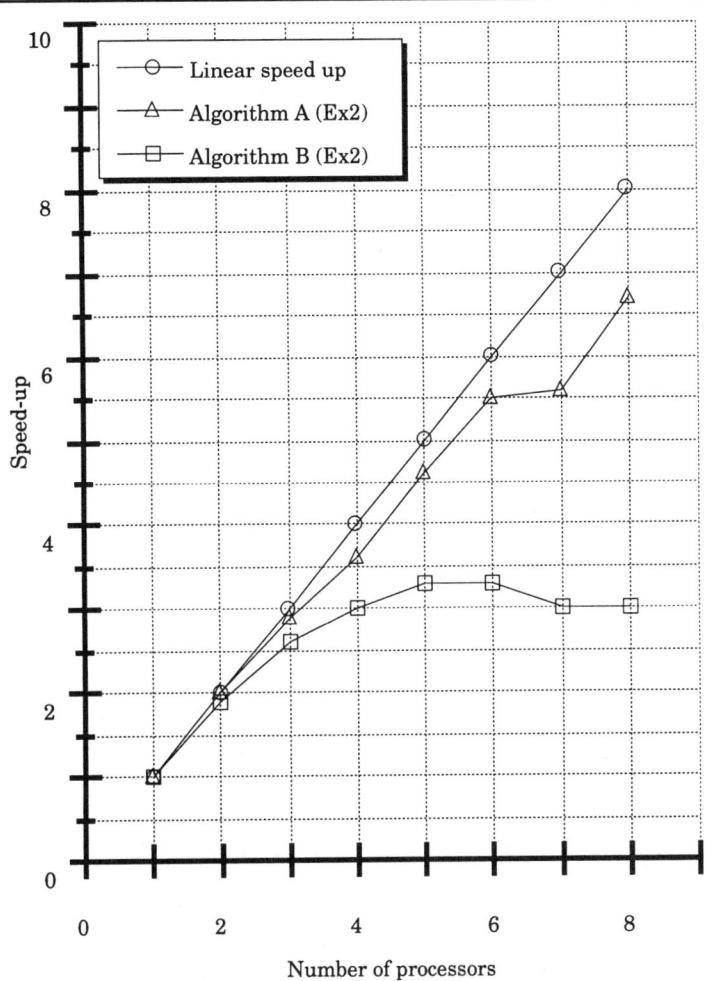

Figure 4–11. The speed-ups for the 7×7 binary image of the numerals 0–9 using algorithms A and B.

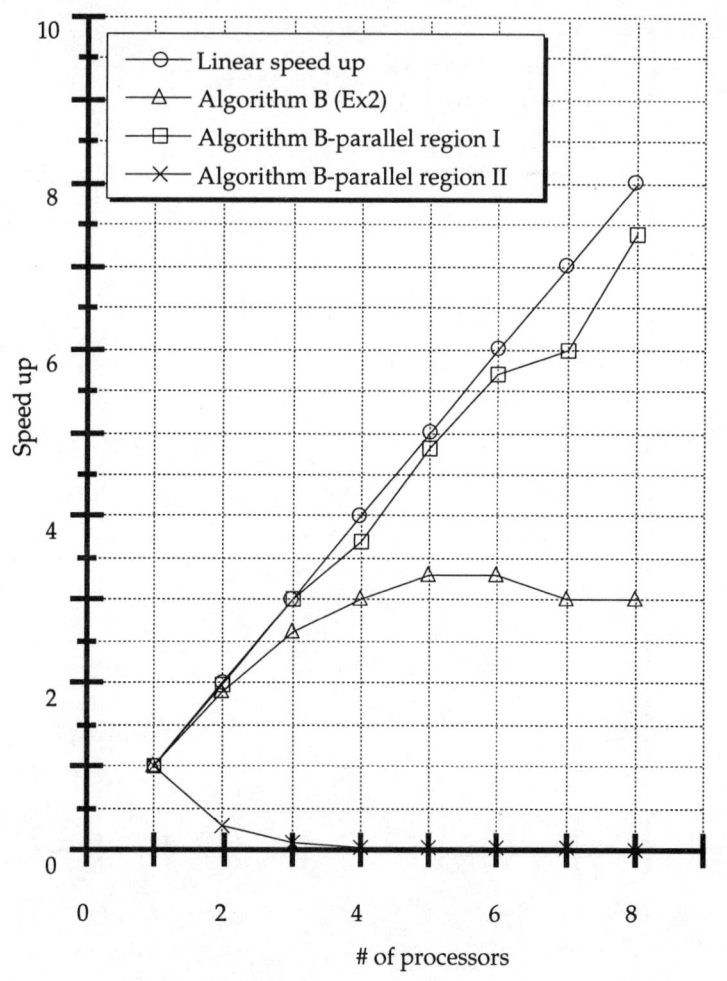

Figure 4-12. The speed-ups of the two individual microtasking regions and the overall code for the 7×7 binary image problem using algorithm B.

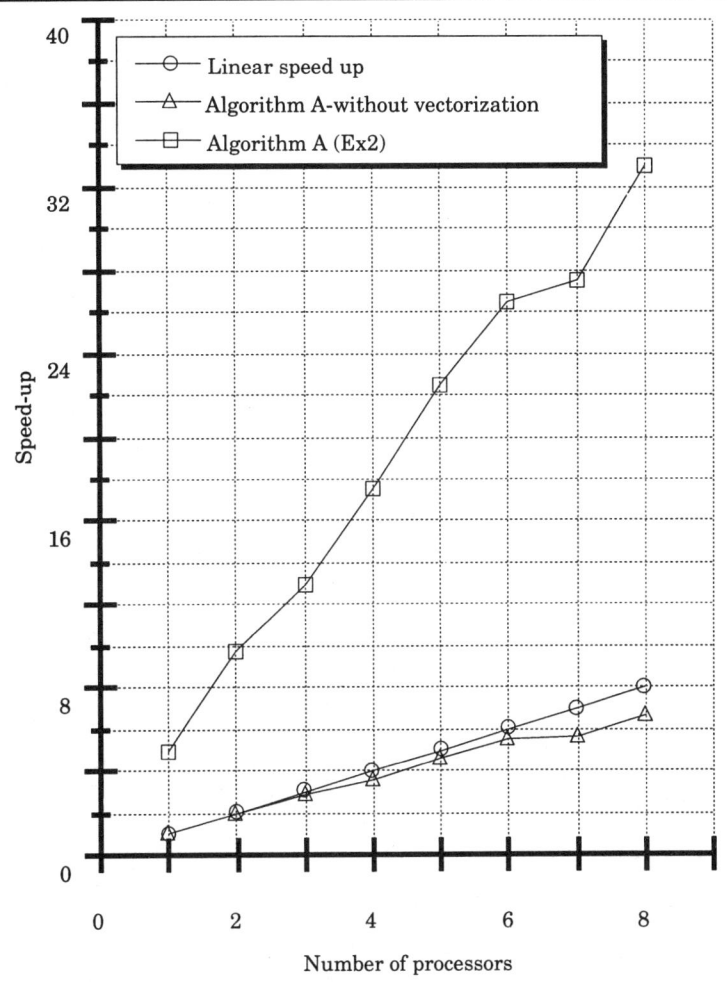

Figure 4-13. The effect of vectorization on the speedup of algorithm A for the 7×7 binary image of the numerals 0-9.

Table 4-2. Mflops for Example 2 on Cray Y-MP8/864 supercomputer.

Vectorized		Nonvectorized	
Algorithm A	Algorithm B	Algorithm A	Algorithm B
93.17	93.19	11.40	11.33

Number of nodes in the input layer: 49.
Number of nodes in the hidden layer: 99.
Number of nodes in the output layer: 10.
Number of links: 5950.
Maximum number of iterations: 2000.

the number of iterations in the outermost loop is 30, which must be balanced among the available processors. When the number of training instances is not a multiple of the number of available processors, a load imbalance inevitably exists that degrades the performance to some extent. This can be seen in the speed-up curve for algorithm A in Figure 4–11 at points of 4 and 7 processors. The performance degradation for algorithm B in this figure is primarily due to the short length of the second parallel region, as explained previously.

With 5950 links, this example uses a large-scale neural network. The average CPU time of the sequential code on a SUN SPARCstation is about 3.6 hours. The nonvectorized and vectorized codes on Cray Y-MP8/864 supercomputer using a single processor on the average take about 3.7 minutes and 43 seconds, respectively.

4.6 CONCLUDING REMARKS

Two concurrent BP neural network learning algorithms were presented and implemented on Cray Y-MP8/864 supercomputer under the UNICOS operating system. The algorithms have been applied to two different domains: engineering design and image recognition. The following observations and conclusions are made:

1. Performance of a concurrent learning algorithm depends on the size of the problem. A concurrent algorithm suitable for a small problem may not perform well for large problems. Our algorithm A is suitable for large neural networks, while algorithm B is suitable for small neural networks.

2. The synchronization section in a concurrent BP algorithm can be reduced to a small portion (about 1 percent). Thus, a high degree of parallelization can be achieved. Using eight processors, we achieved a speed-up of 6.7 for a large example with 5950 links, due to microtasking only.

3. A vector MIMD machine such as Cray Y-MP8/864 provides a more effective environment for achieving maximum performance than parallel machines without vectorization capability. We achieved a speed-up of about 5.0 due to vectorization only on a single processor for a large example with 5950 links. When vectorization was combined with microtasking, a combined speed-up of about 33 was achieved.

4. The image recognition example presented in this chapter is a hard-to-learn problem. That is, a large number of iterations is required to train the network (2000 in our example). Development of learning algorithms with the objective of improving the convergence rate of learning and reducing the required number of iterations will be discussed in the following chapters.

CHAPTER 5

An Adaptive Conjugate Gradient Learning Algorithm for Efficient Training of Neural Networks

Dennis A. Johnston, Ph.D.

5.1 INTRODUCTION

The momentum backpropagation (BP) learning algorithm (Rumelhart et al., 1986) is widely used for training multilayer neural networks for classification problems. This algorithm, however, has a slow rate of learning. In order to improve the convergence rate and reduce the total number of iterations and consequently the execution time, more effective neural network learning algorithms have to be developed. Kollias and Anastassiou (1989) developed an adaptive least-squares learning algorithm for multilayer neural networks. Douglas and Meng (1991) developed an adaptive linearized least-squares learning algorithm for training of multilayer feedforward neural networks. These two algorithms achieved better convergence rate than the momentum BP learning algorithm by using second order derivatives of the error function with respect to the network weights. However, in both of these algorithms the Hessian matrix (H), containing the second order derivatives of the network weights, is needed, requiring a large amount of memory storage and additional computations. These two algorithms are efficient only when the input data set is small.

The conjugate gradient method, originally proposed by Fletcher and Reeves (1964), has been recognized as one of the few practical methods for solving large optimization problems, because it does not require any large matrix storage and its iteration cost is relatively low (Powell, 1986). In this chapter, an adaptive conjugate gradient learning algorithm for training of multilayer feedforward neural networks is presented. The algorithm has been implemented in C on a SUN SPARCstation.

5.2   SUPERVISED LEARNING FOR FEEDFORWARD NEURAL NETWORKS

A classification system is said to be supervised when given a set of objects with known classifications, it can classify unknown objects based on the information acquired by training. Mathematically, it may be stated as follows: Given a set of real input vectors $\mathbf{X}_k \in R^{n_1}$ as well as real output vector $\mathbf{Y}_k \in R^{n_N}$ ($k=1, 2, ..., p$), find the function $f: R^{n_1} \to R^{n_N}$ which maps $\mathbf{X}_k$ to $\mathbf{Y}_k$. The total number of training instances is denoted by p. R^{n_1} and R^{n_N} are sets of real numbers with dimensions n_1 and n_N respectively. In our domain of interest, n_1 and n_N are the total numbers of patterns in the input and output sets, respectively. The mapping process can be classified as a mathematical optimization problem: Find an optimum decision vector, $\mathbf{W}$, to minimize an objective function. The objective function for this optimization problem is the sum of squared error function (the difference between the desired and computed outputs) as follows:

$$E(\mathbf{X}_k, \mathbf{W}) = \frac{1}{2p} \sum_{k=1}^{p} \sum_{m=1}^{n_N} (y_{km} - o_{km})^2 \tag{5-1}$$

where y_{km} and o_{km} are the desired and computed outputs for the mth pattern in output and the kth training instance, respectively.

Feedforward neural networks have been widely used to perform this kind of mapping (Rumelhart et al., 1986, Kollias and Anastassiou, 1989, Douglas and Meng, 1991). A multi-layer feedforward neural network is shown in Figure 5–1. It contains n_1 input nodes, n_N output nodes, and n_i nodes in the $(i-1)$st hidden layer, respectively. The nodes between the ith and $(i+1)$st layers are fully connected. A weight $w_{j,k}$ is assigned to the link between nodes j and k in two connected layers. An input vector is propagated feedforwardly through the network. Except for the nodes of input layer, the input to each node is the sum of the weighted output of the prior layer modified by a nonlinear sigmoidal

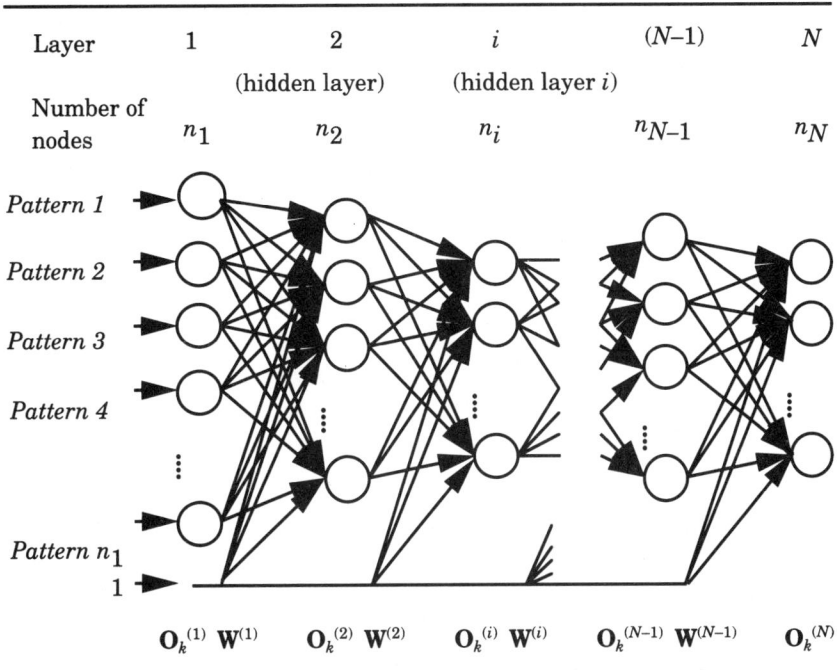

Figure 5–1. A multi-layer feedforward neural network.

function. Following the notation of the neural network in Figure 5–1, the output vectors of the kth training instance for layers 1 to N can be represented by the following equations:

$$\mathbf{O}_k^{(1)} = \begin{bmatrix} \mathbf{X}_k \\ 1 \end{bmatrix} \tag{5-2}$$

$$\mathbf{O}_k^{(i+1)} = \begin{bmatrix} G(\mathbf{W}^{(i)} \cdot \mathbf{O}_k^{(i)}) \\ 1 \end{bmatrix} \quad \text{for } i = 1, 2, ..., N-1 \tag{5-3}$$

The matrix of weights between layers i and $i+1$ can be written as

$$\mathbf{W}^{(i)} = \begin{bmatrix} w_{1,1}^{(i)} & \cdots & w_{1,n_i+1}^{(i)} \\ \vdots & & \vdots \\ w_{n_{i+1},1}^{(i)} & \cdots & w_{n_{i+1},n_i+1}^{(i)} \end{bmatrix}_{(n_{i+1})(n_i+1)} = \begin{bmatrix} \mathbf{W}_1^{(i)T} \\ \vdots \\ \mathbf{W}_{n_{i+1}}^{(i)T} \end{bmatrix} \tag{5-4}$$

where T indicates the transpose of a matrix and $w_{t,n_{i+1}}^{(i)}$ is the threshold value for node t in the ith layer. $\mathbf{W}_j^{(i)T}$ is a row vector containing the weights of the links connected to the jth node in the ith layer. The following sigmoidal function is used as the threshold function:

$$g(u) = \frac{1}{1+e^{-u}} \tag{5-5}$$

Therefore,

$$G\left(\mathbf{W}^{(i)} \cdot \mathbf{O}_k^{(i)}\right) = \begin{bmatrix} g\left(\sum_{j=1}^{n_i+1} \left(w_{1,j}^{(i)} o_{kj}^{(i)}\right)\right) \\ g\left(\sum_{j=1}^{n_i+1} \left(w_{2,j}^{(i)} o_{kj}^{(i)}\right)\right) \\ \vdots \\ g\left(\sum_{j=1}^{n_i+1} \left(w_{n_{i+1},j}^{(i)} o_{kj}^{(i)}\right)\right) \end{bmatrix} \tag{5-6}$$

Now, we define the aforementioned vector $\mathbf{W} \in R^L$ containing all the weights of the feedforward neural network represented in Eq. (5-4) as

$$\mathbf{W} = \left\{ \mathbf{W}_1^{(1)T} \mathbf{W}_2^{(1)T} \dots \mathbf{W}_{n_i}^{(i-1)T} \mathbf{W}_1^{(i)T} \dots \mathbf{W}_{(n_N-1)}^{(N-1)T} \mathbf{W}_{n_N}^{(N-1)T} \right\}^T \tag{5-7}$$

$$\equiv \left\{ w_{1,1}^{(1)} w_{1,2}^{(1)} \dots w_{n_2,n_1+1}^{(1)} w_{1,1}^{(2)} \dots w_{j,k}^{(i)} \dots w_{1,1}^{(N-1)} w_{1,2}^{(N-1)} \dots w_{n_N,n_{N-1}+1)}^{(N-1)} \right\}$$

where L is the total number of links given by

$$L = \sum_{i=1}^{N-1} (n_{i+1})(n_i + 1) \tag{5-8}$$

Note that $\mathbf{W}$ is a column matrix with L elements. The functional mapping between the input vector $\mathbf{X}_k$ and the computed vector $\mathbf{O}_k$ for the kth training instance can be written as follows:

$$f(\mathbf{X}_k, \mathbf{W}) = \mathbf{O}_k \tag{5-9}$$

The vector $\mathbf{W}$ in Eq. (5-9) can be solved either iteratively or directly by finding the pseudoinverse matrix of $\mathbf{X}_k$. However, the latter approach is inconsistent with the biological learning process. The reason is that the learning process in a biological neural network is an improvement process rather than an analytical procedure. Therefore, in order to simulate the human learning process, Eq. (5-9) is solved iteratively in order to find an optimum weight vector $\mathbf{W}^*$, minimizing the total system error represented by Eq. (5-1).

5.3 EFFECT OF LEARNING AND MOMENTUM RATIOS ON CONVERGENCE RATE

Most of the gradient-based nonlinear unconstrained optimization algorithms consist of two stages. One stage is finding the search direction. Determination of the vector of search direction, **d**, is dependent on the chosen optimization algorithm. In the steepest gradient descent search, the vector of search direction is set as the steepest descent direction **d** = $\nabla E(\mathbf{W})$. In this chapter, the search direction is set as the conjugate direction of the steepest descent search direction, as defined in the following section. The other stage is the step length size determination that seeks a scalar λ^* to minimize the function $E(\mathbf{W} + \lambda \mathbf{d})$. Once the search direction is determined, the step size becomes a one-dimensional minimization problem.

In the momentum BP learning algorithm a constant step length (λ) is used to find the direction of search only. Such an algorithm has a slow and irregular convergence rate. Moreover, the convergence rate is highly dependent on the choice of the values of learning ratio (λ) and momentum ratio (α). The proper values of these two ratios are dependent on the type of problem. As an example, the convergence rates for the problem of minimum weight design of steel beams using four different values for the pair (λ, α) are shown in Figure 5–2. It is observed that convergence rate is quite unacceptable for some values of the pair (λ, α).

5.4 INEXACT LINE SEARCH ALGORITHM

The stage of the step length size determination has a great effect on the efficiency of the mathematical optimization algorithm. A very accurate line search algorithm may reduce the total number of iterations but usually needs many function evaluations. Therefore, if the computation of the objective function for the optimization problem is expensive, the performance of an optimization algorithm using an inexact (approximate) line search strategy is better than that of an optimization algorithm using an exact line search strategy. In the previous chapter, we found that the computation of the objective function in the feedforward neural network is the most time-consuming step in each iteration. Therefore, in this chapter, an inexact line search has been utilized.

An inexact (approximate) line search algorithm can determine the search parameter (step length) λ within a small percentage of its true value. Two useful criteria for terminating an inexact line search pro-

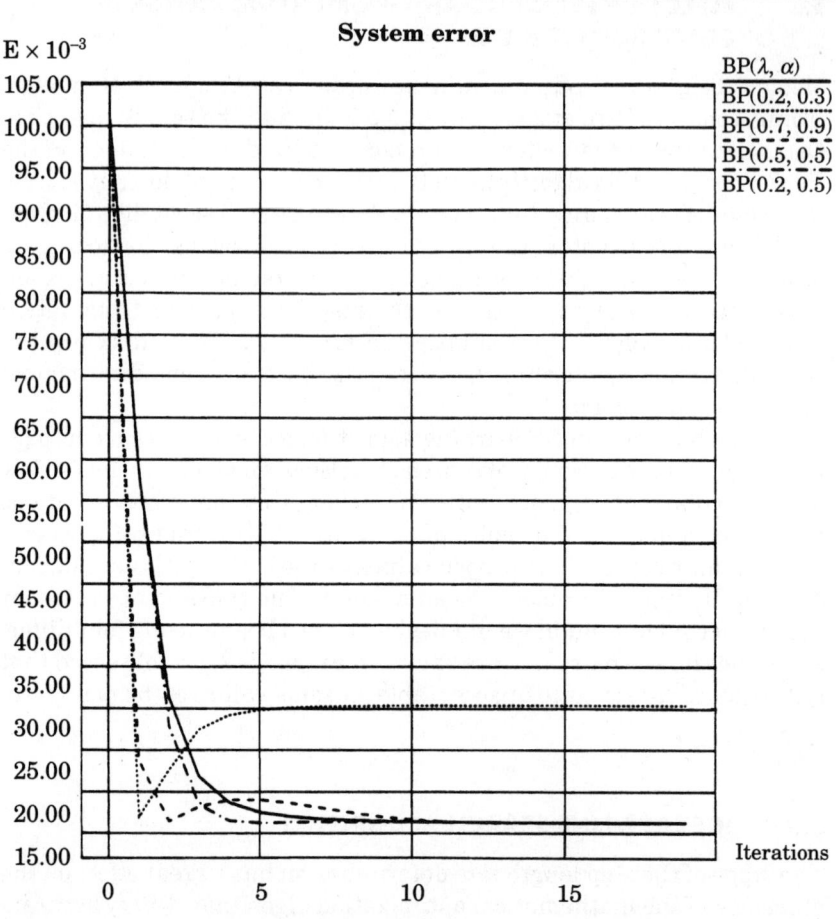

Figure 5–2. Learning performance for the problem of minimum weight design of steel beams by momentum BP learning algorithm with different pairs of (λ, α).

cess have been proposed by Armijo (1966) and Goldstein (1967). These two criteria are used to guarantee that the selected step length λ is neither too large nor too small. According to the first criterion (Armijo, 1966), in order to ensure that the selected step length λ is not too large, it has to satisfy the following condition:

$$E\left(\mathbf{W}^{(k)} + \lambda \mathbf{d}^{(k)}\right) \leq E\left(\mathbf{W}^{(k)}\right) + \beta \lambda \left(\nabla E\left(\mathbf{W}^{(k)}\right)^T \mathbf{d}^{(k)}\right) \quad \beta \in (0, 1) \text{ and } \lambda > 0 \quad (5\text{-}10)$$

The superscript k refers to the kth iteration.

According to the second criterion (Goldstein, 1967), in order to ensure that the selected step length, λ, is not too small, it has to satisfy the following condition:

$$\nabla E\left(\mathbf{W}^{(k)} + \lambda \mathbf{d}^{(k)}\right)^T \mathbf{d}^{(k)} \geq \theta \left(\nabla E\left(\mathbf{W}^{(k)}\right)^T \mathbf{d}^{(k)}\right) \quad \theta \in (\beta, 1) \text{ and } \lambda > 0 \quad (5\text{-}11)$$

The condition, $1 > \theta > \beta > 0$, guarantees that Eqs. (5-10) and (5-11) can be satisfied simultaneously (Dennis and Schnable, 1983).

However, the two conditions represented by Eqs. (5-10) and (5-11) do not guarantee that descent directions are always generated. Therefore, we apply a third condition to ensure that the selected step length λ satisfies the descent condition (Nocedal, 1990):

$$\nabla E\left(\mathbf{W}^{(k)} + \lambda \mathbf{d}^{(k)}\right)^T \mathbf{d}^{(k+1)} < 0 \quad (5\text{-}12)$$

The three aforementioned conditions are described graphically in Figure 5–3. The acceptable step length, λ, is located in a region that satisfies the three conditions. Dennis and Schnable (1983) developed an inexact line search algorithm by backtracking, using successive parabolic and cubic interpolations. Our inexact line search algorithm is based on the integration of Eqs. (5-10) to (5-12) and backtracking by successive parabolic and cubic interpolations.

5.5 AN ADAPTIVE CONJUGATE GRADIENT NEURAL NETWORK LEARNING ALGORITHM

Proposed by Fletcher and Reeves (1964) and modified by Polak and Ribiére (1969), the conjugate gradient method is an effective modification of the steepest descent method. Furthermore, Powell (1986) showed that the unrestarted Polak-Ribiére method with exact line search may fail to converge for non-convex problems, and proposed a more robust algorithm to ensure convergence. We present an adaptive conjugate gradient neural network learning algorithm by using the Powell's modified conjugate gradient algorithm for minimizing the system error in

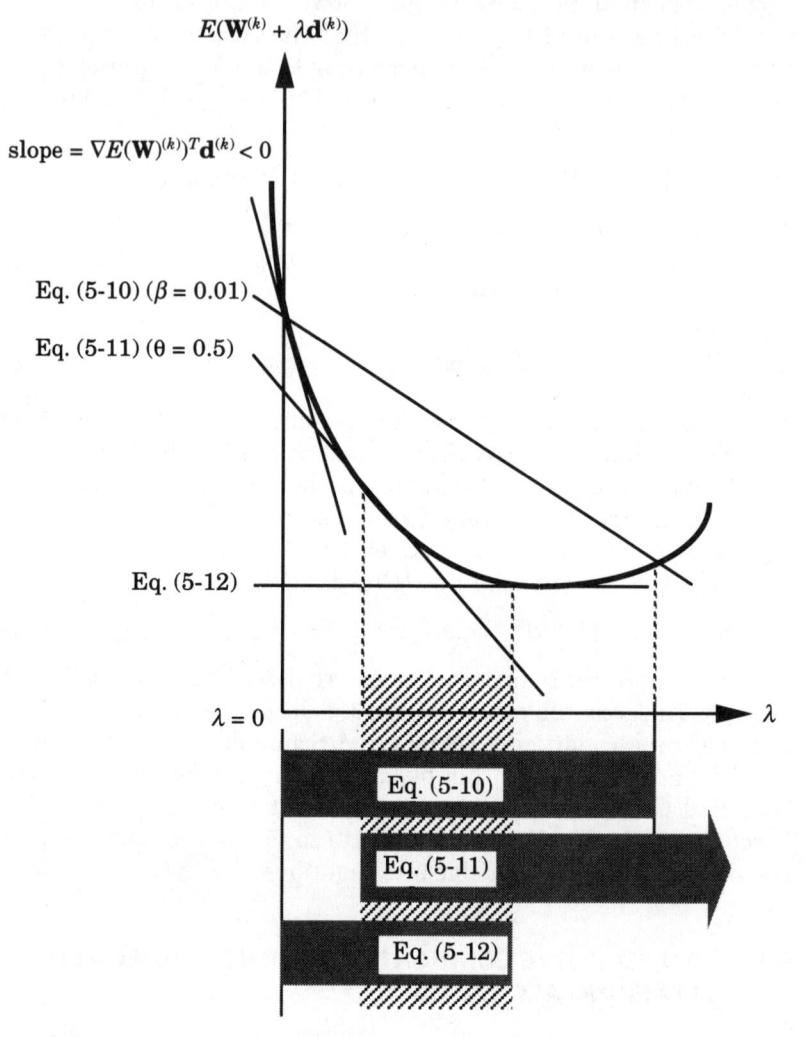

Figure 5-3. Permissible values of λ under three line search conditions.

neural networks with the inexact line search algorithm described in the previous section.

Our optimization problem has L decision variables.

Step 1. Generate a starting weight vector $\mathbf{W} \in R^L$ randomly. Set the iteration counter $n=1$ using three different stopping criteria: the convergence parameter for the gradient vector $\varepsilon (=10^{-6})$, maximum number of iterations (*MaxIter*), and the minimum system error (*minerr*). Set the initial search direction $\mathbf{d}^{(0)}=\{0\}$. Set STOP1=0 and *iter*=0. Set the acceptable minimum and maximum step length as *minlen* (= 0.00001) and *maxlen* (=1000). Set $\beta(=0.9)$ and $\theta(=0.001)$.

Step 2. For $k=1$ to p, perform the following for the kth training instance:

Step 2-1. Perform feedforward procedure of the neural network:

Set $\mathbf{O}_k^{(1)} = \begin{bmatrix} \mathbf{X}_k \\ 1 \end{bmatrix}$

For $i=1$ to $N-1$, calculate the output vector in $(i+1)$st layer:

$$\mathbf{O}_k^{(i+1)} = \begin{bmatrix} G(\mathbf{W}^{(i)} \cdot \mathbf{O}_k^{(i)}) \\ 1 \end{bmatrix} \quad (5\text{-}13)$$

$$G(\mathbf{W}^{(i)} \cdot \mathbf{O}_k^{(i)}) = \begin{bmatrix} \dfrac{1}{1+e^{-\sum_{j=1}^{n_i+1}(w_{1,j}^{(i)} o_{kj}^{(i)})}} \\ \dfrac{1}{1+e^{-\sum_{j=1}^{n_i+1}(w_{2,j}^{(i)} o_{kj}^{(i)})}} \\ \vdots \\ \dfrac{1}{1+e^{-\sum_{j=1}^{n_i+1}(w_{n_{i+1},j}^{(i)} o_{kj}^{(i)})}} \end{bmatrix} \quad (5\text{-}14)$$

Step 2-2. Calculate the system error for the kth training instance:

$$E_k(\mathbf{X}_k, \mathbf{W}) = \sum_{m=1}^{n_N} (y_{km} - o_{km})^2 \quad (5\text{-}15)$$

Step 2-3. Calculate the deltas in the output layer for the kth training instance:

$$\delta_{kr}^{(N)} = \left(y_{kr} - o_{kr}^{(N)}\right)\left(1 - o_{kr}^{(N)}\right)o_{kr}^{(N)} \qquad r=1, 2, \ldots, n_N \qquad (5\text{-}16)$$

Step 2-4. For $r=N-1$ down to 1, calculate the deltas in the hidden layers:

$$\delta_{kr}^{(N)} = \left(y_{kr} - o_{kr}^{(N)}\right)\left(1 - o_{kr}^{(N)}\right)o_{kr}^{(N)} \qquad q=1, 2, \ldots, n_r \qquad (5\text{-}17)$$

Step 2-5. For $i=1$ to $N-1$, calculate the gradient vector for the kth training instance:

$$\nabla E_k(\mathbf{W}^{(n)}) = \frac{\partial E(\mathbf{W})}{\partial w_{q,r}^{(i)}} = \delta_{kq}^{(i+1)} o_{kr}^{(i)}$$

$$q=1, 2, \ldots, n(i+1) \text{ and } r=1, 2, \ldots, n_i + 1 \qquad (5\text{-}18)$$

Step 3. Calculate the total system error:

$$E(\mathbf{X}_k, \mathbf{W}) = \frac{1}{2p} \sum_{k=1}^{p} E_k(\mathbf{X}_k, \mathbf{W}) \qquad (5\text{-}19)$$

If $E(\mathbf{X}_k, \mathbf{W}) < minerr$, set STOP1=1 and go to step 19. Otherwise, go to the next step.

Step 4. Calculate the gradient vector of the total neural network system error:

$$\nabla E(\mathbf{W}^{(n)}) = \sum_{k=1}^{p} \nabla E_k(\mathbf{W}^{(n)}) \qquad (5\text{-}20)$$

Assign the search direction as:

$$\mathbf{d}^{(n)} = -\nabla E\!\left(\mathbf{W}^{(n)}\right) \qquad (5\text{-}21)$$

If $\left|\nabla E\!\left(\mathbf{W}^{(n)}\right)\right| < \varepsilon$, set STOP1=1 and go to step 19. In this case, $\mathbf{W}^{(n)}$ is the optimum solution ($|\mathbf{X}|$ is the length of vector $\mathbf{X}$). Otherwise, continue.

Step 5. Set $iter = iter+1$. If $iter \geq L$, set $iter=0$. If $iter=1$, set $\alpha_n=0$ and go to the next step. Otherwise, calculate the new conjugate direction as:

$$\mathbf{d}^{(n)} = -\nabla E\!\left(\mathbf{W}^{(n)}\right) + \alpha_n \mathbf{d}^{(n-1)} \qquad (5\text{-}22)$$

where

$$\alpha_n = \max\left\{0, \frac{\nabla E\!\left(\mathbf{W}^{(n)}\right)^T \mathbf{v}^{(n-1)}}{\left|\nabla E\!\left(\mathbf{W}^{(n-1)}\right)\right|^2}\right\} \qquad (5\text{-}23)$$

and
$$\mathbf{v}^{(n-1)} = \nabla E(\mathbf{W}^{(n)}) - \nabla E(\mathbf{W}^{(n-1)}) \qquad (5\text{-}24)$$

Step 6. Perform the inexact line search algorithm to calculate λ. Set the stopping criterion STOP2 (= 0). Initialize $\lambda=1$.

Step 7. Calculate $E(\mathbf{W}^{(n)} + \lambda \mathbf{d}^{(n)})$ and $E(\mathbf{W}^{(n)}) + \beta\lambda(\nabla E(\mathbf{W}^{(n)})^T \mathbf{d}^{(n)})$.
If $E(\mathbf{W}^{(n)} + \lambda \mathbf{d}^{(n)}) \leq E(\mathbf{W}^{(n)}) + \beta\lambda(\nabla E(\mathbf{W}^{(n)})^T \mathbf{d}^{(n)})$, go to the next step. Otherwise, go to step 15.

Step 8. Calculate $\nabla E(\mathbf{W}^{(n)} + \lambda \mathbf{d}^{(n)})^T \mathbf{d}^{(n)}$. and $\theta(\nabla E(\mathbf{W}^{(n)})^T \mathbf{d}^{(n)})$.
If $\nabla E(\mathbf{W}^{(n)} + \lambda \mathbf{d}^{(n)})^T \mathbf{d}^{(n)} < \theta(\nabla E(\mathbf{W}^{(n)})^T \mathbf{d}^{(n)})$ go to the next step. Otherwise, go to step 13.

Step 9. If $\lambda=1$, go to step 10. Otherwise, go to step 11.

Step 10. Set $\lambda = \min(2\lambda, maxlen)$.
Calculate the new search direction $\mathbf{d}^{(n+)}$.
Calculate $\nabla E(\mathbf{W}^{(n)} + \lambda \mathbf{d}^{(n)})^T \mathbf{d}^{(n+)}$.
If $(\nabla E(\mathbf{W}^{(n)} + \lambda \mathbf{d}^{(n)})^T \mathbf{d}^{(n+)}) < 0$,
calculate $\nabla E(\mathbf{W}^{(n)} + \lambda \mathbf{d}^{(n)})^T \mathbf{d}^{(n)}$ and $\theta(\nabla E(\mathbf{W}^{(n)})^T \mathbf{d}^{(n)})$.
If $(\nabla E(\mathbf{W}^{(n)} + \lambda \mathbf{d}^{(n)})^T \mathbf{d}^{(n+)}) \geq 0$,
or $(\nabla E(\mathbf{W}^{(n)} + \lambda \mathbf{d}^{(n)})^T \mathbf{d}^{(n)} \geq \theta(\nabla E(\mathbf{W}^{(n)})^T \mathbf{d}^{(n)})$,
or $1 \geq maxlen$, go to step 11. Otherwise, go to step 10.

Step 11. If $\lambda < 1$ or ($\lambda > 1$ and $\nabla E(\mathbf{W}^{(n)} + \lambda \mathbf{d}^{(n)})^T \mathbf{d}^{(n+)} \geq 0$), go to step 12. Otherwise, go to step 17.

Step 12. Perform backtracking using parabolic interpolation to find a new λ.
Calculate $\nabla E(\mathbf{W}^{(n)} + \lambda \mathbf{d}^{(n)})^T \mathbf{d}^{(n)}$ and $\theta(\nabla E(\mathbf{W}^{(n)})^T \mathbf{d}^{(n)})$.
Calculate the new search direction $\mathbf{d}^{(n+)}$.
Calculate $\nabla E(\mathbf{W}^{(n)} + \lambda \mathbf{d}^{(n)})^T \mathbf{d}^{(n+)}$.
If both conditions, $\nabla E(\mathbf{W}^{(n)} + \lambda \mathbf{d}^{(n)})^T \mathbf{d}^{(n)} \geq \theta(\nabla E(\mathbf{W}^{(n)})^T \mathbf{d}^{(n)})$ and $\nabla E(\mathbf{W}^{(n)} + \lambda \mathbf{d}^{(n)})^T \mathbf{d}^{(n+)} < 0$ hold simultaneously, set STOP2=1 and go to step 17. Otherwise, go to the beginning of this step.

Step 13. Calculate the new search direction $\mathbf{d}^{(n+)}$.
Calculate $\nabla E(\mathbf{W}^{(n)} + \lambda \mathbf{d}^{(n)})^T \mathbf{d}^{(n+)}$.
If $\nabla E(\mathbf{W}^{(n)} + \lambda \mathbf{d}^{(n)})^T \mathbf{d}^{(n+)} \geq 0$, go to step 14. Otherwise, set STOP2=1 and go to step 17.

Step 14. Perform backtracking using parabolic interpolation to find a new λ.
Calculate the new search direction $\mathbf{d}^{(n+)}$.
Calculate $\nabla E(\mathbf{W}^{(n)} + \lambda \mathbf{d}^{(n)})^T \mathbf{d}^{(n+)}$.
If $\nabla E(\mathbf{W}^{(n)} + \lambda \mathbf{d}^{(n)})^T \mathbf{d}^{(n+)} < 0$, set STOP2=1 and go to step 17. Otherwise go to the beginning of this step.

Step 15. If $\lambda < minlen$, then set $\lambda=0$, set STOP2=1 and go to step 17. Otherwise, go to the next step.

Step 16. If $\lambda=1$, perform backtracking using parabolic interpolation to find a new λ. Otherwise, perform backtracking using cubic interpolation to find a new λ. Go to the next step.

Step 17. If STOP2 = 1, set $\lambda_n=1$, stop the iterations of inexact line search algorithm, and go to the next step. Otherwise, go to step 7.

Step 18. Update the weight vector as
$$\mathbf{W}^{(n+1)} = \mathbf{W}^{(n)} + \lambda_n \mathbf{d}^{(n)} \quad (5\text{-}25)$$
Set $n = n + 1$. If $n > i$, set STOP1=1 and go to next step.

Step 19. If STOP1=1, stop the iteration of the adaptive conjugate gradient learning algorithm; $\mathbf{W}^{(n)}$ is the optimum weight vector. Otherwise, go to step 2.

The algorithm is restarted every L iterations by setting $\alpha_k = 0$.

5.6 APPLICATIONS

We apply the adaptive conjugate gradient neural network learning algorithm presented in this chapter to the domains of engineering design and image recognition.

Example 1—Engineering Design

This example is the same as Example 3 of Chapter 3, that is, the selection of a minimum weight steel beam from the AISC LRFD wide-flange (W) shape database (AISC, 1989) for a given loading condition. The same four-layer feedforward neural network with two hidden layers shown in Figure 3–10 was used to learn this problem. There are 52 links in this neural network, resulting in 52 decision variables in the corresponding mathematical optimization problem. For the momentum BP learning algorithm, the learning and momentum ratios were chosen as 0.2 and 0.5, respectively. The total number of iterations for the learning process is limited to 20 in this chapter.

Example 2—Image Recognition of 7×7 Binary Images of Numerals 0–9

This example is the same as Example 2 of Chapter 4, that is, recognition of seven by seven (7×7) binary images of the numerals 0 to 9. The same three-layer neural network (with one hidden layer) shown in Figure 4–6 was used to learn this problem. The total number of links in this three-layer neural networks is 5950. Thus, there are 5950 decision variables in the corresponding mathematical optimization problem. This is a very large-scale optimization problem. For the momentum BP learning algorithm, the learning and momentum ratios are chosen as 0.2 and 0.3, respectively. The total number of iterations for the learning process is limited to 200. There are thirty training instances in this example, 10 noiseless and 20 noisy, as shown in Figure 4–5. The value of the threshold function (Eq. 5-5) can vary between 0 (FALSE for the binary output) and 1 (TRUE for the binary output), but can never equal these two values. In implementation, we set g=0.1 and g=0.9 as FALSE and TRUE values, respectively. The outputs can be presented visually in a 3-dimensional contour surface shown in Figure 5–4. The two horizontal axes represent the 10 nodes and 10 possible integer outputs (0 to 9). The vertical axis represents the value of the threshold function. Figure 5–4 represents the desired learning output.

5.7 LEARNING RESULTS

Example 1

The system error for this example using the momentum BP algorithm and the adaptive conjugate gradient neural network (ACGNN) learning algorithm is shown in Figure 5–5. The learning performance of the adaptive conjugate gradient neural network learning algorithm is substantially better than that of the momentum BP learning algorithm. After 20 iterations, the adaptive conjugate gradient neural network learning algorithm converges to a very small value of 10^{-5}. But, after the same number of iterations, the momentum BP algorithm (with $\lambda = 0.2$, $\alpha = 0.5$, the best values among different sets we tried) converges to 0.017.

Example 2

The system error for this example using the momentum BP algorithm with three different pairs of (λ, α) and the adaptive conjugate gradient neural network learning algorithm is shown in Figure 5–6. The system error for the ACGNN learning algorithm is less than 0.1 after 50 itera-

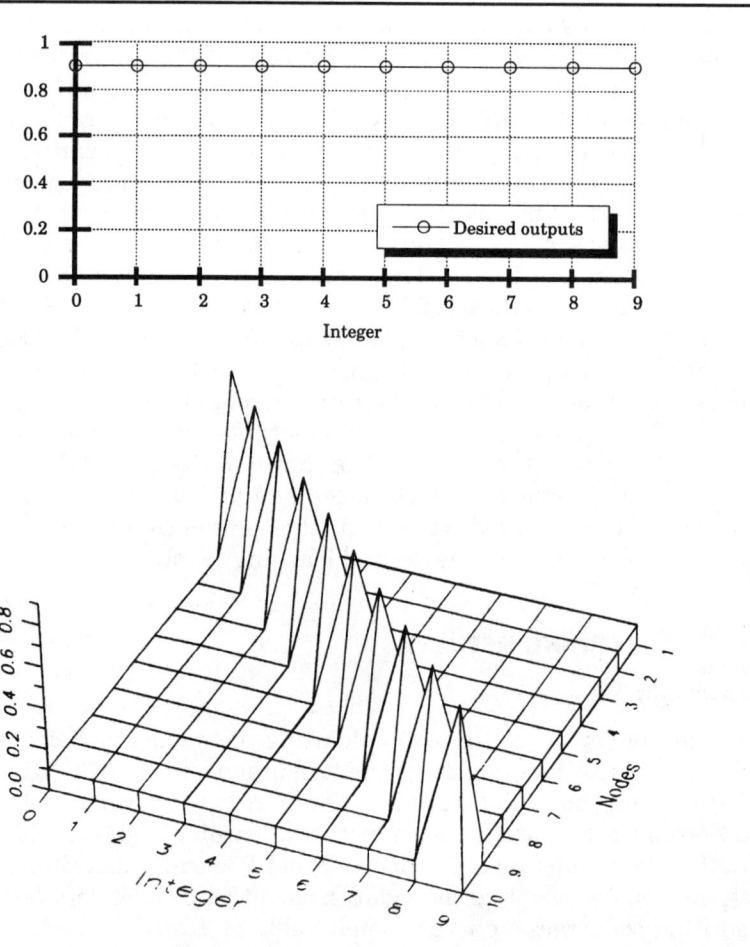

Figure 5–4. 3-dimensional contour surface of the desired outputs for the 7×7 binary image recognition of numerals 0–9.

tions and error-free image recognition is achieved. The computed outputs for the 10 noiseless and twenty noisy training instances given in Figure 4–5 are represented in 3-dimensional contour surfaces in Figures 5–7 to 5–9.

To achieve the same system error with the momentum BP learning algorithm with the best values of the pair (λ, α) requires about 300 iterations. But, using the other values of the pair of (λ, α), the momen-

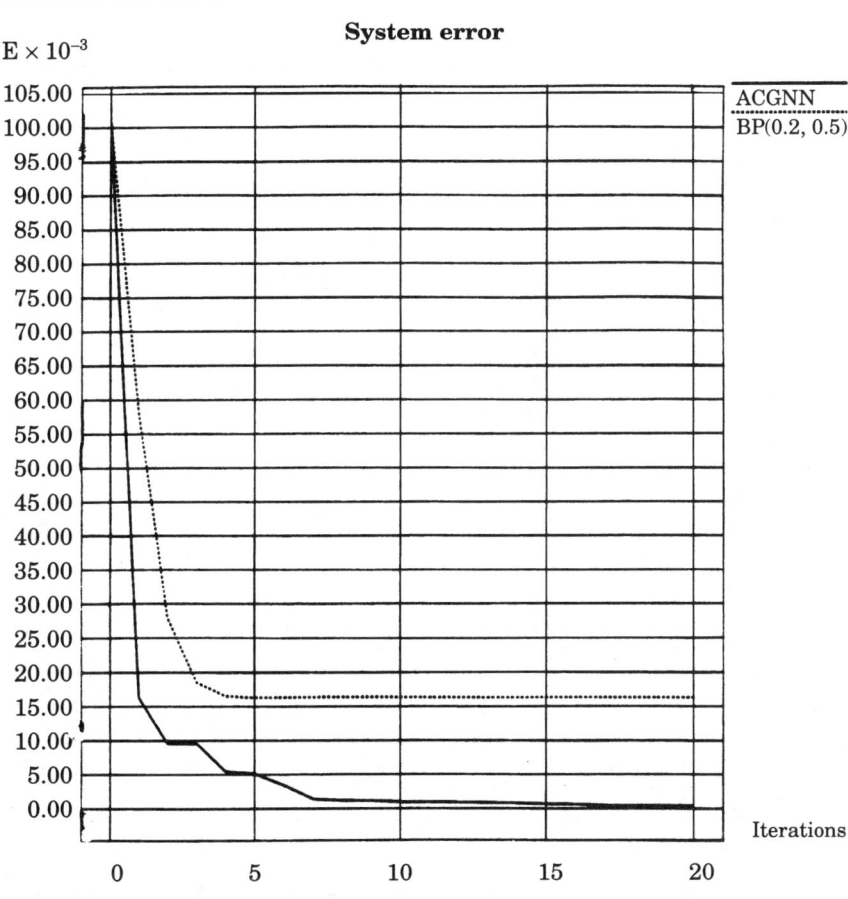

Figure 5–5. System error for the minimum weight steel beam problem.

94 MACHINE LEARNING

tum BP learning algorithm can recognize only 45 percent of the images after 300 iterations, as shown in the example of Figure 5–10.

5.8 CONCLUDING REMARKS

An adaptive conjugate gradient neural network learning algorithm was presented in this chapter. The learning algorithm was applied to two

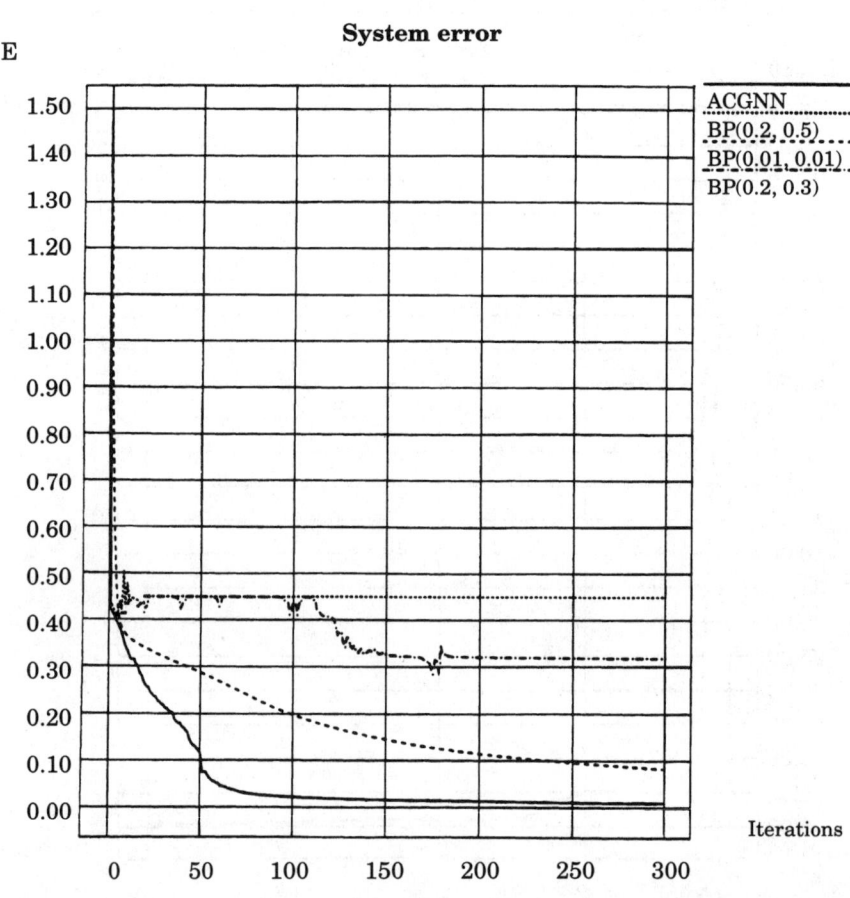

Figure 5–6. System error for the 7×7 binary image recognition of numerals 0–9.

AN ALGORITHM FOR EFFICIENT TRAINING OF NEURAL NETWORKS   95

different domains, engineering design and image recognition. The performance of the algorithm was evaluated by applying it to two examples. The following observations are made and conclusions drawn:

1. The problem of arbitrary trial-and-error selection of the learning ratio (λ) and momentum ratio (α) encountered in the momentum

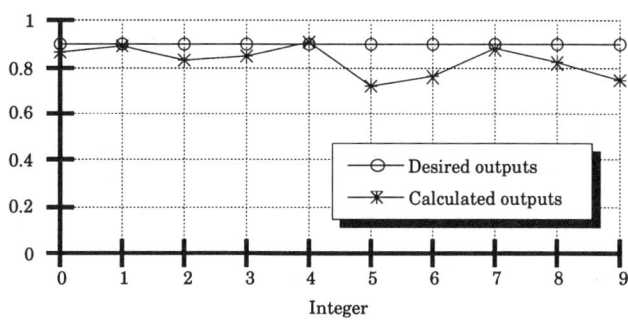

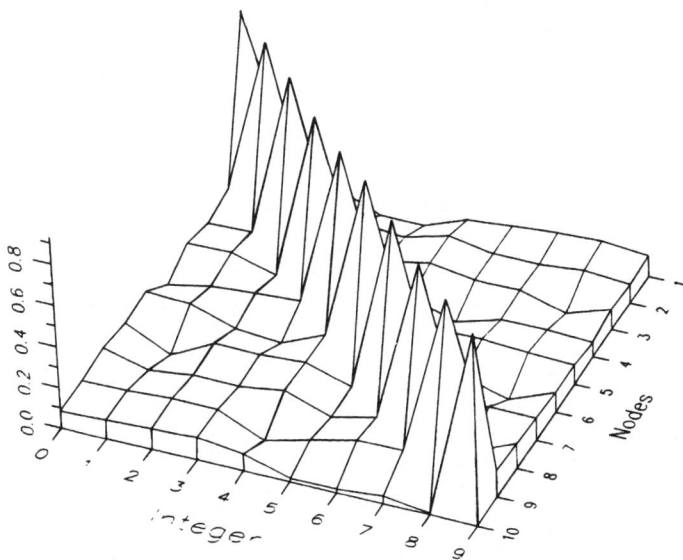

Figure 5–7. 3-dimensional contour surface of the computed outputs for the 10 noiseless training instances shown in Figure 4–5.

backpropagation algorithm is circumvented in the new adaptive algorithm. Instead of constant learning and momentum ratios, the step length in the inexact line search is adapted during the learning process through a mathematical approach. Thus, the new adaptive algorithm provides a more solid mathematical foundation for neural network learning.

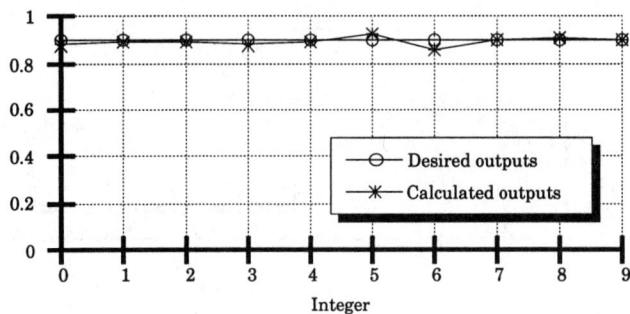

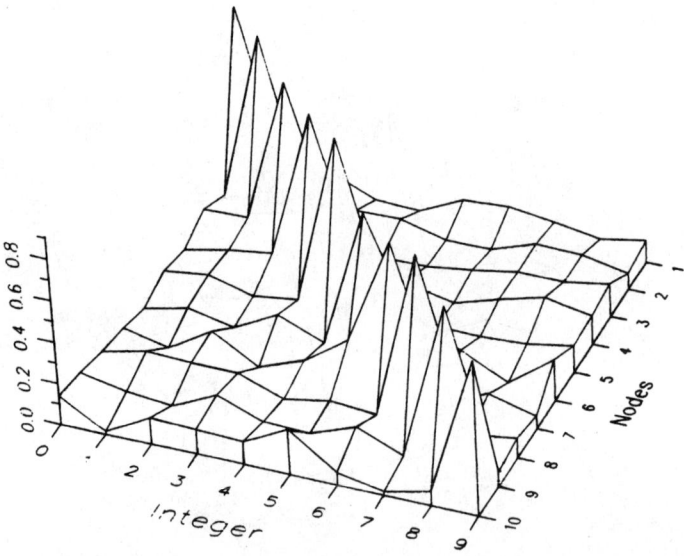

Figure 5–8. 3-dimensional contour surface of the computed outputs for the first ten noisy training instances shown in Figure 4–5.

AN ALGORITHM FOR EFFICIENT TRAINING OF NEURAL NETWORKS   97

2. The adaptive conjugate gradient neural network learning algorithm presented in this chapter converges much faster than the momentum backpropagation algorithm.

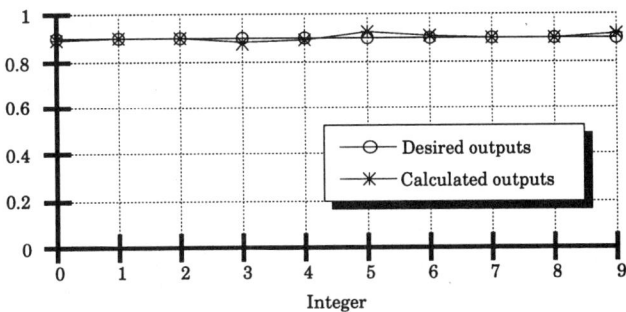

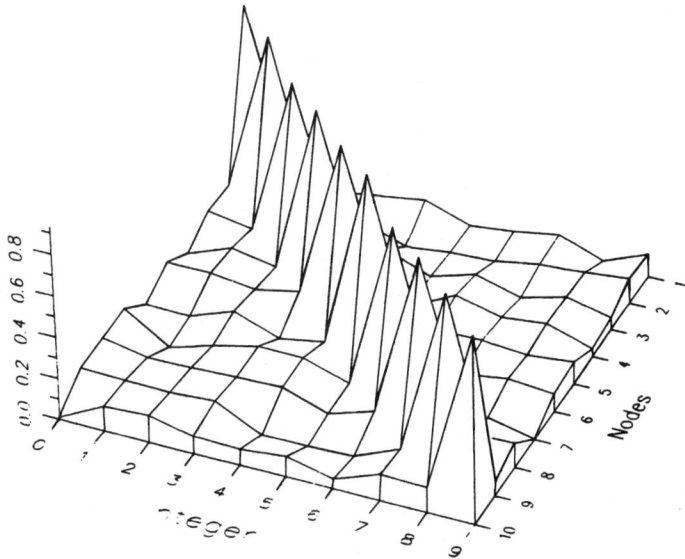

Figure 5-9.   3-dimensional contour surface of the computed outputs for the second ten noisy training instances shown in Figure 4-5.

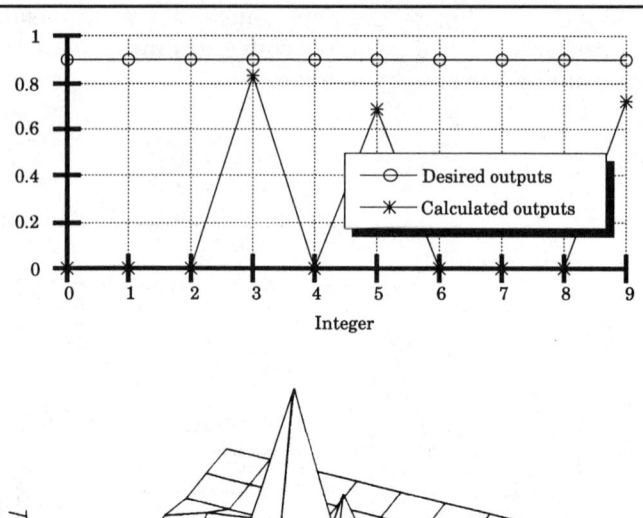
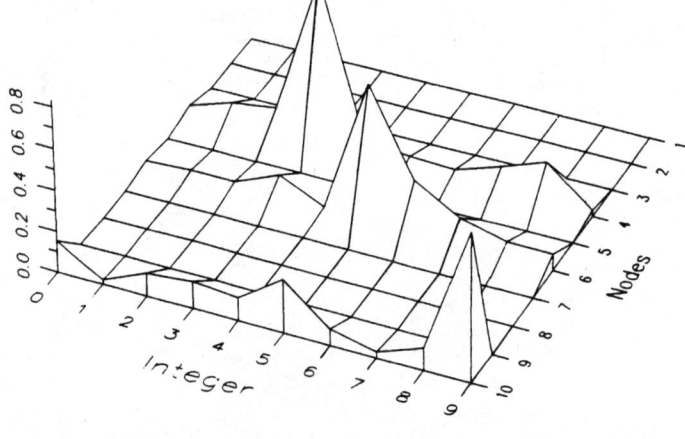

Figure 5–10. 3-dimensional contour surface of the computed outputs for the 10 noiseless training instances (shown in Figure 4–5) using the momentum BP learning algorithm with ($\lambda = 0.2$, $\alpha = 0.5$).

CHAPTER 6

A Concurrent Adaptive Conjugate Gradient Learning Algorithm on MIMD Shared Memory Machines

6.1 INTRODUCTION

Based on a combination of Powell (1986) modified conjugate gradient algorithm with an exact line search algorithm (Dennis and Schnable, 1983; Nocedal, 1990), we presented an adaptive conjugate gradient learning algorithm for training of multilayer feedforward neural networks in Chapter 5. In this chapter, a concurrent adaptive conjugate gradient neural network learning algorithm is presented. The algorithm has been implemented on a vector MIMD shared memory machine (Cray Y-MP8/864 supercomputer under a UNICOS operating system). Two large-scale examples from the domain of image recognition are used to test the performance of the concurrent learning algorithm. Large neural networks with more than 4000 links are used for these examples.

6.2 CONCURRENT CONJUGATE GRADIENT NEURAL NETWORK LEARNING ALGORITHM

Training a large neural network requires large computer processing resources. We present a concurrent conjugate gradient neural network algorithm using the vector processing and multitasking capabilities of a vector MIMD machine, the Cray Y-MP8/864 supercomputer. Multitasking can be performed by microtasking, which is performed at the loop level, or macrotasking that is implemented in the function or procedure level (Cray, 1991; Hsu and Adeli, 1991). In this work, the parallel sections in the concurrent conjugate gradient neural network learning algorithm are implemented using microtasking. As the concurrent learning algorithm is performed iteratively, it cannot be parallelized at the function level effectively using macrotasking. On the other hand, the most time-consuming portions of the concurrent algorithm are the steps of feedforward process and calculation of the system error and the deltas for each instance. These steps are coded in nested loops that can be implemented using a combination of microtasking and vectorization. The algorithm is presented in Tables 6–1 to 6–3. The

Table 6–1. Concurrent adaptive conjugate gradient learning algorithm on Cray Y-MP8/864 supercomputer.

---

1. Initialize the weight vector randomly, set up the topological structure of neural network, and set the counter *cn* to zero.
2. DO
    { Parallel region—entry }
    A. For $i = 1$ to N_s do <u>concurrently</u>
        a. Initialize *sub_system_error* and *sub_delta_weights* to zero.
        b. For $j = 1$ to *chunksize*, do <u>sequentially</u>
            b1. Perform feedforward procedure of the adaptive conjugate gradient learning algorithm.
            b2. Calculate *sub_system_error*.
            b3. Calculate the deltas in output layer.
            b4. Calculate the deltas in hidden layers (from layer *m*-1 to layer 1).
            b5. Calculate the *sub_delta_weights* in hidden layers (from layer *m*-1 to layer 1).
        Next *j*.
        { Guarded section—entry }
        c. Calculate the system error, $E(\mathbf{W})$, by accumulating *sub_system_error*.
        d. Calculate deltas of weights by accumulating the *sub_delta_weights*.
        { **Guarded section—end**}
    Next *i*.
    { Parallel region—end}

Table 6–1. *(Continued)*

B. If $cn \geq 1$, calculate the new conjugate direction.
C. Set $\lambda = 1$ and STOP = 0.
D. DO
    e. Calculate System_error (as in Table 6–2).
    f. If $\left(E(\mathbf{W}+\lambda\mathbf{d}) \leq E(\mathbf{W}) + \beta\lambda\left(\nabla E(\mathbf{W})^T \mathbf{d}\right)\right)$
        f1. Calculate the new gradient vector $\nabla E(\mathbf{W}+\lambda\mathbf{d})$ (as in Table 6–3)
        f2. If $\left(\nabla E(\mathbf{W}+\lambda\mathbf{d})^T \mathbf{d} < \theta\left(\nabla E(\mathbf{W})^T \mathbf{d}\right)\right)$
- If ($\lambda = 1$)
  ·· DO
    ··· $\lambda = \min(2\lambda, maxlen)$.
    ··· Calculate the new gradient vector $\nabla E(\mathbf{W}+\lambda\mathbf{d})$ (as in Table 6–3)
    ··· Calculate the new search direction $\mathbf{d}^{(+)}$.
    ··· Calculate $\nabla E(\mathbf{W}+\lambda\mathbf{d})^T \mathbf{d}^{(+)}$
    ··· If $\nabla E(\mathbf{W}+\lambda\mathbf{d})^T \mathbf{d}^{(+)} < 0$
        Calculate $\nabla E(\mathbf{W}+\lambda\mathbf{d})^T \mathbf{d}$
  WHILE (($\nabla E(\mathbf{W}+\lambda\mathbf{d})^T \mathbf{d}^{(+)} <0$)
  and ($\nabla E(\mathbf{W}+\lambda\mathbf{d})^T \mathbf{d} < \theta(\nabla E(\mathbf{W})^T \mathbf{d})$) and ($\lambda < maxlen$)).
- If ($\lambda < 1$) or (($\lambda > 1$) and $\nabla E(\mathbf{W}+\lambda\mathbf{d})^T \mathbf{d}^{(+)} \geq 0$)
  ·· DO
    ··· Calculate System_error (as in Table 6–2).
    ··· Calculate the new gradient vector $\nabla E(\mathbf{W}+\lambda\mathbf{d})$ (as in Table 6–3)
    ··· Perform backtracking using parabolic interpolation to find a new λ.
  WHILE (~ (($\nabla E(\mathbf{W}+\lambda\mathbf{d})^T \mathbf{d}^{(+)} < 0$) and $\nabla E(\mathbf{W}+\lambda\mathbf{d})^T \mathbf{d}^{(+)}$))
- Set STOP = 1.
        f3. Else
- Calculate the new gradient vector $\nabla E(\mathbf{W}+\lambda\mathbf{d})^T \mathbf{d}^{(+)}$ (as in Table 6–3)
- Calculate the new search direction $\mathbf{d}^{(+)}$.
- Calculate $\nabla E(\mathbf{W}+\lambda\mathbf{d})^T \mathbf{d}^{(+)}$
- If (($\nabla E(\mathbf{W}+\lambda\mathbf{d})^T \mathbf{d}^{(+)}) \geq 0$)
  ·· DO
    ··· Perform backtracking using parabolic interpolation to find a new λ.

–continues

Table 6–1.   *(Continued)*

     ··· Calculate the new search direction $\mathbf{d}^{(+)}$.
     ··· Calculate $\nabla E(\mathbf{W} + \lambda \mathbf{d})^T \mathbf{d}^{(+)}$
    WHILE ($\nabla E(\mathbf{W} + \lambda \mathbf{d})^T \mathbf{d}^{(+)} \geq 0$).
   · Set STOP = 1.
  g. Else If ($\lambda <$ *minlen*), set STOP = 1 and $\lambda = 0$.
  h. Else
    h1. If $\lambda = 1$, Perform backtracking using parabolic interpolation to find a new λ.
    h2. Else, Perform backtracking using cubic interpolation to find a new λ.
   WHILE (STOP = 0).
  E. Set $\lambda^* = \lambda$.
  F. Update the weight vector.
  G. Set *cn* as *cn* + 1.
WHILE (~ stopping criteria).

Table 6–2. Concurrent algorithm for calculation of system error on Cray Y-MP8/864 supercomputer.

/* Procedure System_error */
 { Parallel region—entry }
1. For $i = 1$ to N_s, do <u>concurrently</u>
  A. Initialize *sub_system_error* to zero.
  B. For $j=1$ to *chunksize*, do <u>sequentially</u>
   a. Perform feedforward procedure of the adaptive conjugate gradient learning algorithm.
   b. Calculate *sub_system_error*.
  Next *j*.
  { Guarded section—entry }
  C. Calculate the system error, $E(\mathbf{W})$, by accumulating *sub_system_error*.
  { Guarded section—end}
 Next *i*.
 {Parallel region—end}

Table 6-3. Concurrent algorithm for calculation of gradient vector on Cray Y-MP8/864 supercomputer.

/* Procedure Cal_Gradient */
  { Parallel region—entry }
1. For $i = 1$ to N_s, do <u>concurrently</u>
    A. Initialize *sub_delta_weights* to zero.
    B. For $j = 1$ to *chunksize*, do <u>sequentially</u>
       a. Perform feedforward procedure of the adaptive conjugate gradient learning algorithm.
       b. Calculate the deltas in output layer.
       c. Calculate the deltas in hidden layers. (from layer m-1 to layer 1).
       d. Calculate the *sub_delta_weights* in hidden layers (from layer m-1 to layer 1).
    Next *j*.
  { Guarded section—entry }
    C. Calculate deltas of weights by accumulating the *sub_delta_weights*.
  { Guarded section—end}
  Next *i*.
  { Parallel region—end}

---

glossary of symbols used in the algorithm is presented in Table 6–4. The basic organization of the concurrent learning algorithm is presented schematically in Figure 6–1. The concurrent algorithm has been implemented in C.

In the microtasked conjugate gradient learning algorithm, the steps of feedforward process and calculation of the system error and the deltas for each instance (steps 3 and 6 in Figure 6–1) are performed concurrently, because these are the most time-consuming portions of the algorithm. Steps 5 (calculation of the new conjugate direction) and 7 (updating the weight vector) are vectorized only. In these steps, overhead due to microtasking is large compared with the relatively small amount of the processing time required. In addition, the innermost loops in all steps are vectorized.

We have measured the speed-up of the concurrent algorithm using an expert system tool, called *atexpert* (see Section 4.2.3). The performance is also measured by the value of Mflops.

Table 6–4. The glossary of symbols for the concurrent adaptive conjugate gradient neural network learning algorithm.

i, j	loop index
cn	counter for the number of iterations
$chunksize$	$= p/N_s$; number of instances performed in each processor
d	conjugate gradient search direction
d$^{(+)}$	new conjugate gradient search direction
$E(\mathbf{W})$	system error corresponding to weight vector **W**
$E(\mathbf{W} + \lambda \mathbf{d})$	system error corresponding to weight vector $(\mathbf{W} + \lambda \mathbf{d})$
$\nabla E(\mathbf{W})$	gradient vector corresponding to weight vector **W**
$\nabla E(\mathbf{W} + \lambda \mathbf{d})$	gradient vector corresponding to weight vector $(\mathbf{W} + \lambda \mathbf{d})$
$maxlen$	acceptable maximum step length
$minlen$	acceptable minimum step length
N_s	total number of available processors
p	total number of training instances
STOP	stopping criterion parameter for the inexact line search algorithm
W	weight vector associated with links
β	$\in (0,1)$, constant used in Armijo's criterion for inexact line search algorithm
λ	trial step length in each iteration in the inexact line search algorithm
λ^*	final step length in each iteration
θ	$\in (\beta,1)$, constant used in Goldstein's criterion for inexact line search algorithm

A CONCURRENT ADAPTIVE CONJUGATE GRADIENT LEARNING ALGORITHM   107

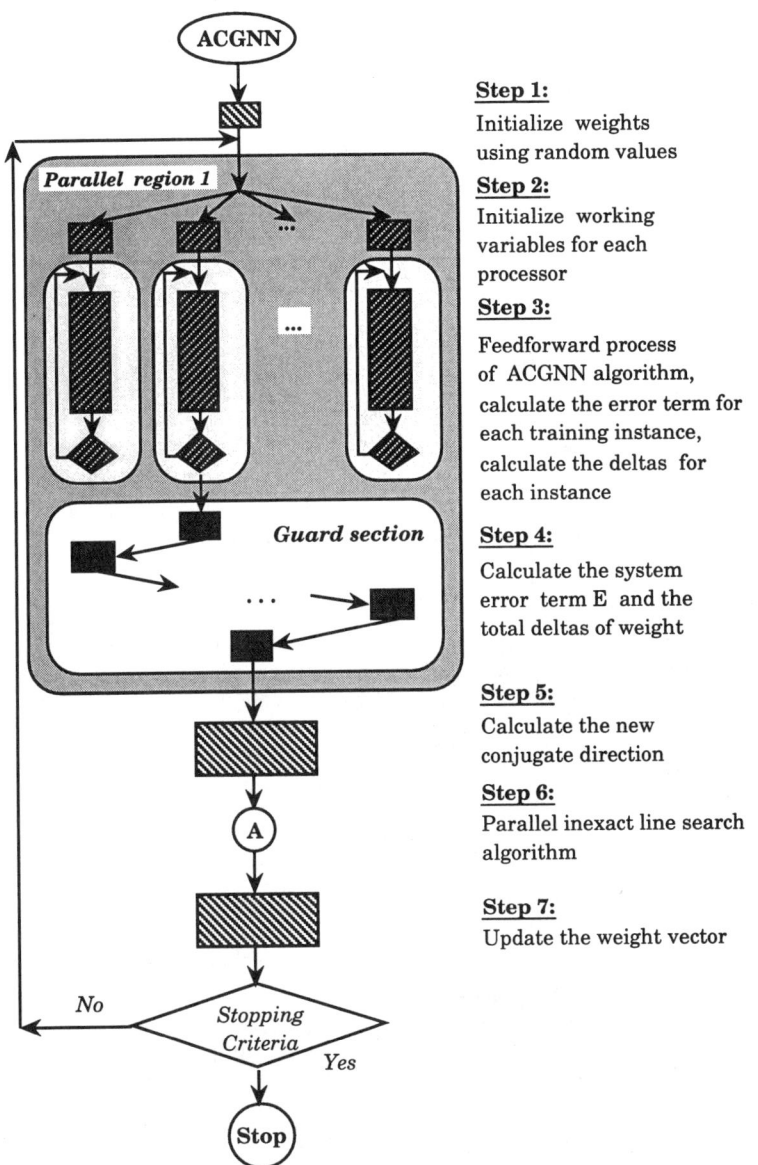

Step 1:
Initialize weights using random values

Step 2:
Initialize working variables for each processor

Step 3:
Feedforward process of ACGNN algorithm, calculate the error term for each training instance, calculate the deltas for each instance

Step 4:
Calculate the system error term E and the total deltas of weight

Step 5:
Calculate the new conjugate direction

Step 6:
Parallel inexact line search algorithm

Step 7:
Update the weight vector

Figure 6–1.   Concurrent adaptive conjugate gradient neural network learning algorithm.

–continues

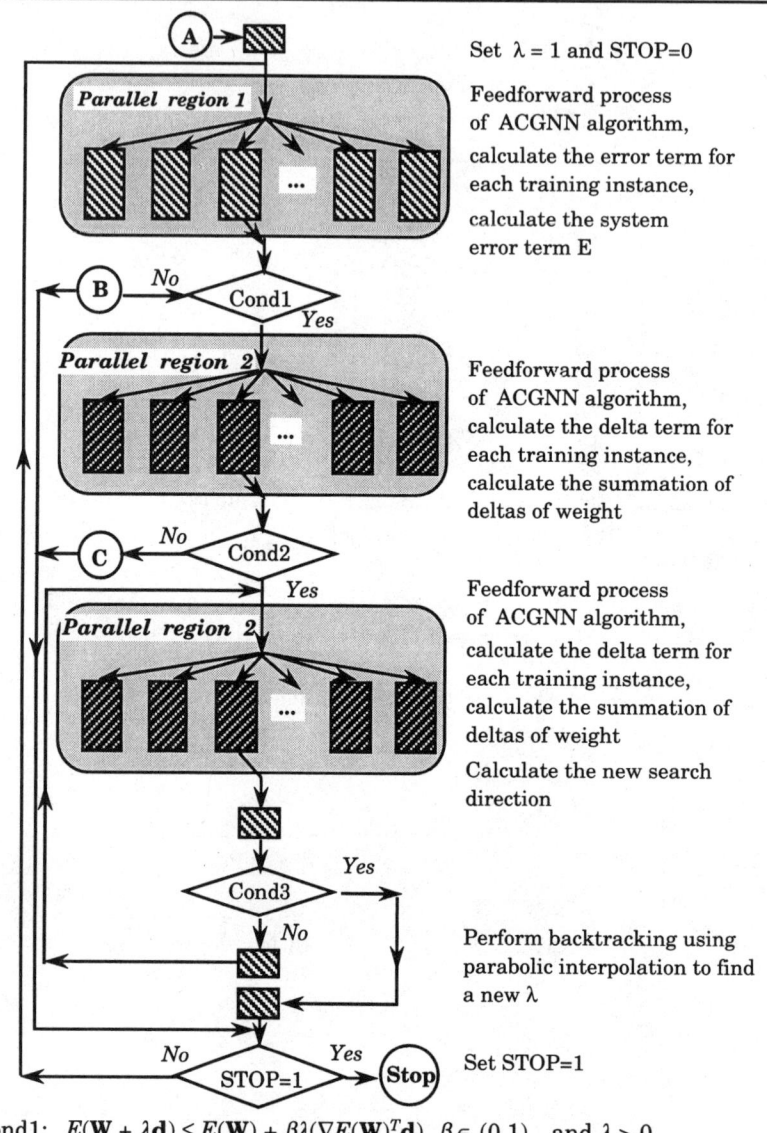

Cond1: $E(\mathbf{W} + \lambda\mathbf{d}) \leq E(\mathbf{W}) + \beta\lambda(\nabla E(\mathbf{W})^T\mathbf{d})$ $\quad \beta \in (0,1) \quad$ and $\lambda > 0$
Cond2: $\nabla E(\mathbf{W} + \lambda\mathbf{d})^T \mathbf{d} \geq \theta(\nabla E(\mathbf{W})^T\mathbf{d})$ $\quad \theta \in (\beta,1) \quad$ and $\lambda > 0$
Cond3: $\nabla E(\mathbf{W} + \lambda\mathbf{d})^T \mathbf{d}^{(+)} < 0$

Figure 6–1. *(Continued)*

A CONCURRENT ADAPTIVE CONJUGATE GRADIENT LEARNING ALGORITHM   109

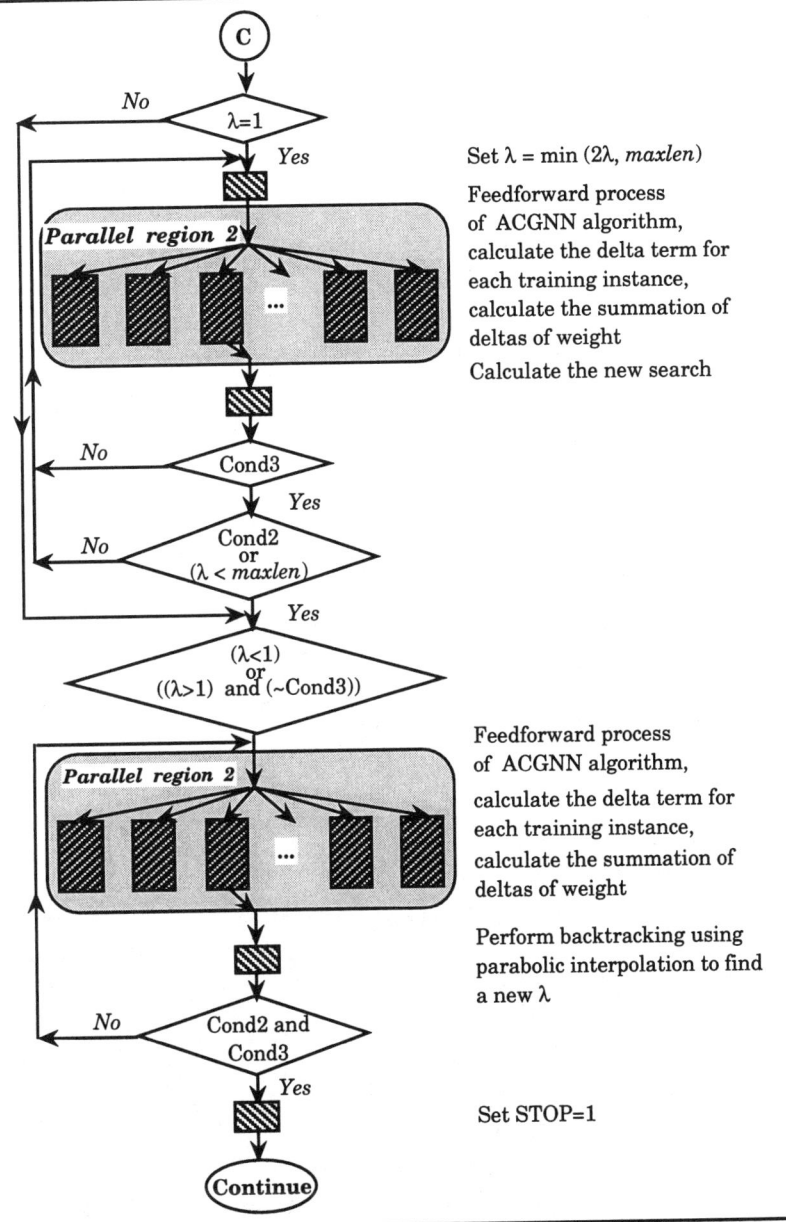

Figure 6–1.   *(Continued)*

–continues

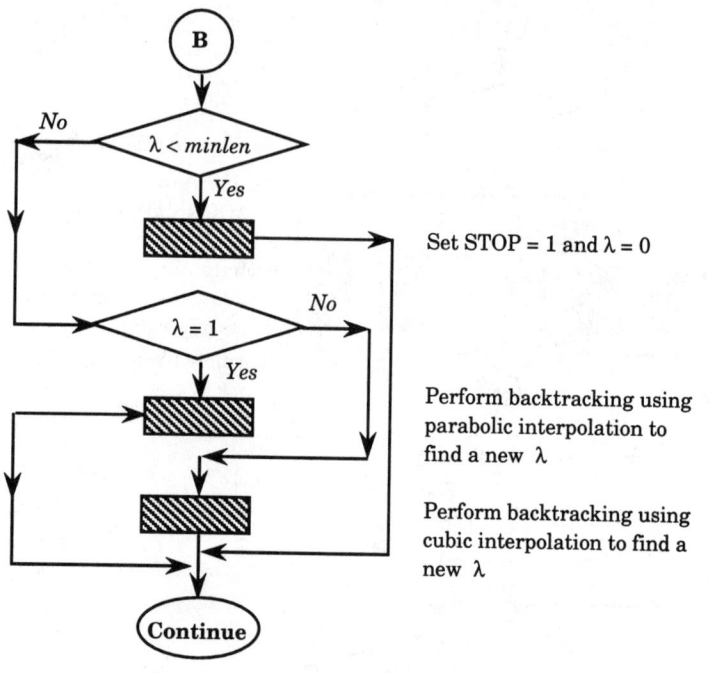

Figure 6–1. *(Continued)*

6.3 APPLICATIONS

We apply the concurrent adaptive conjugate gradient neural network learning algorithm to the domain of image recognition. Two examples are presented: one for face identification and one for image compression.

Example 1—Face Recognition

This example is an image recognition problem, that is, to recognize an 8-bit gray-scale (256 gray levels) of the image known as Lenna image in the literature (Figure 6–2). The gray-scale image (384×384 pixels) is given as a training set to the feedforward neural network. The neural network is trained to regenerate the given Lenna image.

Figure 6–2.   The 8-bit gray-scale (256 levels) Lenna image.

Each training instance is an eight by eight (8×8) square image (Figure 6–3). Thus, the 384×384 pixel Lenna image is decomposed into 2304 training instances used to train the feedforward neural network. The reason to use an 8×8 pixel as a training instance is to balance the size of the neural network and the total number of training instances for maximum processing efficiency. It is possible to decompose the original 384×384 pixel Lenna image into larger square images and reduce the total number of training instances. For instance, it can be decomposed into 576 training instances, each being a sixteen by sixteen (16×16) square image. In this case, however, a very large-scale neural network with 65,792 links is required to train this example. The results would be an unacceptably slow convergence rate and an inordinate amount of computer processing time.

112 MACHINE LEARNING

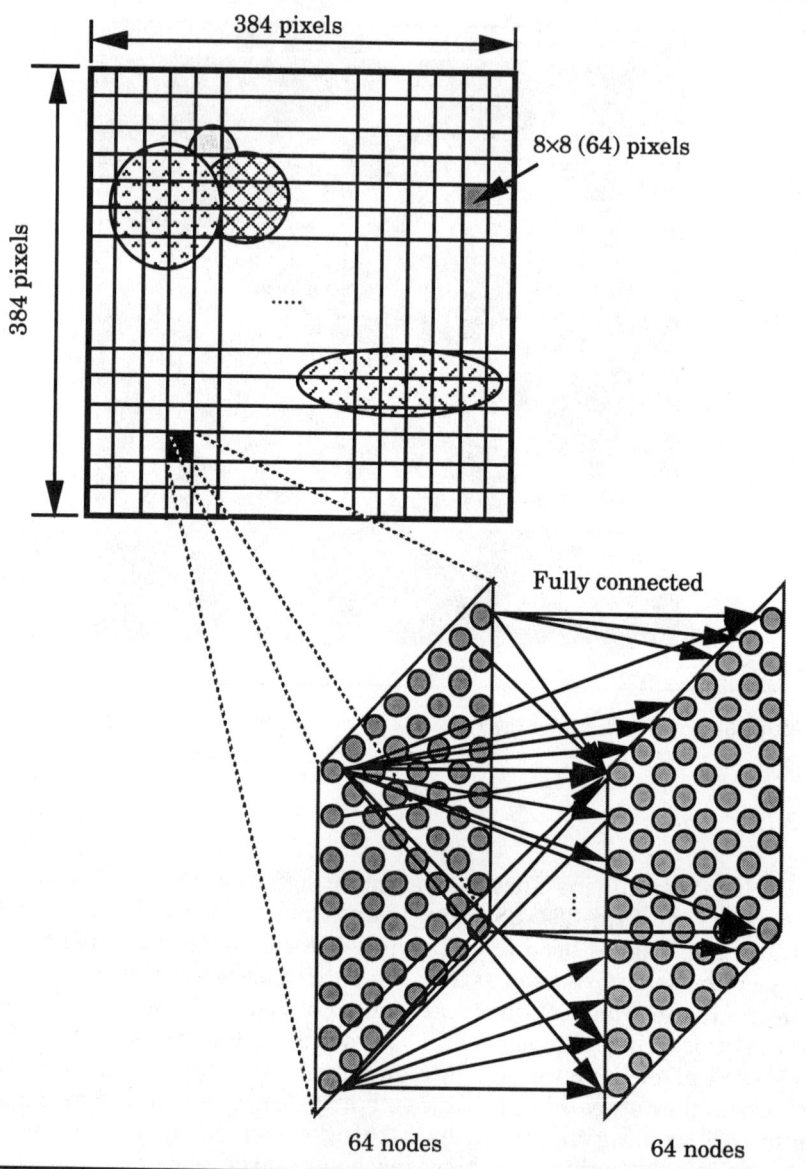

Figure 6–3. Two-layer neural network for the face recognition and image compression problems.

A flat (two-layer) neural network is used to learn this example (Figure 6–3). The number of nodes in both input and output layer is 64. The total number of links in this two-layer neural network is 4160, which is equal to the number of decision variables in the corresponding optimization problem. The learning and momentum ratios for the momentum BP learning algorithm are chosen as 0.001 and 0.001, respectively. The total number of iterations for learning process is limited to 300 for both the adaptive conjugate gradient and momentum BP neural network learning algorithms.

Example 2—Image Compression

This example is also an image recognition problem—to compress the 8-bit gray-scale (256 gray levels) Lenna image into a bitmap (bilevel) Lenna image (Figure 6–4). The gray-scale image training instances of

Figure 6–4.   The bilevel bitmap Lenna image.

Example 1 are used as a training set in the feedforward neural network. In this example, the neural network is trained to regenerate a bilevel (black and white) Lenna image by compression of the gray-scale image using the threshold method. In this method, a gray-scale image is transferred to a bilevel image pixel by pixel. For each pixel, if the value of gray-scale (between 0 and 1) is greater than a given constant threshold value, it is converted to one (black). Otherwise, it is converted to zero (white). Examples 1 and 2 have the same input patterns, but different output patterns. The output pattern for example 1 is a gray-scale image. On the other hand, the output pattern in example 2 is a bilevel image.

Similar to example 1, the 384×384 pixel Lenna image has been decomposed into 2304 training instances. Each training instance is also an eight by eight (8×8) square image. The same topology of the two-layer neural network was used in this example (Figure 6–3). The total number of iterations for the learning process in this example is limited to 200 for both the adaptive conjugate gradient and momentum BP neural network learning algorithms.

6.4 LEARNING RESULTS

6.4.1 Convergence History

Example 1

This example was solved using both the concurrent adaptive conjugate gradient neural network (ACGNN) learning and momentum BP learning algorithms on Cray Y-MP8/864 supercomputer. The system error for this example using the momentum BP algorithm with the values of $\lambda = 0.001$ and $\alpha = 0.001$ (the best of various values we tried), and the adaptive conjugate gradient neural network learning algorithm, are shown in Figure 6–5. The adaptive conjugate gradient neural network learning algorithm regenerated the Lenna image with a system error of 0.5 after 100 iterations. The momentum BP learning algorithm regenerated the Lenna image with the same system error after 289 iterations. The regenerated gray-scale Lenna images using the adaptive conjugate gradient neural network algorithm and the momentum BP algorithm after 300 iterations are presented in Figures 6–6 and 6–7, respectively.

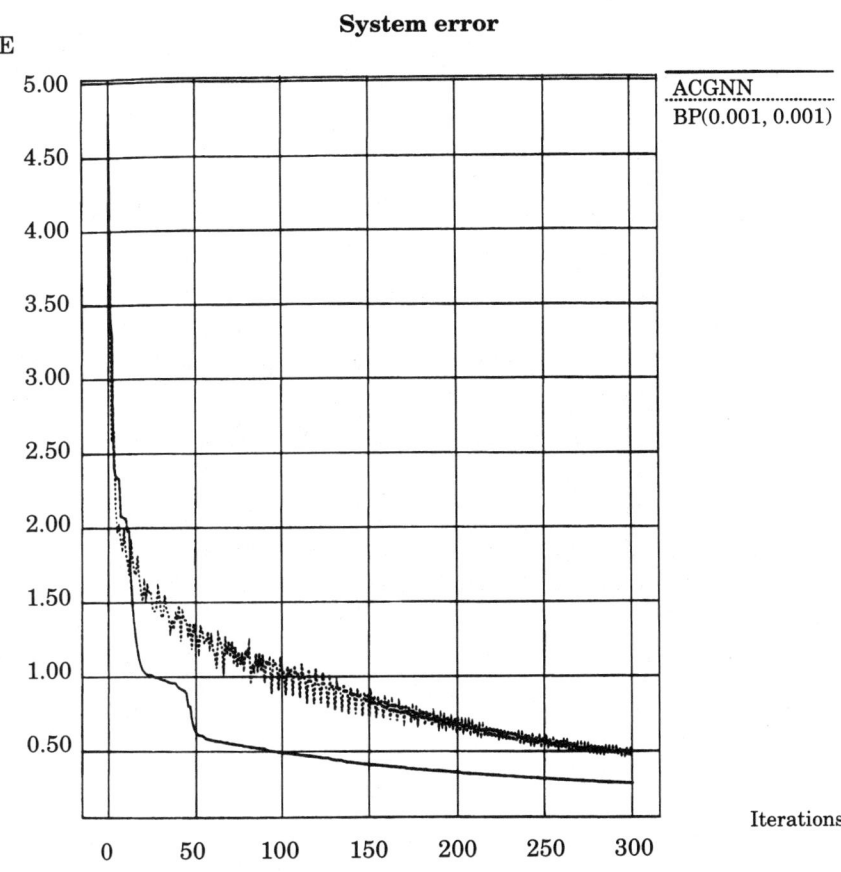

Figure 6–5. System error for the face recognition problem.

Figure 6–6. Gray-scale Lenna image regenerated by the concurrent adaptive conjugate gradient neural network learning algorithm.

Figure 6–7. Gray-scale Lenna image regenerated by the concurrent momentum BP learning algorithm with the pair of ($\lambda = 0.001$, $\alpha = 0.001$).

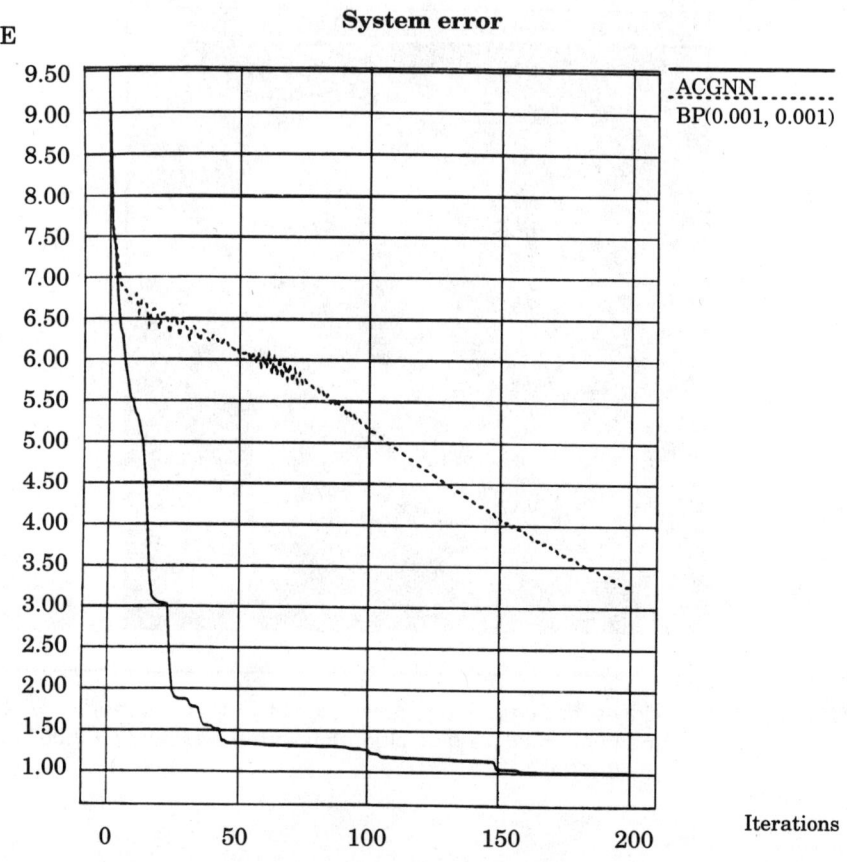

Figure 6–8. System error for the image compression problem.

Example 2

This example was also solved using both the concurrent adaptive conjugate gradient neural network learning algorithm and the concurrent momentum BP learning algorithm. The system error for this example using the momentum BP algorithm with the values of $\lambda = 0.001$ and $\alpha = 0.001$ (the best of various values we tried), and the adaptive conjugate gradient neural network learning algorithm, are shown in Figure 6–8. The adaptive conjugate gradient neural network learning algorithm regenerated the bilevel Lenna image with a system error of 3.25 after 18 iterations. The momentum BP learning algorithm regenerated the bilevel Lenna image with the same system error after 200 iterations. After 200 iterations, the regenerated bilevel Lenna images using the adaptive conjugate gradient neural network algorithm and the momentum BP algorithm are presented in Figures 6–9 and 6–10, respectively.

Figure 6–9. Bilevel Lenna image regenerated by the concurrent adaptive conjugate gradient neural network learning algorithm.

120   MACHINE LEARNING

Figure 6–10.   Bilevel Lenna image regenerated by the concurrent momentum BP learning algorithm with the pair $\lambda = 0.001$ and $\alpha = 0.001$.

6.4.2   Speed-up and the Value of Mflops

A large-scale neural network has been used for Examples 1 and 2 with 4160 links and 2304 training instances. They would require days of CPU time to converge on a serial workstation. Hence, they were solved on a Cray Y-MP8/864 supercomputer using concurrent algorithms. The speed-ups achieved in Examples 1 and 2 using the concurrent adaptive conjugate gradient neural network learning algorithm are presented in Figure 6–11. The speed-ups achieved in Examples 1 and 2 due to combined vectorization and microtasking are presented in Figure 6–12. Using eight processors, the average speed-up in Examples 1 and 2 due

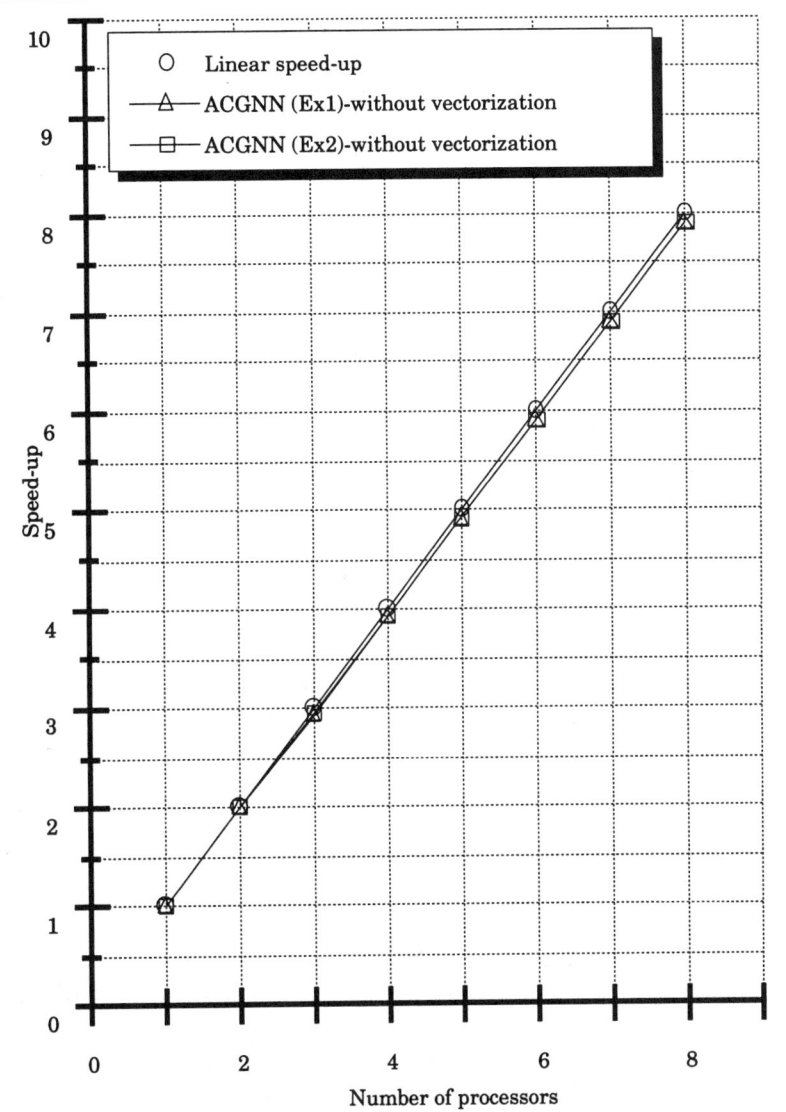

Figure 6–11. Speed-up of the problems of face recognition (Example 1) and image compression (Example 2) using the concurrent adaptive conjugate gradient neural network learning algorithm without vectorization (The curves for the two examples practically coincide).

122 MACHINE LEARNING

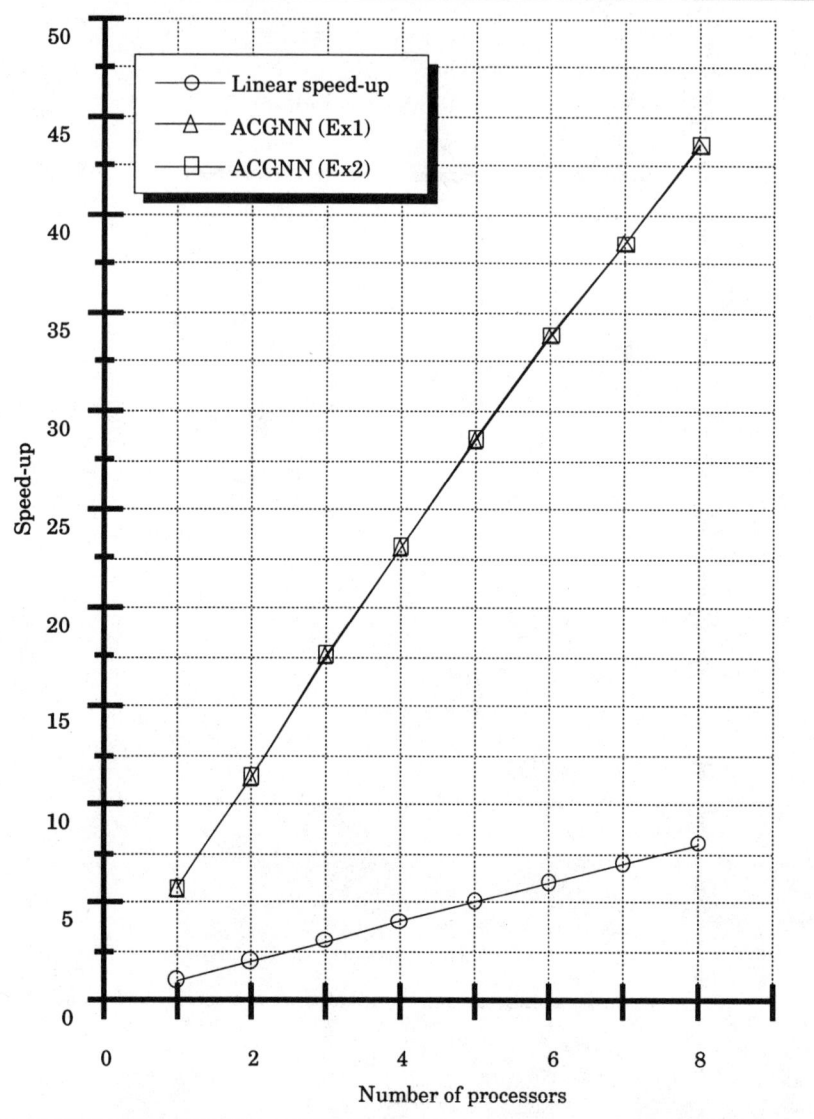

Figure 6–12. Speed-up of the problems of face recognition (Example 1) and image compression (Example 2) using the concurrent adaptive conjugate gradient neural network learning algorithm with vectorization (The curves for the two examples practically coincide).

to microtasking only is about 7.9. A maximum average speed-up of about 44 is achieved when microtasking is combined with vectorization.

The performance achieved in vectorizing the adaptive conjugate gradient neural network learning algorithm using a single processor is measured in terms of Mflops. We achieved a performance of about 130 and 136 Mflops for examples 1 and 2, respectively.

6.5 CONCLUDING REMARKS

A concurrent adaptive conjugate gradient neural network learning algorithm was presented in this chapter. The learning algorithm was applied to the domain of image recognition. The performance of the algorithm was evaluated by applying it to two large-scale training examples. The following observations are made and conclusions drawn:

1. The synchronization section in the concurrent adaptive conjugate gradient neural network learning algorithm is reduced to a small portion. Thus, a high degree of parallelization is achieved. Using eight processors we achieved a speed-up of 7.9 for a large training example (2304 training instances) with 4160 links due to microtasking only.
2. A vector MIMD machine such as Cray Y-MP8/864 provides a more effective environment for achieving maximum performance than parallel machines without vectorization capability. When vectorization was combined with microtasking, a combined speed-up of about 44 was achieved in the examples with 4160 links.

CHAPTER 7

A Concurrent Hybrid Genetic/Neural Network Learning Algorithm for MIMD Shared Memory Machines

7.1   INTRODUCTION

In order to improve the learning performance of neural network learning algorithms, so far we have explored two different approaches. One approach is the development of more effective neural network learning algorithms and the other is the development of learning algorithms on general-purpose parallel computers with the objective of reducing the overall computing time. In the first approach, we presented an adaptive conjugate gradient neural network learning algorithm and applied it to the domains of engineering design and image recognition in Chapter 5.

In the second approach, we presented concurrent backpropagation neural network learning algorithms and a concurrent adaptive conjugate gradient neural network learning algorithm employing the vectorization and microtasking capabilities of vector MIMD machines in Chapters 4, and 6, respectively.

In this chapter, we present a concurrent hybrid learning algorithm by integrating a genetic algorithm with the concurrent adaptive conjugate gradient neural network learning algorithm presented in Chapter 6. The algorithm has been implemented in C on an MIMD machine (Cray

Y-MP8/864 supercomputer). The concurrent hybrid learning algorithm has been applied to two different domains, engineering design and image recognition. Three examples have been used to test the learning performance of the hybrid concurrent learning algorithm.

7.2 GENETIC ALGORITHMS

7.2.1 GA Abstraction

For solution of optimization problems, genetic algorithms have been investigated recently and shown to be effective at exploring a large and complex space in an adaptive way, guided by the equivalent biological evolution mechanisms of reproduction, crossover, and mutation (Goldberg; 1989, Belew, McInerney, and Schrandolph, 1990; Adeli and Cheng, 1993, 1994).

For solution to an optimization problem, five components are required in a genetic algorithm:

1. **Encoding.** This is a way of encoding the decision variables of the optimization problem in a string of binary digits (1's and 0's) called a *chromosome*. If there are m decision variables in an optimization problem and each decision variable is encoded as an n-digit binary number, then a chromosome is a string of $n \times m$ binary digits.
2. **Evaluation or Objective Function.** This function is used to evaluate the given decision variables and return a value. The value of a chromosome's objective function is a fitness of that chromosome. The fitness is used to determine the probability that this chromosome will be selected as a parent chromosome to generate new chromosomes.
3. **Initialization of the Population.** A method of initializing the population of chromosomes is needed. In general, the population of chromosomes is initialized in random.
4. **A Set of Operators to Perform Evolution between Two Consecutive Chromosome Populations.** Genetic algorithms use parent selection techniques that mimic the process of natural selection for selecting chromosomes to create a new generation, where the fittest members reproduce most often. After the parent selection, the process of crossover is applied to recombine two chromosomes and generate two new chromosomes when a random value associated to this pair is greater than a predefined crossover rate.

After the crossover operation, the operation of one-point mutation simply alters one bit in the string (chromosome) when a random value, between 0 to 1, associated to that bit is greater than a predefined mutation rate.

5. **Working Parameters.** A set of parameters is predefined to guide the genetic algorithm, such as the length of each decision variable encoded as a binary string, the number of chromosomes to be generated and operated in each generation, the crossover rate, the mutation rate, and the stopping criterion. The crossover and mutation rates are used as thresholds to determine whether the operators have to be applied to a pair of parent chromosomes or not. In general, the value of crossover and mutation rates are assigned as real numbers, between 0 and 1. The stopping criterion is predefined as the number of iterations or a tolerance value for the objective function.

By having established the five aforementioned components, denoted as $P1$ to $P5$, a genetic algorithm can be described as follows:

1. Encode the decision variables as a chromosome.
2. Initialize a population of chromosomes as the current generation using the method of initialization of population ($P3$).
3. Perform the following iterations until a stopping criterion is met:
   a. Evaluate the objective function values of the current generation population described in $P2$.
   b. Select some chromosomes in the population with the higher fitness value as parent chromosomes to reproduce a new generation of children chromosomes (parent selection in $P4$).
   c. Apply the operators of crossover and mutation ($P5$) to the parent chromosomes selected in the previous step. Operators applied to the parent are determined by random values associated with the parent as well as the predefined crossover and mutation rates defined in $P5$.
   d. Replace the entire population by the children chromosomes as the current generation.

Hoffmeister and Bäck (1991) presented genetic algorithm as an eight-tuple entity. In this work, we extend the aforementioned five components of genetic algorithm and abstract them as a nine-tuple entity:

$$GA = \left(p^0,\ I,\ \lambda,\ L,\ f,\ s,\ c,\ m,\ T\right)$$

where

$$p^0 = (a_1^0, \ldots, a_\lambda^0) = \left(\begin{bmatrix} a_{1,1} \\ \vdots \\ a_{1,L} \end{bmatrix} \cdots \begin{bmatrix} a_{\lambda,1} \\ \vdots \\ a_{\lambda,L} \end{bmatrix} \right) \in I^\lambda \quad \text{Initial population}$$

$I = \{0, 1\}^L$	Encoding of chromosomes
$\lambda \in N$	Population size
$L \in N$	Length of chromosome
$f : I \to R$	Fitness function
$s : I^\lambda \to I$	Parent-selection operation
$c : I^2 \to I^2$	Crossover operation
$m : I \to I$	Mutation operation
$T : I^\lambda \to \{0, 1\}$	Termination criterion

There are λ chromosomes in each population. The initial population of chromosomes, p^0, is generated randomly. The entity α_k^t denotes the kth chromosome in the tth generation of population, p^t. A chromosome, I, is encoded as a string of binary digits, 1's and 0's. If there are v decision variables in an optimization problem and each decision variable is

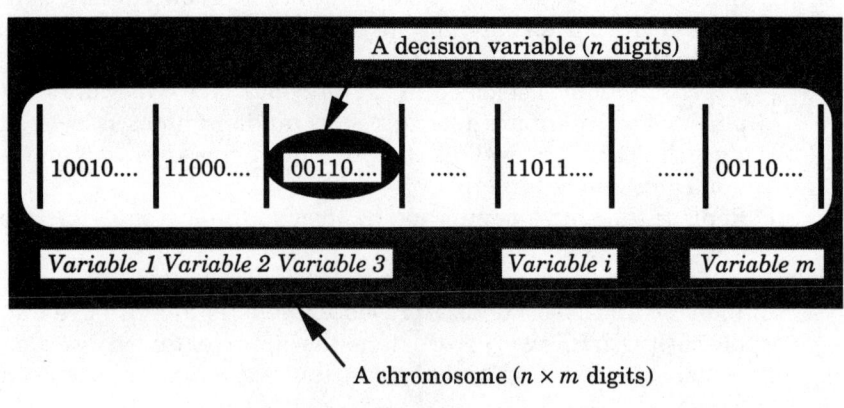

Figure 7–1. Encoding decision variables as a chromosome.

GENETIC/NEURAL NETWORK LEARNING ALGORITHM 131

encoded as an n-digit binary number, then a chromosome is a string of $L = v \times n$ binary digits (Figure 7–1) and represented as a column vector $[a_{k,1}, ..., a_{k,L}]^T$. The term $g : X \rightarrow Y$ denotes a function g maps x to y where $x \in X$ and $y \in Y$. Variables N and R are sets of integer and real numbers, respectively. The evolution process of genetic algorithm is continued ($T = 0$) until one of the termination criteria is met ($T = 1$).

7.2.2 Parent Selection

The parent selection operation, s, produces an intermediate population $p'^t = (a_1'^t, ..., a_\lambda'^t)$ from the population $p^t = (a_1^t, ..., a_\lambda^t)$ in the tth generation. Any $a_i'^t = a_q^t = s(p^t)$ in p'^t is selected by a given random real number a_i satisfying the following condition:

$$0 \le \alpha_i \le \sum_{j=1}^{\lambda} f(a_j^t) \tag{7-1}$$

The index q is obtained from

$$q = \min\left\{ k \mid \forall k \in \{1,...,\lambda\}, \text{ s.t. } \alpha_i \le \sum_{k=1}^{\lambda} f(a_k^t) \right\} \tag{7-2}$$

7.2.3 Crossover Operation

For any pair of selected chromosomes in a population p^t, an associated real value, $0 \le r \le 1$, is generated randomly. If r is greater than the predefined crossover threshold, r_c, the crossover operator is applied to this pair of chromosomes. Three different crossover strategies have been applied in this work. The first one is two-point crossover, c_{tp}, that produces an intermediate population p'^t from the population p^t and is defined as:

$$\begin{aligned}\left\{\begin{matrix}a_i'^t \\ a_{(i+1)}'^t\end{matrix}\right\} &= c_{tp}\left(\left\{\begin{matrix}a_i^t \\ a_{(i+1)}^t\end{matrix}\right\}\right) \quad \forall i \in \{1,3,\cdots,2k+1,\cdots,\lambda-1\} \\ &= \left\{\begin{matrix}[a_{(i+1),1}, a_{(i+1),2}, ..., a_{(i+1),\rho_1}, a_{i,(\rho_1+1)}, ..., a_{i,\rho_2}, a_{(i+1),(\rho_2+1)}, ..., a_{(i+1),L}]^T \\ [a_{i,1}, a_{i,2}, ..., a_{i,\rho_1}, a_{(i+1),(\rho_1+1)}, ..., a_{(i+1),\rho_2}, a_{i,(\rho_2+1)}, ..., a_{i,L}]^T\end{matrix}\right.\end{aligned} \tag{7-3}$$

where $1 \le \rho_1 < \rho_2 \le L$. In this crossover strategy, two positions in a pair of chromosomes are selected. The pair of chromosomes is divided into three sub-chromosomes by these two points and crossed over to each other by swapping the first and third sub-chromosomes.

The second crossover strategy is multi-point crossover, c_{mp}, that produces an intermediate population p'^t from the population p^t and is defined as:

$$\begin{Bmatrix} a_i^{'t} \\ a_{(i+1)}^{'t} \end{Bmatrix} = c_{mp}\left(\begin{Bmatrix} a_i^t \\ a_{(i+1)}^t \end{Bmatrix}\right) \quad \forall i \in \{1, 3, \cdots, 2k+1, \cdots, \lambda - 1\}$$

$$= \bigcup_{k=1}^{L} \left\{ \begin{bmatrix} a_{i,k} \\ a_{(i+1),k} \end{bmatrix}, \text{ if } \rho_k \geq \rho_{mp} \right) \vee \left(\begin{bmatrix} a_{(i+1),k} \\ a_{i,k} \end{bmatrix}, \text{ if } r_k < r_{mp} \right) \right\} \quad (7\text{-}4)$$

where $0 \leq \rho_k, \rho_{mp} \leq 1$. In this crossover strategy, more than one crossover point is selected in a pair of chromosomes. The crossover operator is performed in bit level (allele in a chromosome). That is, the process of crossover is performed bit by bit. The numbers of crossover points and crossover positions in each pair of chromosomes are selected randomly, distinctly from each other.

The third crossover strategy is uniform crossover, c_{un}, that produces an intermediate population p'^t from the population p^t. First, a mask, a binary array with length L, is generated. L real values, $0 \leq r_j \leq 1$, ($j = 1, 2, \ldots, L$), are generated randomly. If the jth random number, r_j, is greater than or equal to the predefined threshold value, r_{ma}, the value of the jth element in the binary array is set as 1. Otherwise, it is set as 0. The mask, ma, is defined as:

$$ma = \bigcup_{j=1}^{L} \left\{ ([1], \text{ if } r_j \geq \rho_{ma}) \vee ([0], \text{ if } r_j < \rho_{ma}) \right\} \quad (7\text{-}5)$$

The uniform crossover is defined as:

$$\begin{Bmatrix} a_i^{'t} \\ a_{(i+1)}^{'t} \end{Bmatrix} = c_{un}\left(\begin{Bmatrix} a_i^t \\ a_{(i+1)}^t \end{Bmatrix}\right) \quad \forall i \in \{1, 3, \cdots, 2k+1, \cdots, \lambda - 1\}$$

$$= \bigcup_{k=1}^{L} \left\{ \begin{bmatrix} a_{i,k} \\ a_{(i+1),k} \end{bmatrix}, \text{ if } ma_k = 0 \right) \vee \left(\begin{bmatrix} a_{(i+1),k} \\ a_{i,k} \end{bmatrix}, \text{ if } ma_k = 1 \right) \right\} \quad (7\text{-}6)$$

Similar to the multi-point crossover strategy, the process of uniform crossover is performed bit by bit in a pair of chromosomes. In the uniform crossover strategy, the crossover positions are predefined in a mask. All chromosomes in a population are crossed over in the same positions. On the other hand, in the multi-point crossover strategy, each pair of chromosomes are crossed over at different points because no predefined mask is used. Three aforementioned crossover operators are shown schematically in Figure 7–2.

7.2.4 Mutation Operation

For any chromosome in a population p^t, an associated real value, $0 \le r \le 1$, is generated randomly. If r is less than the predefined mutation threshold, r_m, the mutation operator is applied to this chromosome. The mutation operator simply alters one bit from 0 to 1 (or 1 to 0) in a chromosome. As the mutation operator is not guided by the fitness (objective) function, the result of mutation operator can make an instant change between two successive generations. The operator of mutation, m, produces an intermediate population p'' from the population p^t and is defined as:

$$a_i^{'t} = m(a_i^t) \qquad \forall i \in \{1,...,\lambda\}$$

$$a'_{i,k} = \begin{cases} a_{i,k} & \text{for } k \in \{1,2,\cdots,p-1,p+1,\cdots,L\} \\ \overline{a}_{i,k} & \text{for } k = p \end{cases} \qquad (7\text{-}7)$$

where $1 \le p < L$.

By having established the five aforementioned components, a genetic algorithm can be described as follows:

Step 1. Encode the decision variables as a chromosome (Figure 7–1).

Step 2. Initialize a population of chromosomes as current generation randomly.

Step 3. Perform the following steps until one of the stopping criteria is met:

Step 3-1. Evaluate the fitness (objective) function values of the current generation population.

Step 3-2. Select chromosomes in the population with the higher fitness value as parent chromosomes to reproduce a new generation of children chromosomes.

Step 3-3. Apply the operators of two-point, multi-point, or uniform crossover and one-point mutation to the chil-

134 MACHINE LEARNING

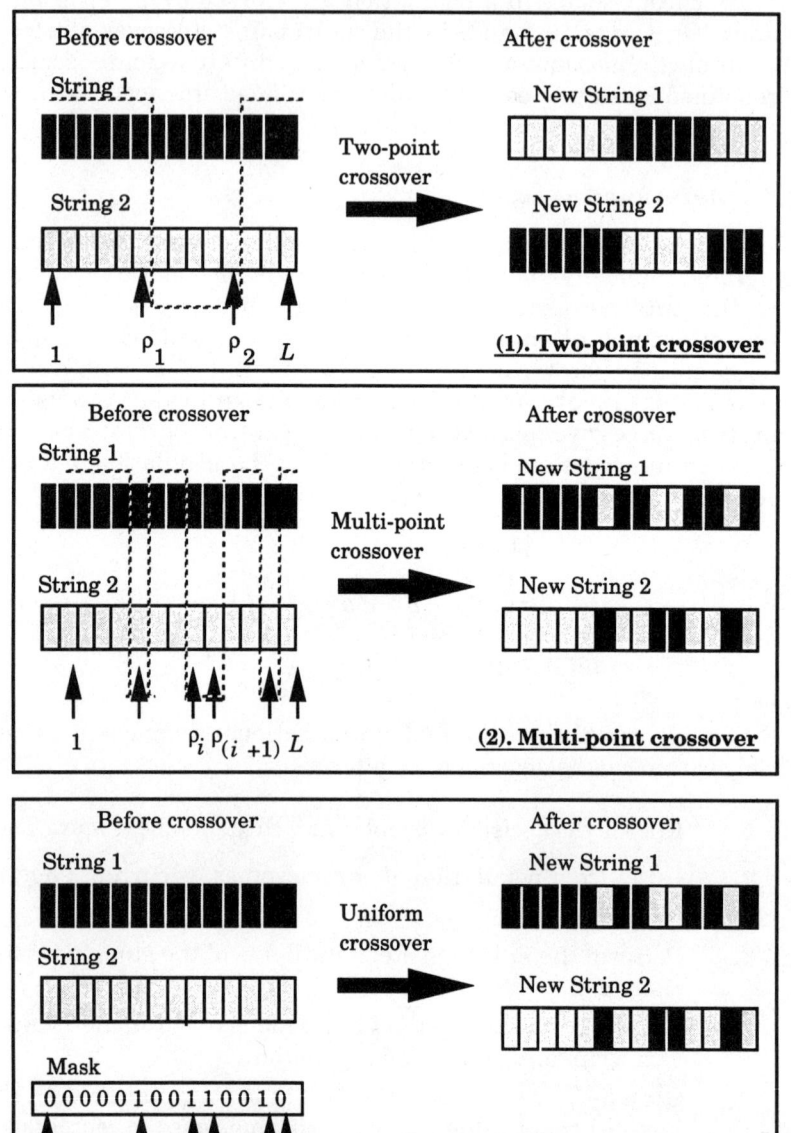

Figure 7–2. Two-point, multi-point, and uniform crossovers.

dren chromosomes selected in the previous step. Operators applied to the children are determined by random values associated to the children as well as the predefined crossover and mutation rates.

Step 3-4. Replace the entire population by the children chromosomes as the current generation. Go to step 3.

7.3   A HYBRID NEURAL NETWORK LEARNING ALGORITHM

A hybrid learning algorithm using genetic algorithm with adaptive conjugate gradient multilayer neural networks is presented in Figure 7–3. It consists of two learning stages. The first learning stage is used to accelerate the whole learning process by using a genetic algorithm with the feedforward step of the adaptive conjugate gradient neural network (ACGNN) learning algorithm. The genetic algorithm performs global search and seeks a near-optimal initial point (weight vector) for the second stage. In this stage, each chromosome is used to encode the weights of neural network. The fitness (objective) function for the genetic algorithm is defined as the average squared system error of the corresponding neural network. Therefore, it becomes an unconstrained optimization problem: Find a set of decision variables minimizing the objective function. The best fitness function value in a population is defined as the smallest value of the objective function in the current population.

The process of global search using genetic algorithm is schematically presented in Figure 7–4. Consider three consecutive generations, t1, t2, and t3. The chromosomes in t1 generation perform local search in some discrete domain. After applying the crossover and mutation operators to the t1 generation, the chromosomes with lower fitness function are selected as the parents, the chromosomes with higher fitness function are discarded, some new chromosomes are generated via the selected parent chromosomes, and the t1 generation is replaced by the new population of chromosomes called t2 generation. In the t2 generation, the chromosomes perform local search in a larger domain than the t1 generation, and approach some local minimums with lower fitness function values. In the t3 generation, the chromosomes with lower fitness function in the t2 generation are selected, and new chromosomes are generated that cover the whole bounded domain. In this last gen-

136 MACHINE LEARNING

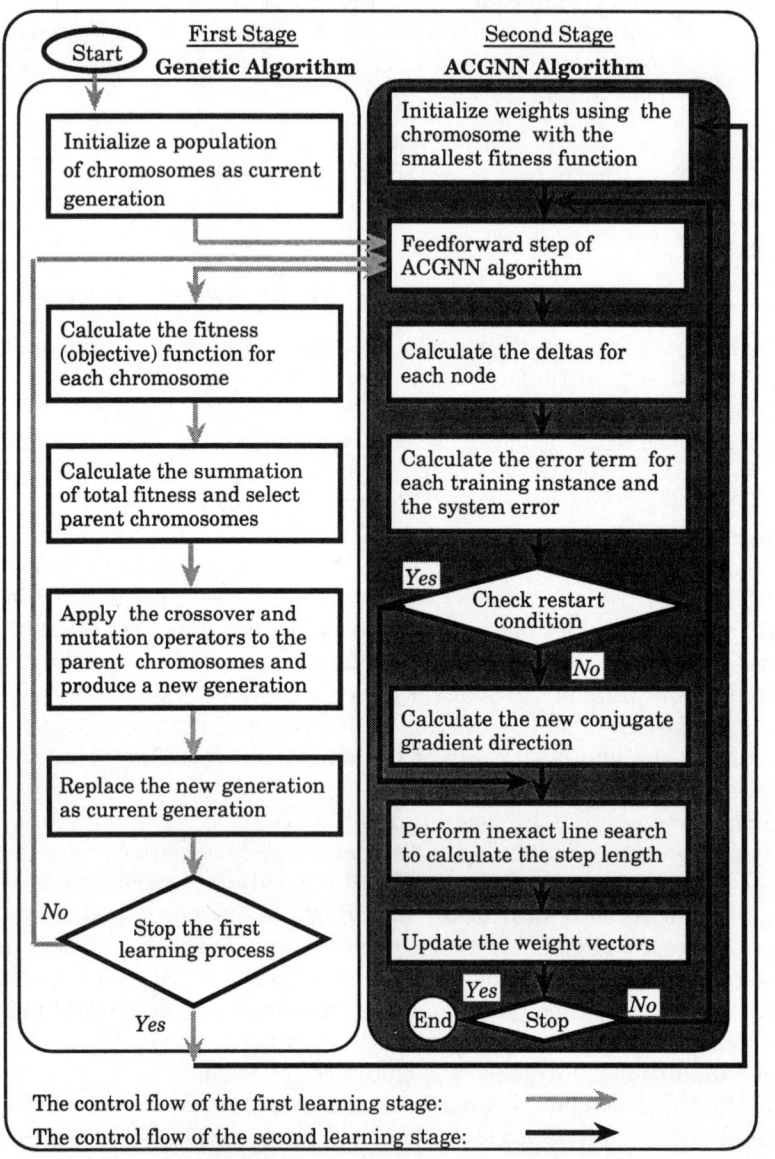

Figure 7-3. A hybrid learning algorithm using a genetic algorithm with adaptive conjugate gradient neural network learning algorithm.

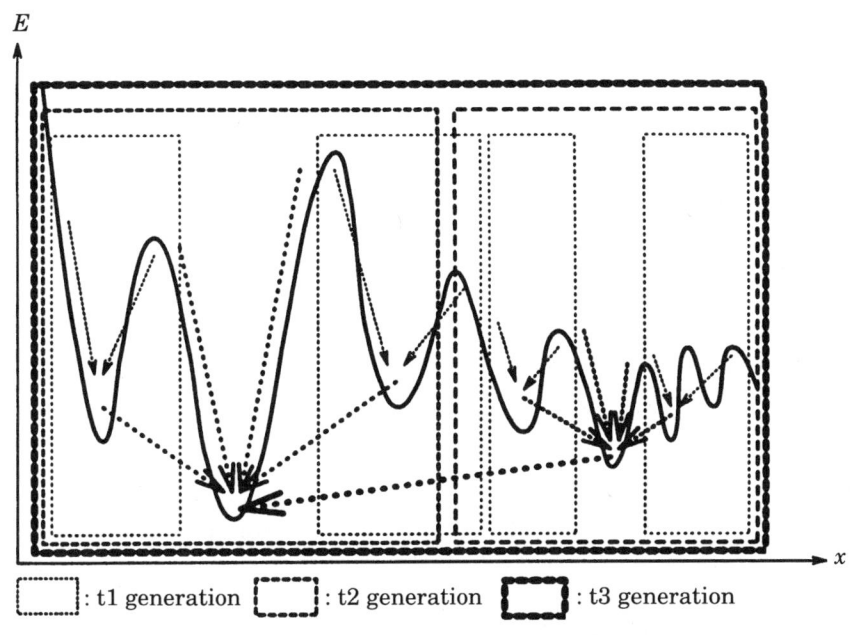

Figure 7–4. Global search using genetic algorithm.

eration, the chromosomes perform global search in the whole bounded domain and approach the global minimum in the domain.

After performing several iterations and meeting one of the stopping criteria, the first learning stage is terminated and the chromosome returning the minimum objective function (the best seed) is considered as the initial weight of the neural network in the second stage. Next, the adaptive conjugate gradient learning algorithm performs the second learning process until the terminal condition is satisfied.

In order to reduce the memory storage requirement and increase the computational efficiency, the allele (binary digit) of each chromosomes in a population is encoded as a bit rather than an integer. In this case, the length of each chromosome is equal to the length of an integer, such as 16 bits on a SUN SPARCstation. Hence, the memory storage used for each chromosome is an integer rather than a sixteen-element integer array. Since we encode the chromosome as an integer, the operations of crossover and mutation can be performed using bitwise operators that are directly performed via computer hardware.

Consider a multilayer neural network with $N[i]$ nodes in layer i. The learning problem is mapped from $N[1]$ input nodes to $N[m]$ output nodes and a number of N_s instances are given as training examples. The total number of weights and nodes are denoted by N_w and N_n, respectively. For the genetic algorithm, we assume N_p chromosomes are generated and operated on in each iteration. The operators and other features of the genetic algorithm are the same as those defined previously.

The first learning stage is a combination of the genetic algorithm with the feedforward process of the adaptive conjugate gradient learning algorithm. In each iteration of this learning stage, the chromosome with the smallest value of objective function is saved as *sub_best_chromosome* and compared with the one saved in the previous iteration, called *best_chromosome*. After the first learning stage is terminated, the *best_chromosome* is used as the initial weight vector for the second learning stage. In order to reduce redundant computations in this learning stage, three different stopping criteria are employed to terminate this learning process. If one of these three stopping criteria is met, the first learning stage is terminated:

- The smallest value of the objective functions in a population is less than the acceptable predefined value.
- The fitness ratio, defined as the value of the *best_chromosome*'s objective function to the average value of objective functions, is greater than 0.95.
- If the fitness function of the *best_chromosome* does not change in a predefined number of consecutive iterations (in this work, a value of 10 is used for this number).

The first stage of the concurrent hybrid learning algorithm is presented in Table 7–1 and shown schematically in Figure 7–5.

The second learning stage is a stand-alone adaptive conjugate gradient neural network learning algorithm (see Chapters 5 and 6). A number of N_s tasks are created and executed concurrently. The second stage of the concurrent hybrid neural network learning algorithm is presented in Table 7–2 and shown schematically in Figure 7–6. The step C, for performing inexact line search to calculate the step length, is presented in detail in Chapter 5.

Table 7–1. The first stage of the concurrent hybrid learning algorithm.

/*First Learning Stage */

1. Initialize the chromosomes randomly as current generation, initialize working parameters, and set the first chromosome as the *best_chromosome*.

   { Parallel region 1—entry }

2. For $i = 1$ to N_p, do <u>concurrently</u>

   A. Initialize *sub_total_fitness* to zero and *sub_best_chromosome* as *null*.

   B. For $j = 1$ to *chunksize*, do <u>sequentially</u>

      a. For $k = 1$ to N_s, do <u>sequentially</u>

         a.1. Perform feedforward procedure of the adaptive conjugate gradient learning algorithm.

         a.2. Calculate the objective function (system error for the neural network).

      Next *k*.

      b. Calculate the *sub_total_fitness* by accumulating objective function of each chromosome.

      c. Store the best chromosome as *sub_best_chromosome*.

   Next *j*

   { Guarded section 1—entry }

   C. Calculate the *total_fitness* by accumulating *sub_total_fitness*.

   D. Compare the *sub_best_chromosome* with each other and set the best *sub_best_chromosome* as the *best_chromosome*.

   { Guarded section 1—end}

   Next *i*

   { Parallel region 1—end }

3. DO

   { Parallel region 2—entry }

   E. For $i = 1$ to $(N_p/2)$, do <u>concurrently</u>

      d. Initialize *sub_total_fitness* to zero and *sub_best_chromosome* as *null*.

–continues

Table 7–1. *(Continued)*

---

    e. For $j = 1$ to *chunksize*, do <u>sequentially</u>

        e1. Select parents using roulette wheel parent selection.

        e2. Apply two-point, multi-point, or uniform crossovers and mutation to the parents.

        e3. For $k = 1$ to N_s, do <u>sequentially</u>

            e3.1. Perform feedforward procedure of the adaptive conjugate gradient learning algorithm to parent chromosomes.

            e3.2. Calculate the objective function (system error for the neural network) for parent chromosomes.

    Next *k*

        e4. Calculate the *sub_total_fitness* by accumulating objective function of each chromosome.

        e5. Store the best chromosome as *sub_best_chromosome*.

    Next *j*

    { Guarded section 2—entry }

    f. Calculate the *total_fitness* by accumulating *sub_total_fitness*.

    g. Compare the *sub_best_chromosome* to each other and set the best *sub_best_chromosome* as the *best_chromosome*.

    { Guarded section 2—end}

    Next *i*

    { Parallel region 2— end }

    F. Replace the old generation by the new generation.

WHILE (~stopping criteria).

GENETIC/NEURAL NETWORK LEARNING ALGORITHM 141

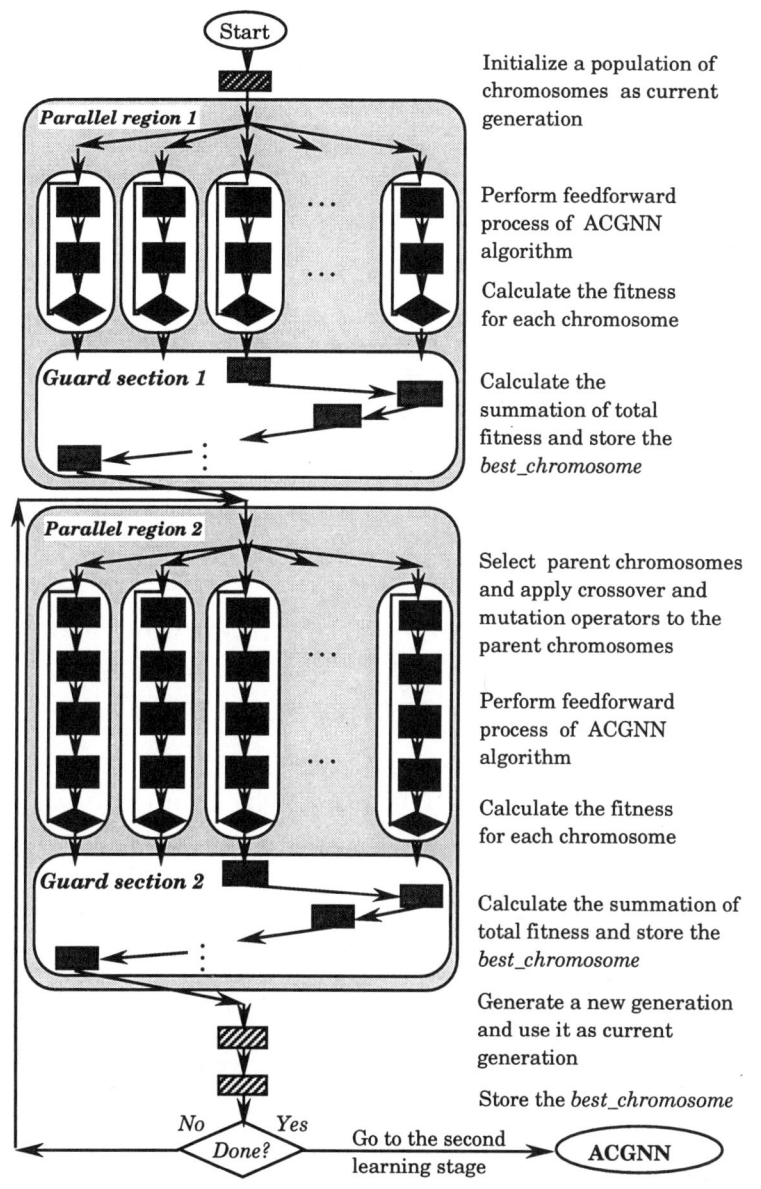

Figure 7-5. The first learning stage of the concurrent hybrid neural network learning algorithm.

Table 7–2. The second stage of the concurrent hybrid learning algorithm.

/* Second Learning Stage */

1. Set the *best_chromosome* as the initial weight vector, set up the topological structure of neural network, and set the counter *cnt* to zero.

2. DO

    { Parallel region—entry }

    A. For $i = 1$ to N_s, do <u>concurrently</u>

       a. Initialize *sub_system_error* and *sub_delta_weights* to zero.

       b. For $j = 1$ to *chunksize*, do <u>sequentially</u>

          b1. Perform feedforward procedure of the adaptive conjugate gradient learning algorithm.

          b2. Calculate *sub_system_error*.

          b3. Calculate the deltas in output layer.

          b4. Calculate the deltas in hidden layers (from layer m-1 to layer 1).

          b5. Calculate the *sub_delta_weights* in hidden layers (from layer m-1 to layer 1).

       Next *j*.

       { Guarded section—entry }

       c. Calculate the system error, *E*, by accumulating *sub_system_error*.

       d. Calculate deltas of weights by accumulating the *sub_delta_weights*.

       { Guarded section—end}

    Next *i*.

    { Parallel region—end}

    B. If $cnt \geq 1$, calculate the new conjugate gradient direction.

    C. Perform inexact line search to calculate the step length.

    D. Update the weight vector.

    E. Set *cnt* as *cnt* +1.

   WHILE (~ stop criteria).

GENETIC/NEURAL NETWORK LEARNING ALGORITHM 143

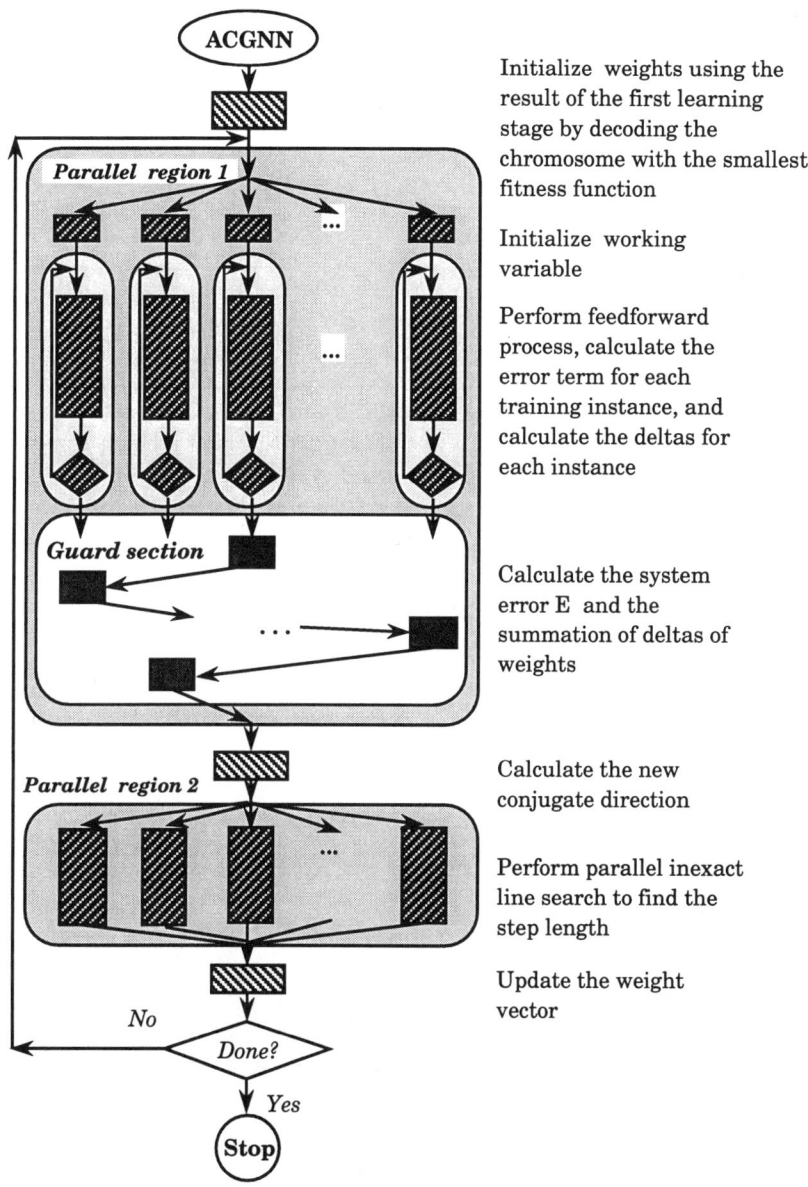

Figure 7–6. The second learning stage of the concurrent hybrid neural network learning algorithm.

144 MACHINE LEARNING

7.4 APPLICATIONS

We apply the concurrent hybrid neural network learning algorithm to two different domains: engineering design and image recognition. Three examples presented in the previous chapters are again used in this chapter, one in the domain of engineering design and two in the domain of image recognition.

Example 1—Engineering Design

This example is the same as Example 3 of Chapter 3—selection of a minimum weight steel beam from the AISC LRFD wide-flange (*W*) shape database (AISC, 1989) for a given loading condition. A four-layer feedforward neural network with two hidden layers was used to learn this problem (see Figure 3–10). In this chapter, the total number of iterations for learning process is limited to 100. The working parameters for the first stage of learning (genetic algorithm) are given as:

Population size: 4000

Length of decision variable: 16 bits

Chromosome length: 832 (52×16) bits

Crossover rate: 0.8

Mutation rate: 0.08

Range of decision variables: −5 to 5

Example 2—Image Recognition of 7×7 Binary Images of Numerals 0–9

This example is the same as Example 2 of Chapter 4—recognition of seven by seven (7×7) binary images of the numerals 0 to 9 (Figure 4–5). A three-layer neural network with one hidden layer was used to learn this problem (Figure 4–6). In this chapter, the total number of iterations for learning process is limited to 100. The working parameters for the first stage of learning (genetic algorithm) are as follows:

Population size: 250

Length of decision variable: 16 bits

Chromosome length: 95,200 (5,950×16) bits

Crossover rate: 0.8
Mutation rate: 0.08
Range of decision variables: −1 to 1

Example 3—Image Recognition (Lenna image)

This example is the same as Example 1 of Chapter 6—recognition of an 8-bit gray-scale (256 gray levels) of the Lenna image (Figure 6–2). The same flat (two-layer) neural network was used to learn this example (Figure 6–3). In this chapter, the total number of iterations for learning process is limited to 50. The working parameters for the first stage of learning (genetic algorithm) are as follows:

Population size: 250
Length of decision variable: 16 bits
Chromosome length: 66,560 (4,160×16) bits
Crossover rate: 0.9
Mutation rate: 0.095
Range of decision variables: −1 to 1

7.5   COMPUTATION RESULTS

7.5.1   Convergence History

Example 1

The system error for this example, using the adaptive conjugate gradient neural network learning algorithm and the hybrid genetic/neural network algorithm, is shown in Figure 7–7. After 12 iterations of learning process, the first learning stage of the hybrid genetic/neural network learning algorithm met one of the stopping criteria. The best fitness function value was about 0.0023. The result of the first learning stage is used as an initial weight vector in the second learning stage. After a total of 100 iterations of the learning process, the system error in the hybrid genetic/neural network learning algorithm converges to a value 7.5×10^{-5}. The stand-alone adaptive conjugate gradient neural network learning algorithm converges to 1.84×10^{-4} after 100 iterations of the learning process.

146 MACHINE LEARNING

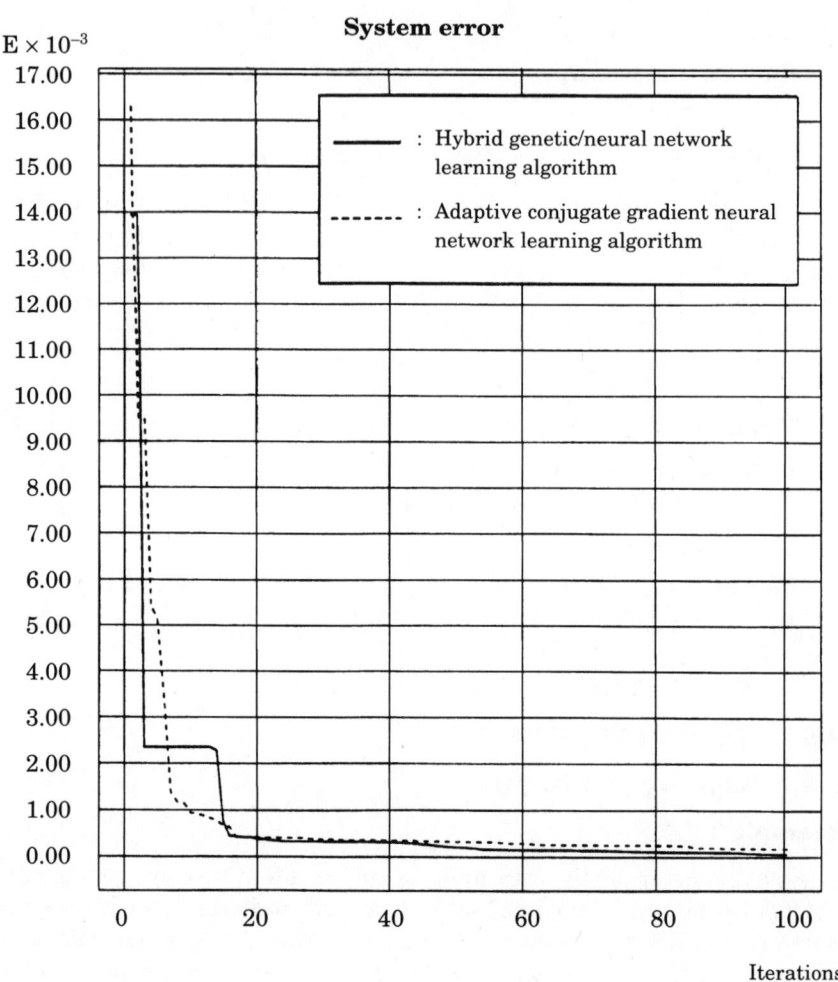

Figure 7-7. System error for the minimum weight steel beam design.

Example 2

The system error for this example, using the adaptive conjugate gradient neural network learning algorithm and the hybrid genetic/neural network learning algorithm, is shown in Figure 7-8. After 18 itera-

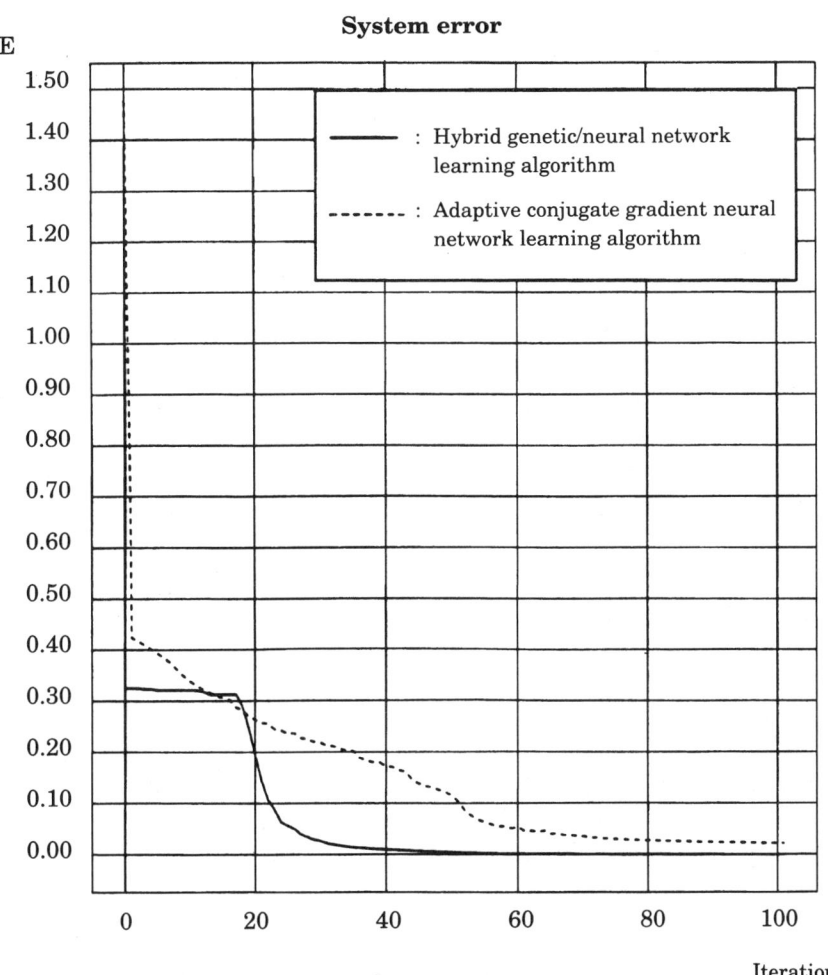

Figure 7-8. System error for the 7×7 binary image recognition of numerals 0-9.

tions, the first learning stage of the hybrid genetic/neural network learning algorithm met one of the stopping criteria. The best fitness function has a value of about 0.3. The result of the first learning stage is used as an initial weight vector for the second learning stage. After 82 more iterations, the system error in the hybrid genetic/neural network learning algorithm converges to a value of less than 0.001 and the algorithm achieves 100 percent recognition of all the 30 training instances.

After the same number of iterations, the stand-alone adaptive conjugate gradient neural network learning algorithm converges to a value of 0.017 and recognizes about 63 percent (19 out of 30) of the training set.

Example 3

The system error for this example, using the adaptive conjugate gradient neural network learning algorithm and the hybrid genetic/neural network learning algorithm, is shown in Figure 7–9. After 8 iterations of learning process, the first learning stage of the hybrid genetic/neural network learning algorithm met one of the stopping criteria. The best fitness function value was about 4.4. The result of the first learning stage is used as an initial weight vector for the second learning stage. After 42 more iterations, the system error in the hybrid genetic/neural network learning algorithm converges to a value of 0.10. The stand-alone adaptive conjugate gradient neural network learning algorithm converges to a value of 0.15 after 50 iterations.

7.5.2 Speed-up

The speed-up is measured by using an expert system tool, called *atexpert* (see Section 4.2.3). A neural network with 52 links is used in Example 1. In the first learning stage of the concurrent hybrid genetic/neural network learning algorithm, 4000 chromosomes are operated on in each learning iteration. That is, 4000 tasks are created and performed concurrently in this stage. Each concurrent task performs the computation of a stand-alone neural network with 10 training instances. The overall speed-up achieved by the concurrent hybrid genetic/neural network learning algorithm for Example 1 is dominated by the first learning stage. As the genetic algorithm is an intrinsically parallel algorithm, the maximum speed-up of Example 1 due to microtasking is about 7.9, using eight processors of the Cray Y-MP8/864 supercomputer (Figure 7–10). A maximum average speed-up of about 9 is achieved when microtasking is combined with vectorization using eight processors of the Cray machine (Figure 7–11). In this example, the value of speed-up due to a combination of microtasking and vectorization is not high, because the loop performed by vector operation is short.

GENETIC/NEURAL NETWORK LEARNING ALGORITHM 149

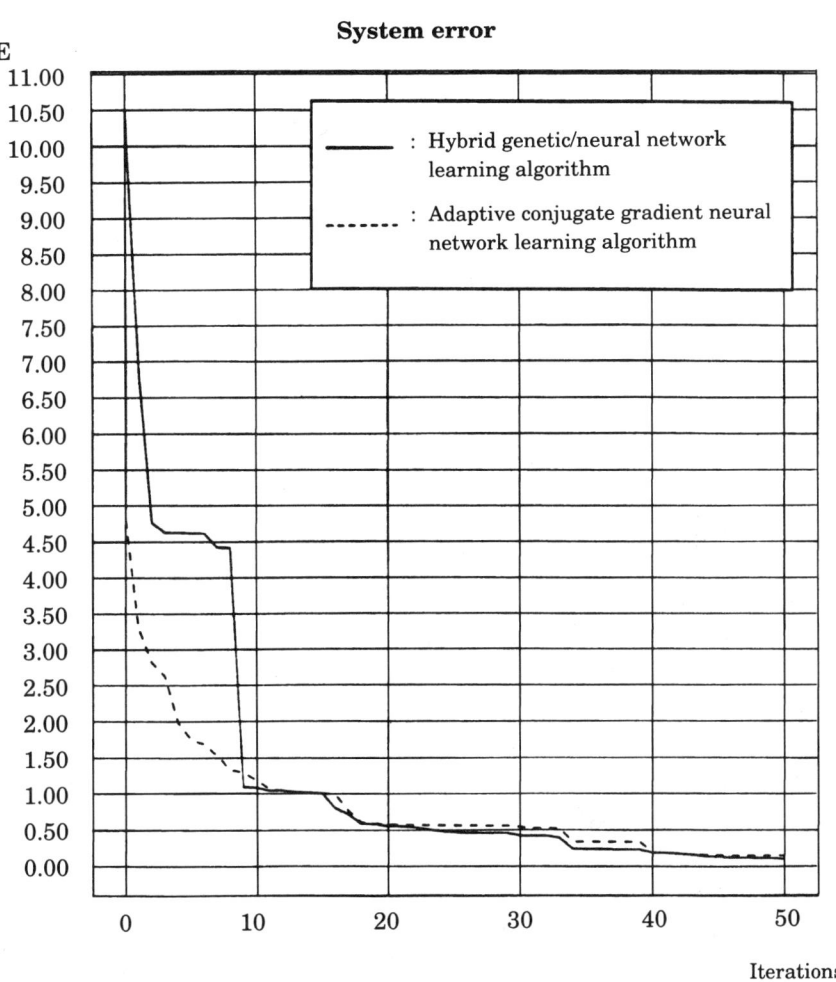

Figure 7-9. System error for the Lenna image recognition problem.

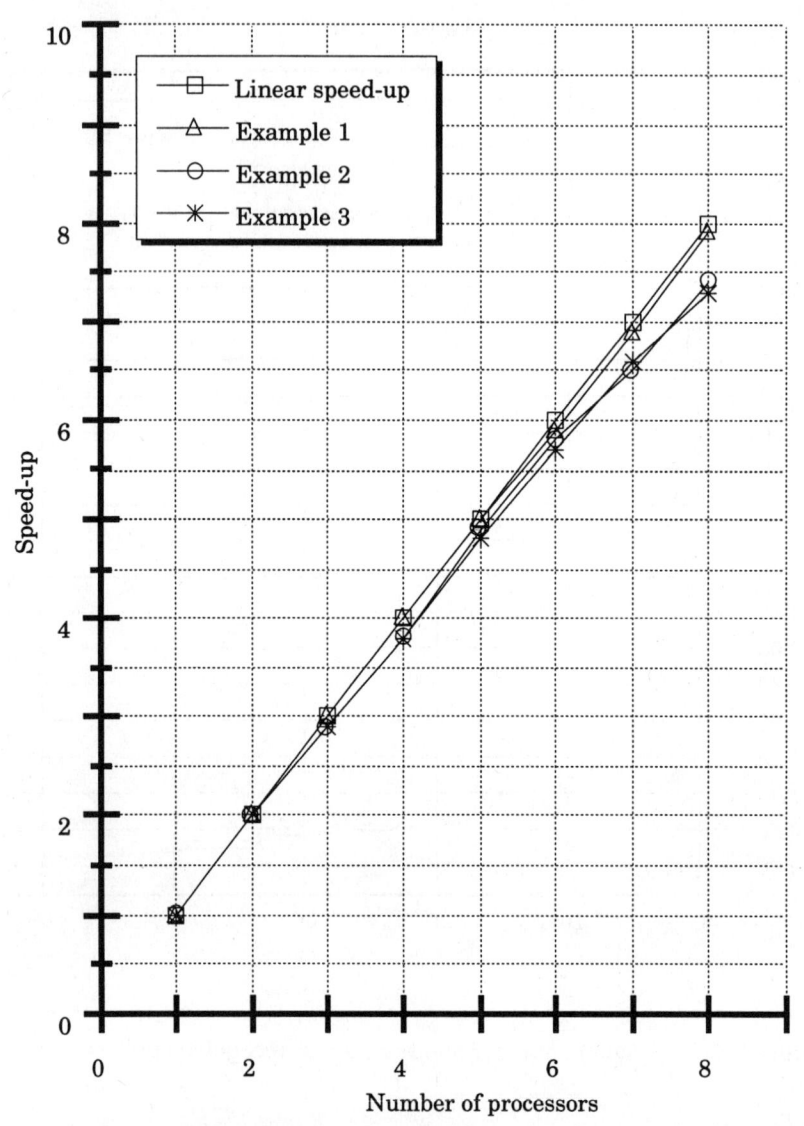

Figure 7–10. Speed-up for Examples 1, 2, and 3 using the concurrent hybrid genetic/neural network learning algorithm without vectorization.

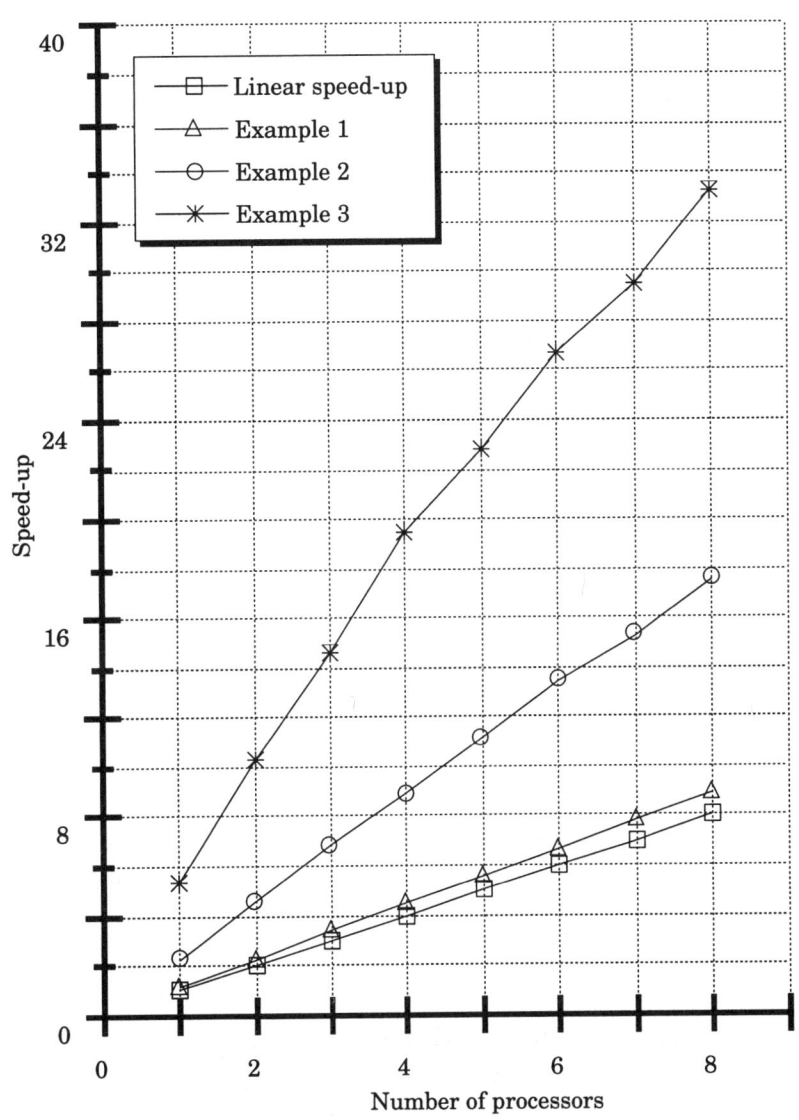

Figure 7-11. Speed-up for Examples 1, 2, and 3 using the concurrent hybrid genetic/neural network learning algorithm with vectorization.

A very large neural network with 5950 links is used in Example 2. Two hundred fifty (250) chromosomes are operated on in each learning iteration. That is, 250 tasks are created and performed concurrently in this learning stage. Each concurrent task performs the computation of a stand-alone neural network with 30 training instances. The overall speed-up achieved by the concurrent hybrid neural network learning algorithm for Example 2 is also dominated by the first learning stage. The maximum speed-up due to microtasking is about 7.4, using eight processors of the Cray Y-MP8/864 supercomputer (Figure 7–10). A maximum average speed-up of about 17.6 is achieved due to a combination of microtasking with vectorization (Figure 7–11).

A very large neural network with 4160 links is used in Example 3 with 2304 training instances. Two hundred fifty (250) chromosomes are operated on in each learning iteration. The maximum speed-up due to microtasking is about 7.3, using eight processors of the Cray Y-MP8/864 supercomputer (Figure 7–10). A maximum average speed-up of about 33 is achieved when microtasking is combined with vectorization (Figure 7–11).

7.6 CONCLUDING REMARKS

We presented a concurrent hybrid genetic/neural network learning algorithm by integrating genetic algorithm with the adaptive conjugate gradient neural network learning algorithm developed previously. The following observations are made and conclusions drawn:

1. The results of neural network learning are sensitive to the initial value of the weight vector. In this chapter, a genetic algorithm is employed to perform global search and seek a good starting weight vector for the subsequent neural network learning algorithm. The result is an improvement in the convergence speed of the algorithm.

2. The problem of entrapment in a local minimum is encountered in gradient-based neural network learning algorithms. In the hybrid learning algorithm presented in this chapter, this problem is circumvented by using a genetic algorithm which is guided by the fitness function of a population rather than gradient direction. After several iterations of the global search, the first learning stage returns a near-global optimum point that is used as the initial weight vector for the second learning stage.

3. A large-scale multi-layer neural network requires substantial computing processing time in order to converge to an acceptably small system error value. By developing efficient concurrent learning algorithms on multiprocessor computers, we can increase the computational speed-up by an order of magnitude.

CHAPTER 8

A Hybrid Learning Algorithm for Distributed Memory Multicomputors

8.1 INTRODUCTION

In this chapter we present a hybrid neural network learning algorithm for distributed multicomputer systems. It is based on integration of a genetic algorithm (see Section 7.2.1) with error backpropagation multilayer neural network learning algorithm.

8.2 DISTRIBUTED MEMORY MULTICOMPUTER WITH TROLLIUS OPERATION SYSTEM

Initially developed at Cornell University and extended at the Center of Research Computing at the Ohio State University, Trollius is a programming environment designed for distributed memory multicomputers, consisting of a host node based on Unix operating system and a group of node computers (Burns, 1989; Trollius, 1991). A computer node is defined as a processor with its own associated memory. Nodes are linked through communication channels. The topology of the multicomputer is declared by the *spread* command which describes the number, type, and identification of multicomputer nodes.

As a programming environment, Trollius includes three components: an operating system, a command line user interface, and C and FORTRAN libraries. The main function of the operating system is to handle synchronization message passing among nodes. The user interface provides a man-machine interface to declare the topology of multicomputer, boot Trollius on the nodes, load parallel programs, and provide information on running processors.

The C and FORTRAN on Trollius, unlike C and FORTRAN supported by Cray UNICOS, do not provide any type of automatic task parallelization (such as autotasking in Cray FORTRAN). Rather, the parallelization of the task is performed by calling message passing functions in the Trollius libraries. The key issue of programming on the multicomputer is message passing among nodes.

The hybrid concurrent algorithm has been implemented in C on a transputer multicomputer system. The host of the transputer multicomputer system is a SUN 3 workstation. There are two separate transputer systems. One system has 4 T800 32-bit processors (T node) each with 1MB memory and the other has 8 T800 processors each with 2 MB memory (Figure 8–1). The 4-node system can be configured in any topology possible with 4 nodes. Each node can have a maximum of 4 links. The 8-node system can be connected as a 2×4 array (shown in Figure 8–1), a 1×8 array, a ring, hypercube, etc.

8.3 A HYBRID NEURAL NETWORK LEARNING ALGORITHM

A hybrid learning algorithm using genetic algorithm with error backpropagation multilayer neural networks is presented in Figure 8–2. It consists of two learning stages. The first learning stage is to accelerate the learning process by using a genetic algorithm with the feedforward step of the backpropagation learning algorithm. In this stage, the weights of the neural network are encoded on chromosomes as decision variables. The objective function for the genetic algorithm is defined as the average squared system error. Therefore, it becomes an unconstrained optimization problem: Find a set of decision variables minimizing the objective function.

After performing several iterations and meeting the stopping criterion, the first learning stage is terminated and the chromosome returning the minimum objective function is considered as the initial weight

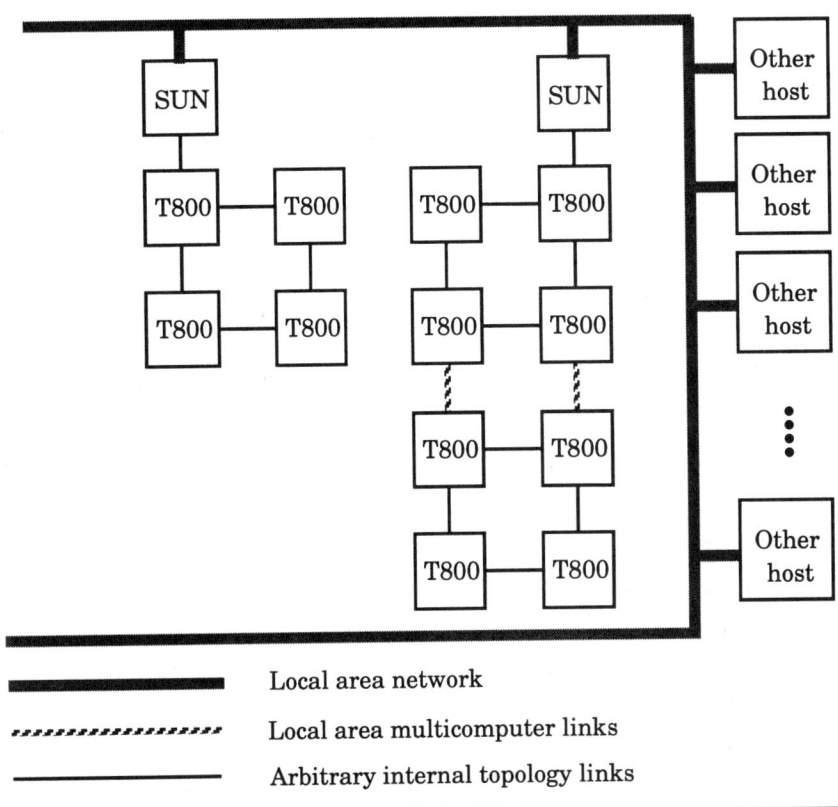

Figure 8–1. The layout of a transputer distributed memory multicomputer system.

160 MACHINE LEARNING

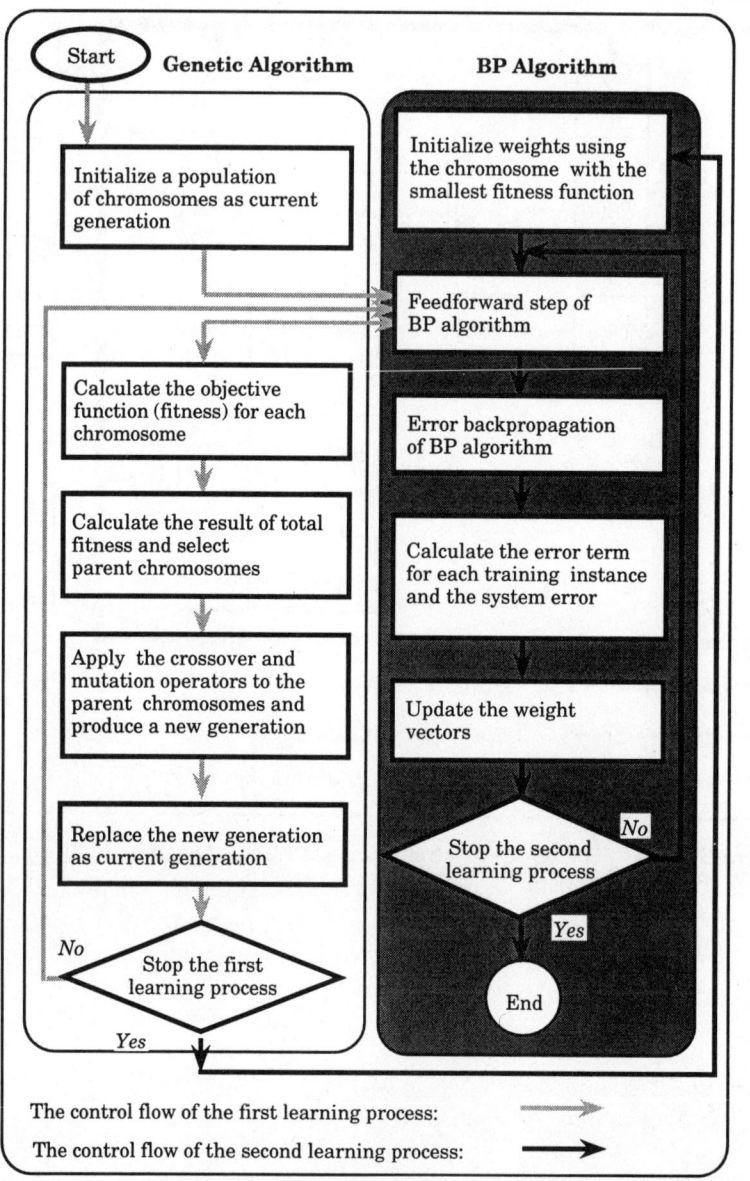

Figure 8–2. A hybrid learning algorithm using a genetic algorithm with an error backpropagation neural network learning algorithm.

of the neural network in the second stage. Next, the backpropagation learning algorithm performs the second learning stage until the terminal condition is satisfied.

8.4 A CONCURRENT LEARNING ALGORITHM FOR DISTRIBUTED MEMORY MULTICOMPUTERS

Consider the topology of a multilayer neural network shown in Figure 4–3. The number of input and output nodes connected in layer i are $N[i - 1]$ and $N[i]$, respectively. In addition, the learning problem is mapped from $N[0]$ input nodes to $N[m]$ output nodes, and a number of N_s instances are given as training samples. The total number of the weights and nodes are denoted by N_w and N_n, respectively. For the genetic algorithm, we assume N_p chromosomes are generated and operated on in each iteration. The operators and other features of the genetic algorithm are the same as those defined in Section 7.2.1.

Suppose the distributed memory multicomputer transputer system is configured as a $1 \times N$ linear array topology. Therefore, there are one host and N nodes in the system. The parallelization of the task performed on the system is achieved by message passing among nodes using the commands *nsend* and *nreceive* (Trollius, 1991).

The concurrent hybrid learning algorithm for a distributed memory multicomputer transputer is shown schematically in Figures 8–3 and 8–4. As tasks executed on the host and nodes are different, the learning algorithm is divided into two components and presented in the following paragraphs.

As a controller, the host program contains not only the same procedures executed on the nodes, but also the procedure controlling the whole task. The main processes included in the host program are: initializing the problem, sending message to the nodes, performing the first and second learning stages on the host and nodes simultaneously, and receiving the messages sent from nodes. The pseudocode of the host program is listed in Table 8–1.

The procedures in the node program are almost the same as those in the host except for the procedures of initializing the problem and sending message to the nodes. The main processes in the node program are: receiving message from the host, performing the task on each node and the host simultaneously, and sending messages to the host. The pseudo code of the node program (for node n) is listed in Table 8–2.

162 MACHINE LEARNING

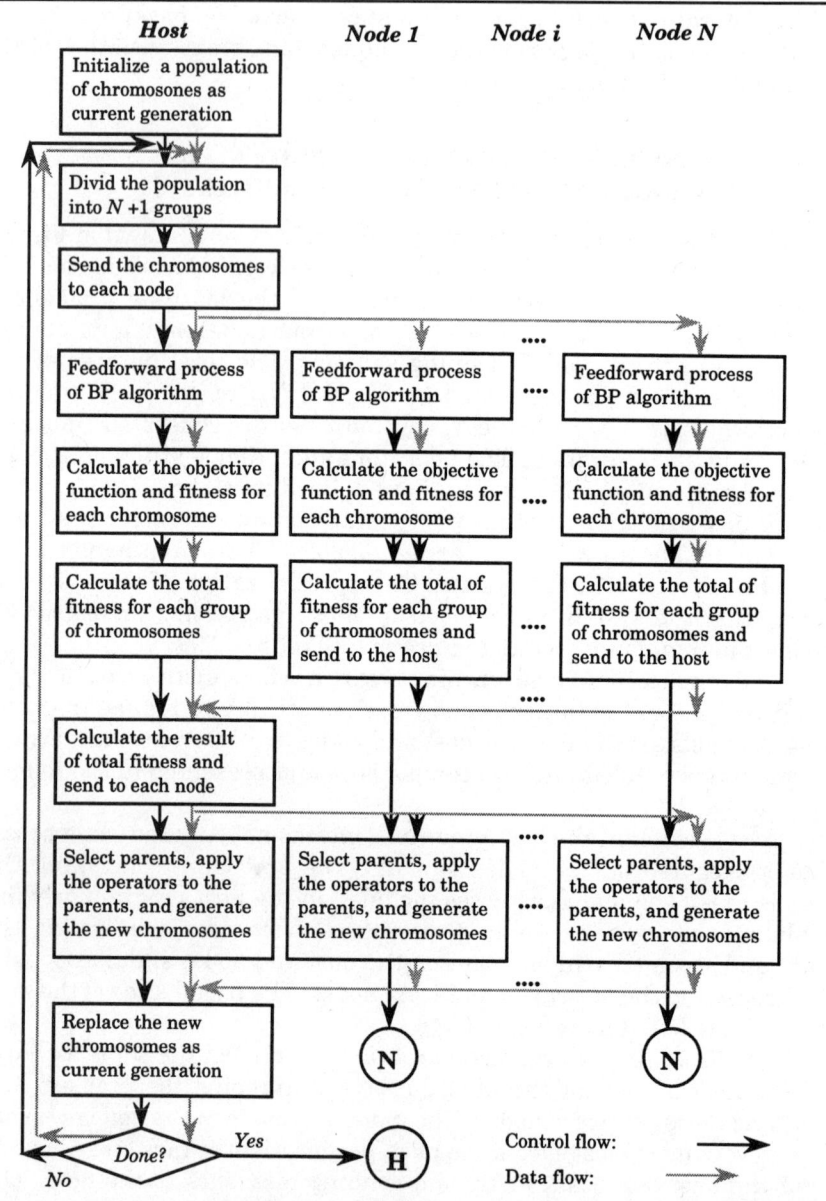

Figure 8-3. The host and node programs of the first learning stage on the distributed memory system.

A HYBRID LEARNING ALGORITHM   163

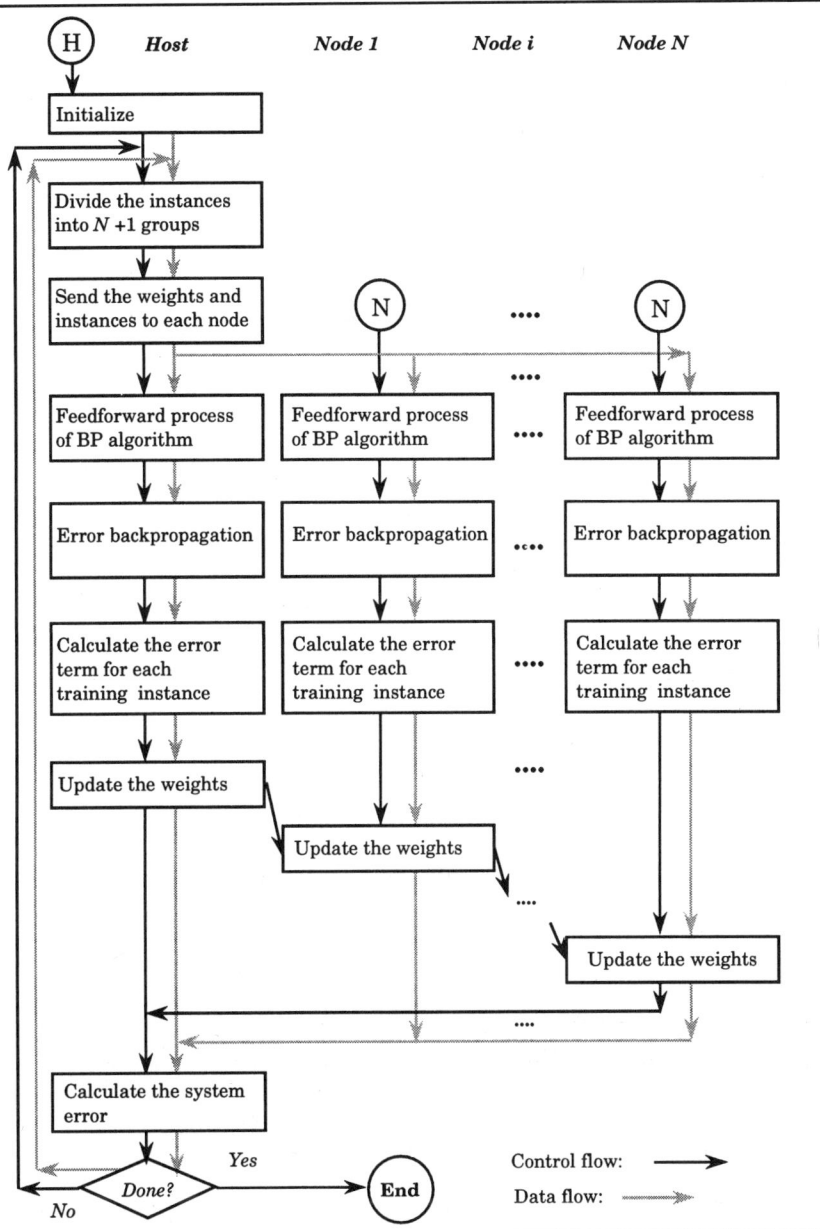

Figure 8-4. The host and node programs of the second learning stage on the distributed memory system.

Table 8-1. Parallel learning algorithm for a distributed memory system (program on the host).

/* The first learning stage */

For $i = 1$ to N_p, do <u>serially</u>

   a. Initialize the chromosome in random as current generation.

Next i.

DO

   a. Divide N_p chromosomes into $N + 1$ groups $[n_p = N_p/(N + 1)]$ and assign to each group $n_p + 1$ or n_p chromosomes.

   b. Send $tag = GA$ to each node.

   c. Send group 2 to $N + 1$ to node 1 to N, respectively.

For $i = 1$ to n_p, do <u>concurrently</u>

   For $j = 1$ to N_s, do <u>serially</u>

     a. Feedforward process of BP learning algorithm.

   Next j.

     a. Evaluate the objective function.

Next i.

   d. Receive the value of objective function from node 1 to N.

For $i = 1$ to n_p, do <u>concurrently</u>

   a. Select parents using roulette wheel parent selection technique.

   b. Apply reproduction, crossover, and mutation to the parents.

Next i.

For $i = 1$ to N, do <u>serially</u>

   a. Receive the new generation from node i.

Next i.

   e. Replace the new chromosomes as current generation.

WHILE (~stop criterion).

Table 8–1.   *(continued)*

/* The second learning stage */

a. Initialize weights of the network.
b. Divide N_s instances into $N + 1$ groups and assign to each group $n_s + 1$ or n_s instances.
c. Send *tag* = BP and *proc* = 1 to each node.
d. Send group 2 to $N + 1$ to node 1 to N, respectively.

DO

    a. Send *tag* = BP and *proc* = 2 to each node.
    b. Send the weights of the network to nodes 1 to N.

    For $i = 1$ to n_s, do <u>concurrently</u>

        a. Perform feedforward procedure of the BP learning algorithm.
        b. Calculate the value of the system error.
        c. Calculate the delta in the output layer, (*m*).

        For $j = m - 1$ to 1, do <u>serially</u>

            a. Calculate the delta in hidden layer, (*j*).
            b. Update the weights of the network.
            c. Send a signal to node 1.

        Next *j*.

    Next *i*.

    For $i = 1$ to N, do <u>serially</u>

        a. Receive the sub-sum of the system error from node 1 to N and accumulate the system error.

    Next *i*.

WHILE (~ stop criterion).

Table 8–2. Parallel learning algorithm for a distributed memory system (for node n).

/* The first learning stage */

   a. Receive *tag* from the host.

   If *tag* = GA then

      a. Receive the $N+1$ groups of chromosomes and the variable n_p from the host.

      For $i = 1$ to n_p, do <u>concurrently</u>

         For $j = 1$ to n_s, do <u>serially</u>

            a. Feedforward process of BP learning algorithm.

         Next *j*.

         a. Evaluate the objective function for each chromosome.

      Next *i*.

      b. Send the value of objective function to the host.

      For $i = 1$ to n_s, do <u>concurrently</u>

         a. Select parents using roulette wheel parent selection technique.

         b. Apply reproduction, crossover, and mutation to the parents.

      Next *i*.

      c. Send the new chromosomes to the host.

      Next *i*.

   End_If.

Table 8–2.   *(Continued)*

```
/* The second learning step */
```

If $(tag = BP)$ and $(proc = 1)$ then

    a. Receive the $N + 1$ groups of instances from the host.

End_If.

If $(tag = BP)$ and $(proc = 2)$ then

    a. Receive the weights of the network from the host.

    For $i = 1$ to n_s, do <u>concurrently</u>

        a. Perform feedforward procedure of the BP learning algorithm.

        b. Calculate the value of the system error.

        c. Calculate the delta in the output layer (m).

    For $j = m - 1$ to 1, do <u>serially</u>

        a. Calculate the delta in hidden layer (j).

        b. If $n <> 1$, wait for the signal sent from the node $n - 1$. Otherwise, wait for the signal sent from the host.

        c. Update the weights of the network.

    Next j.

    Next i.

    b. Send the sub-sum of the system error to the host.

End_if.

CHAPTER 9

A Fuzzy Neural Network Learning Model

9.1   INTRODUCTION

In this chapter, a fuzzy neural network learning model is presented by integrating an unsupervised fuzzy neural network classification algorithm, a genetic algorithm, and an adaptive conjugate gradient neural network learning algorithm. The fuzzy neural network learning model has been implemented in C on a vector MIMD shared memory machine, the Cray Y-MP8/864 supercomputer. A large-scale example from the domain of image recognition has been used to test the performance of the new fuzzy learning model.

9.2   SUPERVISED AND UNSUPERVISED CLASSIFICATION ALGORITHMS

The problem of data classification can be solved by supervised or unsupervised classification algorithms. If the input and output pairs of training data sets are provided, a supervised classification algorithm can be used to solve the problem. Using the given input data, the algorithm computes the output data and compares them with the given output data. The objective of the algorithm is to reduce the error between the given and calculated output data as much as possible. Hence, a supervised classification problem can be mapped to a corresponding unconstrained mathematical optimization problem.

On the other hand, if only the input data of training set are provided, an unsupervised classification algorithm should be used to solve the problem. Unsupervised classification algorithms are often based on a concept called data clustering or feature abstraction. The objective of the clustering process is to classify a given training set into a certain number of homogeneous clusters or classes based on a predefined feature in the training data. A cluster is called homogeneous when the elements in the cluster each have the same weight. The elements in each cluster are chosen to be as similar as possible to each other and dissimilar to those in the other clusters.

Supervised neural network learning algorithms have been widely employed for solving classification problems. The learning process in a supervised neural network is to update the weight vector guided by a learning rule, usually iteratively. Thousands of iterations are often required for training a neural network to solve the problem using a supervised neural network learning algorithm (Adeli and Yeh, 1989, 1990; Hung and Adeli, 1991a).

A commonly used technique for unsupervised learning is called competitive learning (Carpenter and Grossberg, 1988). The learning process in a competitive neural network learning is to update the weight vector using the following steps. First, training instances are inputted one by one through the network and the output data are calculated for each one. Then, the output nodes compete with each other to become active, guided by a predefined function. Finally, the weights associated with the links between the input and output nodes are modified using a learning rule.

9.3   FUZZY SETS

The theory of fuzzy sets has been developed as a complete set of mathematical abstractions for representing and operating the fuzzy logic (Zadeh, 1978) and applied in various domains. The fundamental idea behind the theory of fuzzy sets is based on the observation that human thinking is not just two-valued or multi-valued logic, but logic with fuzzy truths.

A fuzzy set, $\tilde{A}$, for a set of objects $\mathbf{X} = \{x_1, x_2, \cdots, x_n\}$ is defined as a collection of ordered pairs:

$$\tilde{A} = \{(x_i, \mu_{\tilde{A}}(x_i)), i = 1, 2, \cdots, n\} \tag{9-1}$$

The entity $\mu_{\tilde{A}}(x_i)$, a real number in the interval [0, 1], is called the membership function. It is used to represent the membership grade of x_i in $\tilde{A}$. A subset of objects in $\mathbf{X}$ with positive values of membership function, $\mu_{\tilde{A}}(x_i)$, is called the supports of $\tilde{A}$. A value of one for $\mu_{\tilde{A}}(x_i)$ indicates the support x_i is completely in $\tilde{A}$. On the other hand, if x_i does not belong to $\tilde{A}$, the value of $\mu_{\tilde{A}}(x_i)$ is equal to zero. If the supports $\mathbf{X}_{\text{sup}} = \{x_1, x_2, \ldots, x_s\}$ are discrete in the domain, the fuzzy set with the set of discrete support $\mathbf{X}_{\text{sup}}$ can be expressed as:

$$\tilde{A} = \mu_1/x_1 \cup \mu_2/x_2 \cup \cdots \cup \mu_s/x_s \qquad s \leq n \tag{9-2}$$
$$= \bigcup_{i=1}^{s} \mu_i/x_i$$

where $\cup$ denotes the operator of union. The entity μ_s/x_s denotes an object x_s with a membership value of μ_s in $\tilde{A}$. We model the image recognition problem as a discrete domain.

Though there are several different approaches for expressing the membership function in a fuzzy set, the unique evaluation of membership function of a fuzzy set is still one of the main subjects of debate in the application of fuzzy sets (Pal and Dutta Majumder, 1986; Li, 1990; Chang, Hasegawa, and Ibbs, 1991). We use a triangular-shaped membership function to express the degree of membership in a fuzzy set. We found this function to be simple for mathematical manipulation and adequate for the domain of interest. The triangular membership function shown in Figure 9–1 is expressed mathematically as:

$$\mu_j(x) = \begin{cases} 0 & \text{if } x < a_1 \\ \dfrac{x - a_1}{a_2 - a_1} & \text{if } a_1 \leq x < a_2 \\ 1 & \text{if } x = a_2 \\ \dfrac{a_3 - x}{a_3 - a_2} & \text{if } a_2 < x \leq a_3 \\ 0 & \text{if } x > a_3 \end{cases} \tag{9-3}$$

where a_1, a_2, and a_3 are predefined parameters identified in Figure 9–1.

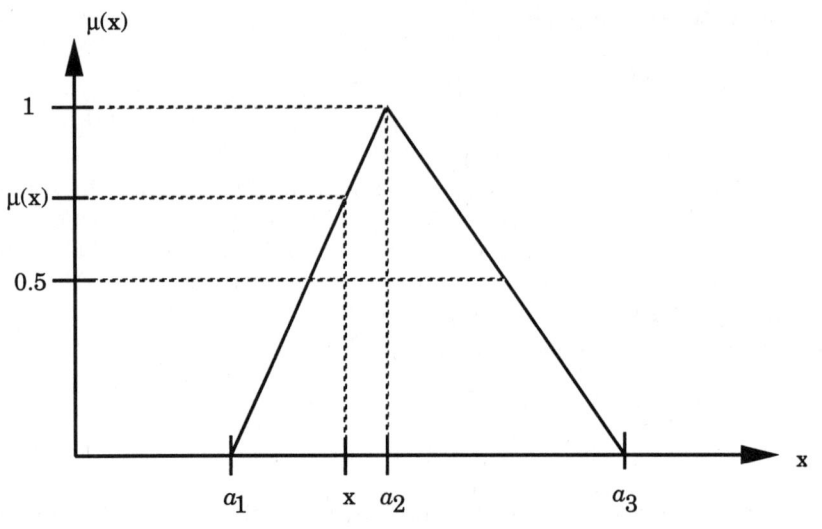

Figure 9–1. A triangular-shaped fuzzy membership function.

9.4 AN UNSUPERVISED FUZZY NEURAL NETWORK CLASSIFICATION ALGORITHM

In this section, an unsupervised fuzzy neural network classification algorithm is presented. The algorithm is based on integration of a recursive estimate algorithm, a topology&weight-change neural network, and the theory of fuzzy sets. The recursive estimate algorithm has been used as a tool for successive estimation of an unknown parameter (Pal and Dutta Majumder, 1986). Suppose there are N training instances $\mathbf{X}_1, \mathbf{X}_2, ..., \mathbf{X}_N$ and there are M patterns in each training instance, $\mathbf{X}_i = [x_{i1}, x_{i2}, ..., x_{iM}]$. The mean vector of these instances is defined as:

$$\overline{\mathbf{X}}_N = \frac{1}{N} \sum_{i=1}^{N} \mathbf{X}_i \tag{9-4}$$

The mean vector of $N + 1$ training instances can be found using a successive estimation from the mean $\overline{\mathbf{X}}_N$ and the instance $\mathbf{X}_{N+1}$ as follows:

$$\overline{\mathbf{X}}_{N+1} = \frac{1}{N+1}\sum_{i=1}^{N+1}\mathbf{X}_i$$

$$= \frac{1}{N+1}\left(\sum_{i=1}^{N}\mathbf{X}_i + \mathbf{X}_{N+1}\right) \tag{9-5}$$

$$= \left(\frac{1}{N+1}\right)\left(N\overline{\mathbf{X}}_N + \mathbf{X}_{N+1}\right)$$

$$= \left(\frac{N}{N+1}\right)\overline{\mathbf{X}}_N + \left(\frac{1}{N+1}\right)\mathbf{X}_{N+1}$$

The process of unsupervised classification is performed using a topology&weight-change two-layer (flat) neural network. The number of input nodes is equal to the number of patterns (M) in each training instance. The number of output nodes is equal to the number of clusters. Since the number of clusters is determined through the classification process, the topology of the neural network is changed and self-organized dynamically during the classification process. The training instances are classified one by one. First, a neural network with M input nodes and one output node, denoted as $\Phi(M, 1)$, is generated and the first training instance is inputted. At this point, the first training instance belongs to the first cluster. Then, the second training instance is inputted through the network. If the second instance is classified to the first cluster, the output node, representing the first cluster, becomes active. In this case, the topology of the neural network does not change, but the weights associated with the links are updated using the aforementioned recursive estimate algorithm. The topology of the neural network is still a $\Phi(M, 1)$ network. On the other hand, if the second training instance is classified as a new cluster, an additional output node is added to the neural network. The values of weights in the original neural network do not alter. In this case, the topology of the neural network is modified as a $\Phi(M, 2)$ network. The classification process follows this procedure until all the training instances are classified. This unsupervised classification process is shown schematically in Figure 9–2.

The classification of a training instance into an existing cluster or a new cluster is based on the concept of maximum likelihood. We define a function $\mathit{diff}(\mathbf{X}, \mathbf{C})$, called the degree of difference, to represent the difference between a training instance $\mathbf{X}$ and a cluster $\mathbf{C}$ in a $\Phi(M, P)$ neural network. This function maps two given vectors ($\mathbf{X}$ and $\mathbf{C}$) to a real number (diff). The patterns of each cluster (means of the patterns

176 MACHINE LEARNING

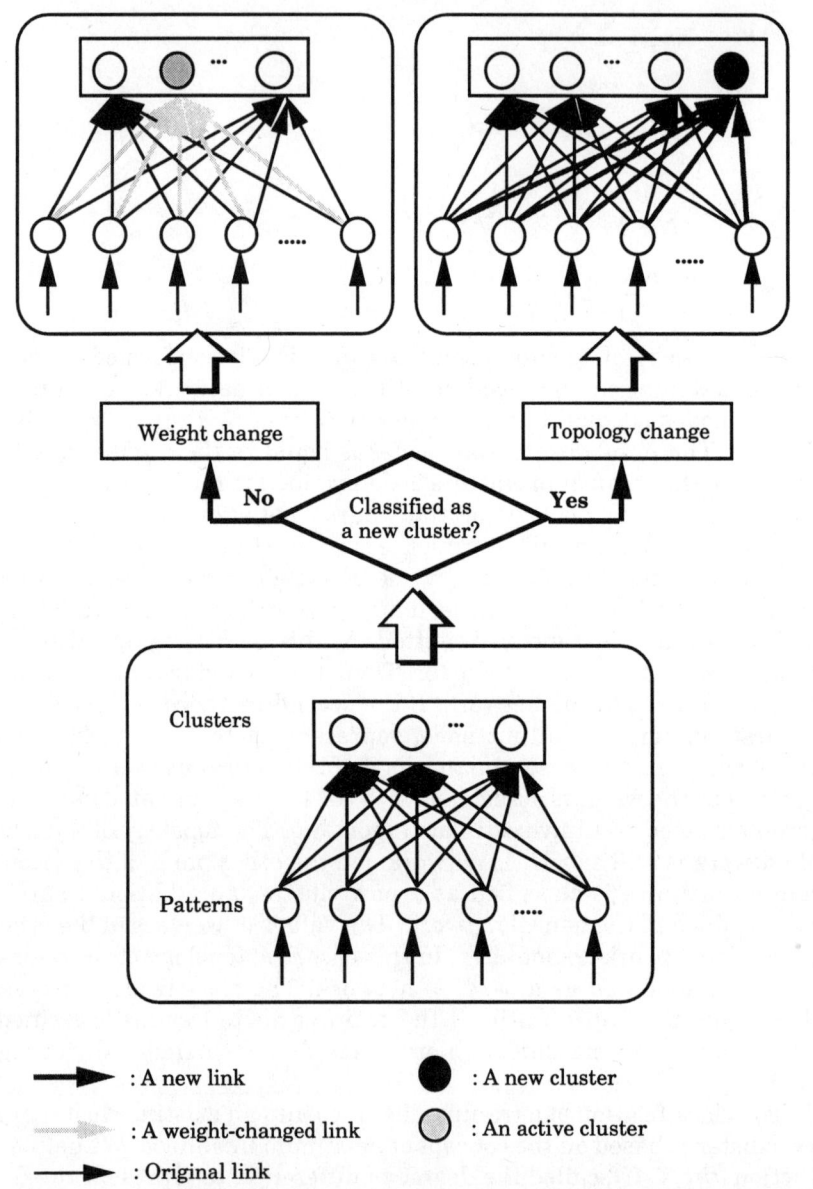

Figure 9–2. The classification process of topology&weight-change neural network.

of the instances in the cluster) are stored in the links (weights) of neural network during the classification process. We use the following scheme for classifying a training instance into an active or new cluster:

1. Calculate the degree of difference, $diff(\mathbf{X}, \mathbf{C}_i)$, between the training instance, $\mathbf{X}$, and each cluster, $\mathbf{C}_i$. For the image recognition problem, the function $diff(\mathbf{X}, \mathbf{C})$ is defined as the Euclidean distance represented by:

$$diff(\mathbf{X},\mathbf{C}_i) = \left[\sum_{j=1}^{M}(x_j - c_{ij})^2\right]^{1/2} \qquad (9\text{-}6)$$

2. Find the smallest degree of difference, $diff_{min}$, and assign the cluster with the smallest degree of difference as an active cluster:

$$\mathbf{C}_{active} = \{\mathbf{C}_i \mid \min\{diff(\mathbf{X},\mathbf{C}_i)\}, \ i = 1,2,\cdots,P\} \qquad (9\text{-}7)$$

3. Compare the value of $diff_{min}$ with a predefined threshold value κ. If the value of $diff_{min}$ is greater than the predefined threshold value κ, the training instance is classified as a new cluster:

$$\mathbf{C}_{new} = \mathbf{X} \qquad \text{if } \kappa < \min\{diff(\mathbf{X},\mathbf{C}_i), \ i = 1,2,\cdots,P\} \qquad (9\text{-}8)$$

After the process of classification is completed, classified clusters may be disjoint or partly overlapping (see Figure 9–3). Suppose the given N training instances have been classified into P clusters. The entity $\mathbf{C}_j$ denotes the jth cluster and $\mathbf{U}$ is the set of all clusters. If the clusters are completely disjoint, each given instance in the training set belongs to only one of the classified clusters. A binary matrix $\mathbf{Z}$ can be used to record the cluster of each instance. If the instance i belongs to the jth cluster, $z_{ij} = 1$, otherwise $z_{ij} = 0$. Let f_j be the number of instances in cluster j, then the following relations hold:

$$\sum_{p=1}^{P} f_p = N,$$

$$\bigcup_{p=1}^{P} \mathbf{C}_p = \mathbf{U}$$

$$\mathbf{C}_i \bigcap_{i \neq j} \mathbf{C}_j = \varnothing$$

where $\varnothing$ denotes an empty set. However, if the classified clusters are partly overlapping, a given instance in the training set may belong to

178 MACHINE LEARNING

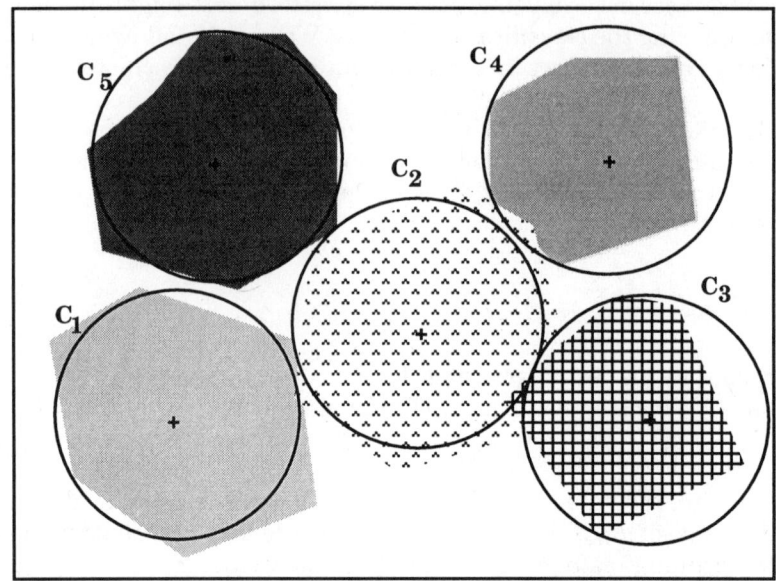

(a) A collection of disjoint clusters

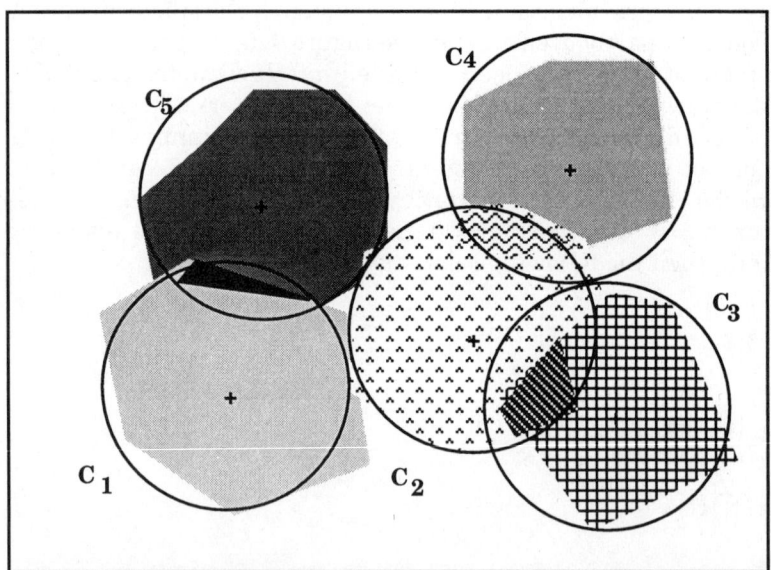

(b) A collection of partly overlapping clusters

Figure 9–3. A collection of clusters with crisp and fuzzy boundaries.

more than one cluster. In this case, the boundaries of the classified clusters are fuzzy rather than crisp (see Figure 9–3). The same binary matrix **Z** is used to record the cluster of each instance. Let n_j be the number of instances completely or partly in cluster j, then the following conditions hold:

$$\sum_{j=1}^{P} z_{ij} \geq 1 \qquad i = 1, 2, \cdots, N,$$

$$\sum_{p=1}^{P} n_p \geq N,$$

$$\bigcup_{p=1}^{P} \mathbf{C}_p = \mathbf{U},$$

$$\mathbf{C}_i \bigcap_{i \neq j} \mathbf{C}_j \neq \emptyset \qquad \text{for some } i, j = 1, 2, \cdots, M$$

The algorithm we use for evaluating the membership function is based on the hypothesis that there is a prototype for each cluster, defined as the mean of all instances in that cluster, and the degree of membership of each instance in the cluster is based on how similar this instance is to the prototype one. The "similarity" can be defined as a function of distance between the instance and the prototype of the cluster. Suppose there are n_p instances in a cluster p. The patterns vector of the ith instance in the cluster p is $\mathbf{X}_i^p = [x_{i1}^p, x_{i2}^p, \cdots, x_{iM}^p]$. Then, the patterns vector of the prototype instance (mean of all instances) in the cluster p is defined as:

$$\mathbf{C}_p = [c_{p1}, c_{p2}, \cdots, c_{pM}] = \frac{1}{n_p} \sum_{i=1}^{n_p} \mathbf{X}_i^p \qquad (9\text{-}9)$$

$$\text{where} \quad c_{pj} = \frac{1}{n_p} \sum_{i=1}^{n_p} x_{ij}^p \qquad (j = 1, 2, \cdots, M). \qquad (9\text{-}10)$$

Based on the aforementioned triangular-shaped membership function, the fuzzy membership value of the ith instance in the cluster p is defined as:

$$\mu_p(\mathbf{X}_i^p) = f(D^w(\mathbf{X}_i^p, \mathbf{C}_p)) = \begin{cases} 0 & \text{if } D^w(\mathbf{X}_i^p, \mathbf{C}_p) > \kappa \\ 1 - \frac{D^w(\mathbf{X}_i^p, \mathbf{C}_p)}{\kappa} & \text{if } D^w(\mathbf{X}_i^p, \mathbf{C}_p) \leq \kappa \end{cases} \qquad (9\text{-}11)$$

The predefined threshold value κ is used as a crossover value. The similarity function is defined as the weighted norm $D^w(\mathbf{X}_i^p, \mathbf{C}_p)$. In this book, the weighted norm is defined as the Euclidean distance and expressed by:

$$D^w(\mathbf{X}_i^p, \mathbf{C}_p) = \|w_p(\mathbf{X}_i^p - \mathbf{C}_p)\|^w = \left[\sum_{j=1}^{M}(x_{ij}^p - c_{pj})^2\right]^{1/2} \qquad (9\text{-}12)$$

A value of one is used for the weight parameters w and w_p for the image recognition problem. If the Euclidean distance for a given instance is less than the crossover value κ, the instance belongs to the cluster p and the fuzzy membership value is between zero and one. Otherwise, the instance does not belong to the cluster and the fuzzy membership value is equal to zero. Figure 9–4 shows four clusters $\mathbf{C}_1$, $\mathbf{C}_2$, $\mathbf{C}_3$, and $\mathbf{C}_4$ and their corresponding membership functions. The instance $\mathbf{X}_i$ in this figure belongs to the clusters $\mathbf{C}_1$, $\mathbf{C}_2$, and $\mathbf{C}_3$ with its corresponding membership values μ_1, μ_2, and μ_3, respectively. In this case, the clusters $\mathbf{C}_1$, $\mathbf{C}_2$, and $\mathbf{C}_3$ are the supports of instance $\mathbf{X}_i$ and the cluster $\mathbf{C}_4$ is not.

We have found the Euclidean distance to be a good measurement for the membership function in the domain of image recognition. Suppose each pixel in an 8×8 binary image instance is represented as a 3-dimensional point $(p_x, p_y, g_{x,y})$. The entities p_x and p_y are the x and y coordinates of the point and $g_{x,y}$ is the gray-scale integer value for this pixel (varying between 0 and 255 in the example to be presented subsequently in this chapter). The patterns vector for training instance i is $\mathbf{X}_i = [g_{1,1}^i, g_{1,2}^i, \cdots, g_{8,7}^i, g_{8,8}^i]$. Hence, the degree of similarity of two images can be defined as a function of gray-scale value, $g_{x,y}$, only. Since each pixel in the image has the same weight ($w = 1$ and $w_p = 1$ in Eq. 9-12), the simple Euclidean distance function can express the fuzzy membership value effectively.

Our fuzzy neural network classification algorithm consists of two stages. The first stage is an unsupervised neural network classification process. In this stage, the algorithm classifies the training instances into a certain number of clusters determined dynamically. After all the training instances have been classified, the values of the mean vector (prototype) for each cluster are stored in the weights associated with the links between the input and output nodes. The second stage is a fuzzification process. In this stage, the fuzzy membership values for each training instance in the set of supports, classified clusters, are evaluated.

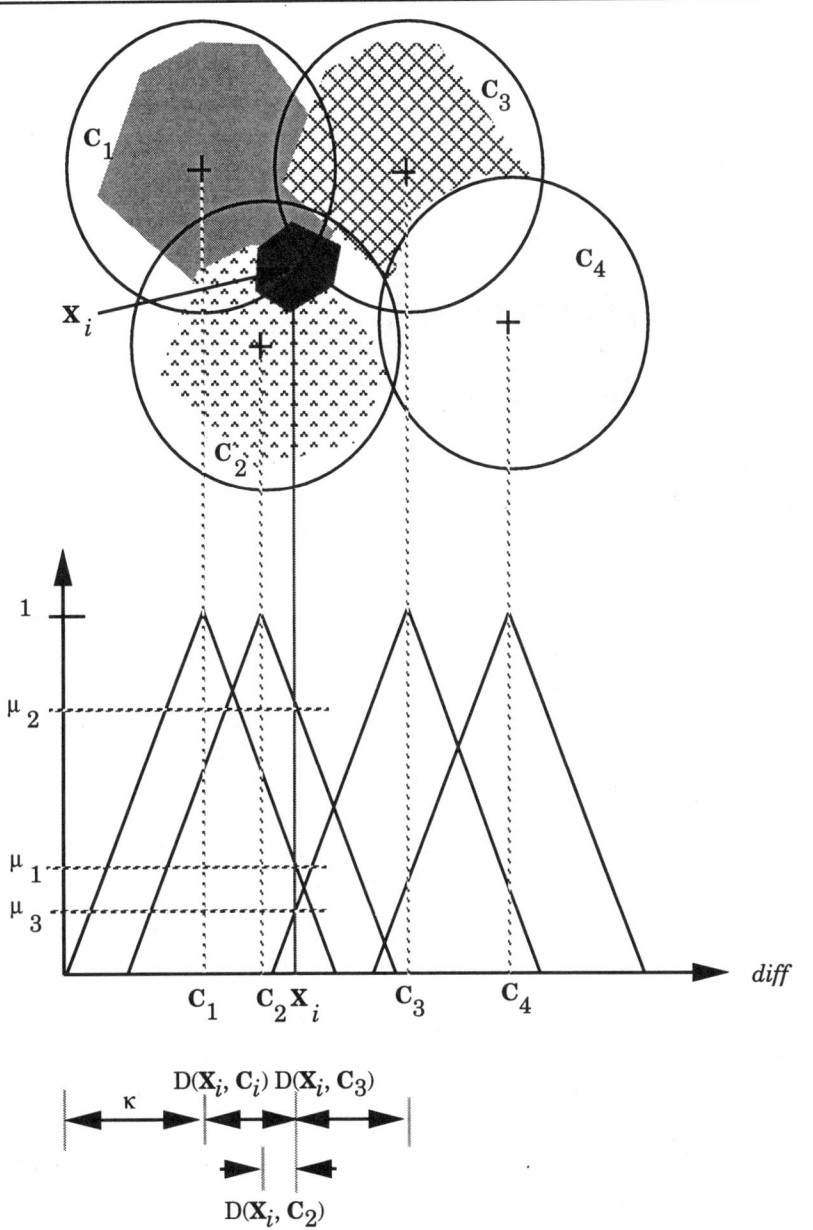

Figure 9-4. A collection of clusters with their triangular fuzzy membership functions.

For a set of N training instances with M input patterns for each training instance, the unsupervised fuzzy neural network classification algorithm is presented as follows:

Step 1. Set the counter of outer loop $i = 1$. Generate a two-layer neural network with a topology of M input nodes and one output node, $\Phi(M, 1)$, set the number of clusters, c, equal to 1, set the number of elements in cluster one, n_1, equal to 1, and the number of elements in other clusters $n_2, n_3, ..., n_N$ equal to zero. Set the weights of the $\Phi(M, 1)$ network, z_{1j}, equal to the instance patterns vector x_{1j} ($j = 1, 2, ..., M$). Set the value of crossover parameter, κ.

Step 2. Set $i = 2$ and perform the following steps to classify the given training instances, $\mathbf{X}_i$, into a certain number of clusters.

Step 2.1 Set the counter of inner loop, k, equal to one and perform the following steps to determine an active cluster:

Step 2.1.1 Calculate the Euclidean distance

$$D_k = \sqrt{\sum_{j=1}^{M}(z_{ij} - x_{ij})^2}$$

between the ith training instance and the kth cluster.

Step 2.1.2 If $k = 1$, set the working parameter, D_s, equal to D_k. Otherwise compare the value of D_k with the value of D_s. If $D_k < D_s$, set D_s equal to D_k and index s equal to k, otherwise continue.

Step 2.1.3 Set $k \leftarrow k + 1$. If $k \geq c$, go to the next step. Otherwise go to Step 2.1.1.

Step 2.2 Compare the value of D_s with the predefined crossover value, κ. If $D_s \leq \kappa$, assign the training instance $\mathbf{X}_i$ to the sth cluster and go to the next step. Otherwise, set $c \leftarrow c + 1$, set $n_c = 1$, modify the topology of the neural network as $\Phi(M, c)$ by adding an additional output node, set the new weights, z_{cj}, equal to the input patterns $\mathbf{X}_i$, and go to Step 2.4.

Step 2.3 Update the weight z_{sj}:

$$z_{sj} = \left(\frac{n_s}{n_s + 1}\right)z_{sj} + \left(\frac{1}{n_s + 1}\right)x_{ij} \quad j = 1, 2, ..., M$$

Set $n_s \leftarrow n_s + 1$ and go to the next step.

Step 2.4   Set $i \leftarrow i + 1$. If $i > N$ stop the stage of classification and go to the next step. Otherwise go to Step 2.1.

Step 3.   Set the counter of outer loop, i, equal to one and perform the following steps to calculate the associated fuzzy membership values for each instance.

Step 3.1   Set a counter $t = 0$.

Step 3.2   Set $k = 1$ and perform the following steps.

Step 3.2.1 Calculate the Euclidean distance D_{ik}. If D_{ik} is less than the predefined crossover value, κ, calculate the fuzzy membership value

$$\mu_k = 1 - \frac{D_{ik}}{\kappa} \quad \text{and set } t \leftarrow t + 1.$$

Step 3.2.2 Set $k \leftarrow k + 1$. If $k > c$ go to the next step, otherwise go to Step 3.2.1.

Step 3.3   If $t = 0$, create a new cluster for the ith instance. Set $c \leftarrow c + 1$, the weight, z_{cj}, equal to x_{ij}, and the fuzzy membership value $\mu_1 = 1$. Otherwise, go to the next step.

Step 3.4   Set $i \leftarrow i + 1$. If $i > N$ stop the second stage, otherwise go to Step 3.1.

9.5   A FUZZY NEURAL NETWORK LEARNING MODEL

A fuzzy neural network learning model is presented by integrating the unsupervised fuzzy neural network classification algorithm described in the previous section with the hybrid genetic/adaptive conjugate gradient neural network (ACGNN) algorithm. As shown schematically in Figure 9–5, it consists of three major stages. Suppose there are N training instances and each instance consists of M patterns. The collection of training instances is represented as an $N \times M$ matrix $\mathbf{T}$:

$$\mathbf{T} = \begin{bmatrix} \mathbf{X}_1 \\ \mathbf{X}_2 \\ \vdots \\ \mathbf{X}_{N-1} \\ \mathbf{X}_N \end{bmatrix} = \begin{bmatrix} x_{11} & x_{12} & \cdots & x_{1(M-1)} & x_{1M} \\ x_{21} & x_{22} & \cdots & x_{2(M-1)} & x_{2M} \\ \vdots & \vdots & \ddots & \vdots & \vdots \\ x_{(N-1)1} & x_{(N-1)2} & \cdots & x_{(N-1)(M-1)} & x_{(N-1)M} \\ x_{N1} & x_{N2} & \cdots & x_{N(M-1)} & x_{NM} \end{bmatrix}_{N \times M} \quad (9\text{-}13)$$

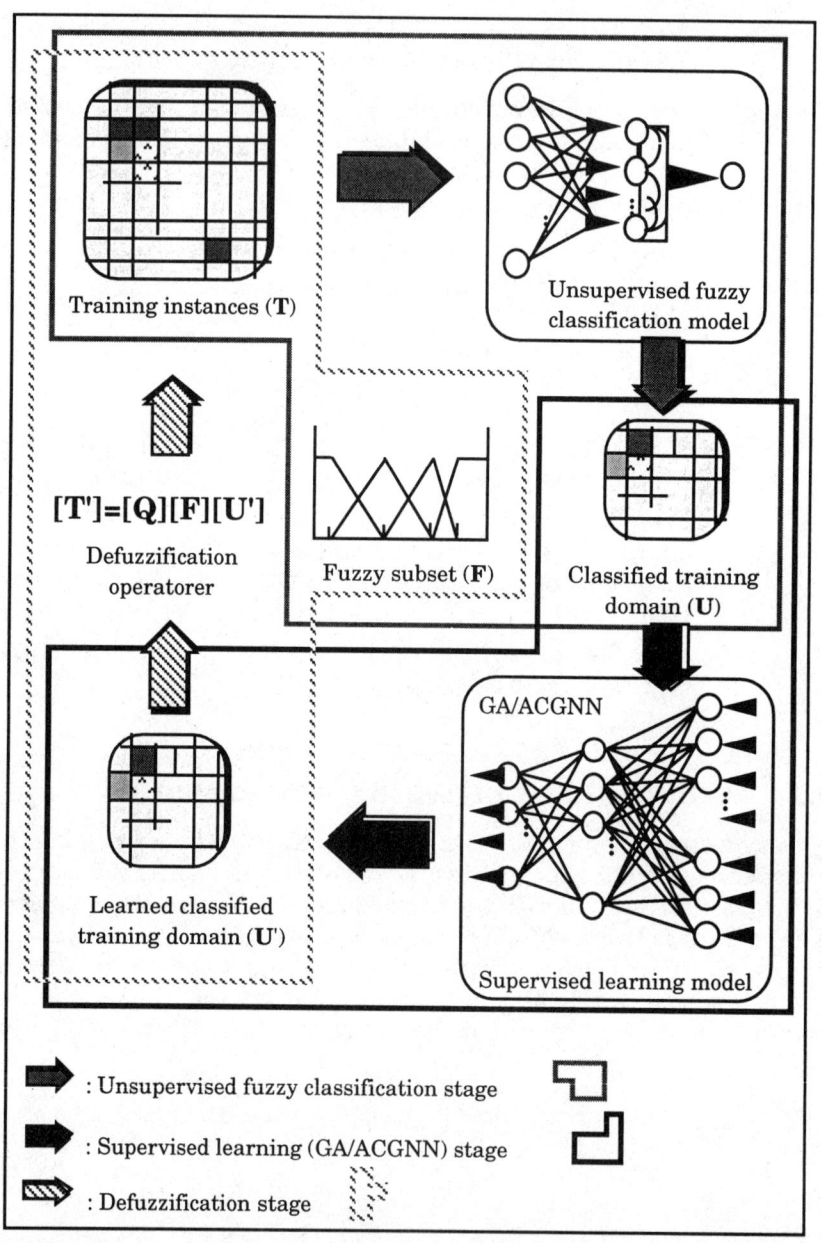

Figure 9-5. A fuzzy neural network learning model.

where the row vector $\mathbf{X}_N$ is the Nth training instance and the entity $x_{N[M-1]}$ is the $(M-1)$st pattern in the Nth training instance.

The first major learning stage is used to classify the given training instances into a small number, say $P \le N$, clusters using the unsupervised fuzzy neural network classification algorithm presented in the previous section. This step is used as a preprocessor to perform fuzzy classification with the objective of reducing the total number of training instances for the second learning stage. These classified clusters can be represented as a matrix $\mathbf{U}$ with $P \times M$ elements:

$$\mathbf{U} = \begin{bmatrix} \mathbf{C}_1 \\ \mathbf{C}_2 \\ \vdots \\ \mathbf{C}_{P-1} \\ \mathbf{C}_P \end{bmatrix} = \begin{bmatrix} c_{11} & c_{12} & \cdots & c_{1(M-1)} & c_{1M} \\ c_{21} & c_{22} & \cdots & c_{2(M-1)} & c_{2M} \\ \vdots & \vdots & \ddots & \vdots & \vdots \\ c_{(P-1)1} & c_{(P-1)2} & \cdots & c_{(P-1)(M-1)} & c_{(P-1)M} \\ c_{P1} & c_{P2} & \cdots & c_{P(M-1)} & c_{PM} \end{bmatrix}_{P \times M} \qquad (9\text{-}14)$$

Since these clusters are not completely disjoint, a set of fuzzy membership values are generated and used to represent the relationship among the given training instances with these classified clusters (supports). The fuzzy membership values are stored in a matrix $\mathbf{F}$ with $N \times P$ elements:

$$\mathbf{F} = \begin{bmatrix} \Theta_1 \\ \Theta_2 \\ \vdots \\ \Theta_{(N-1)} \\ \Theta_N \end{bmatrix} = \begin{bmatrix} \mu_{11} & \mu_{12} & \cdots & \mu_{1(P-1)} & \mu_{1P} \\ \mu_{21} & \mu_{22} & \cdots & \mu_{2(P-1)} & \mu_{2P} \\ \vdots & \vdots & \ddots & \vdots & \vdots \\ \mu_{(N-1)1} & \mu_{(N-1)2} & \cdots & \mu_{(N-1)(P-1)} & \mu_{(N-1)P} \\ \mu_{N1} & \mu_{N2} & \cdots & \mu_{N(P-1)} & \mu_{NP} \end{bmatrix}_{N \times P} \qquad (9\text{-}15)$$

After classifying the given training instances, $\mathbf{T}$, into a number of fuzzy clusters, $\mathbf{U}$, the first learning stage is completed. The second stage is a supervised neural network learning model using the classified clusters $\mathbf{U}$ as training instances. The computed outputs are denoted as $\mathbf{U}'$. Since the hybrid genetic/adaptive conjugate gradient learning algorithm presented in Chapter 7 has superior convergence property compared with the momentum backpropagation learning algorithm, it is employed in the new fuzzy learning model. The genetic algorithm is used to accelerate the whole learning process in the hybrid learning algorithm (Hung and Adeli, 1994b). It performs global search and seeks a near-optimal initial point for the adaptive conjugate gradient learning algorithm. The objective of this supervised learning stage is to reduce the difference (error) between the desired outputs, **U**, and the computed outputs, **U'**. In this work, we define the system error as follows:

$$E_{system} = \frac{1}{2 \times P \times M} \sum_{i=1}^{P} \left(\sum_{j=1}^{M} (c_{ij} - c'_{ij})^2 \right) \tag{9-16}$$

After the completion of the supervised learning process, the neural network has been trained to regenerate the input instances (classified clusters). The third stage is the process of defuzzification. A defuzzification operator is used to regenerate the input training instances using the output of the second stage, **U'**, and the fuzzy membership values calculated in the first learning stage, **F**. In each training instance, the values of the fuzzy membership values specify a possible distribution of clusters. The defuzzification operator is defined in the form of a matrix multiplier:

$$\mathbf{T'} = defuzzifier(\mathbf{U'}, \mathbf{F}) = \mathbf{QFU'} \tag{9-17}$$

The matrix **Q** is a diagonal matrix used to normalize the matrix **F**. The $N \times N$ matrix **Q** is defined as:

$$\mathbf{Q} = \begin{bmatrix} \left(\sum_{k=1}^{P} \mu_{1i}\right)^{-1} & 0 & \cdots & 0 \\ 0 & \ddots & 0 & \vdots \\ \vdots & 0 & \left(\sum_{k=1}^{P} \mu_{(N-1)k}\right)^{-1} & 0 \\ 0 & \cdots & 0 & \left(\sum_{k=1}^{P} \mu_{Nk}\right)^{-1} \end{bmatrix}_{N \times N} \tag{9-18}$$

The matrix **T'** contains the final learning results. Any training instance, **T'**$_i$, is regenerated using its own supports (clusters) and the associated fuzzy membership functions as follows:

$$\mathbf{T'}_i = \frac{1}{\sum_{k=1}^{s} \mu_{ik}} (\mu_{i1} \mathbf{C'}_1 + \mu_{i2} \mathbf{C'}_2 + \cdots + \mu_{is} \mathbf{C'}_s) \tag{9-19}$$

The process of defuzzification is shown schematically in Figure 9–6.

9.6 APPLICATIONS

We apply the new fuzzy neural network learning model to the domain of image recognition. This example is the same as Example 1 of Chapter 6—recognition of an 8-bit gray-scale (256 gray levels) Lenna image

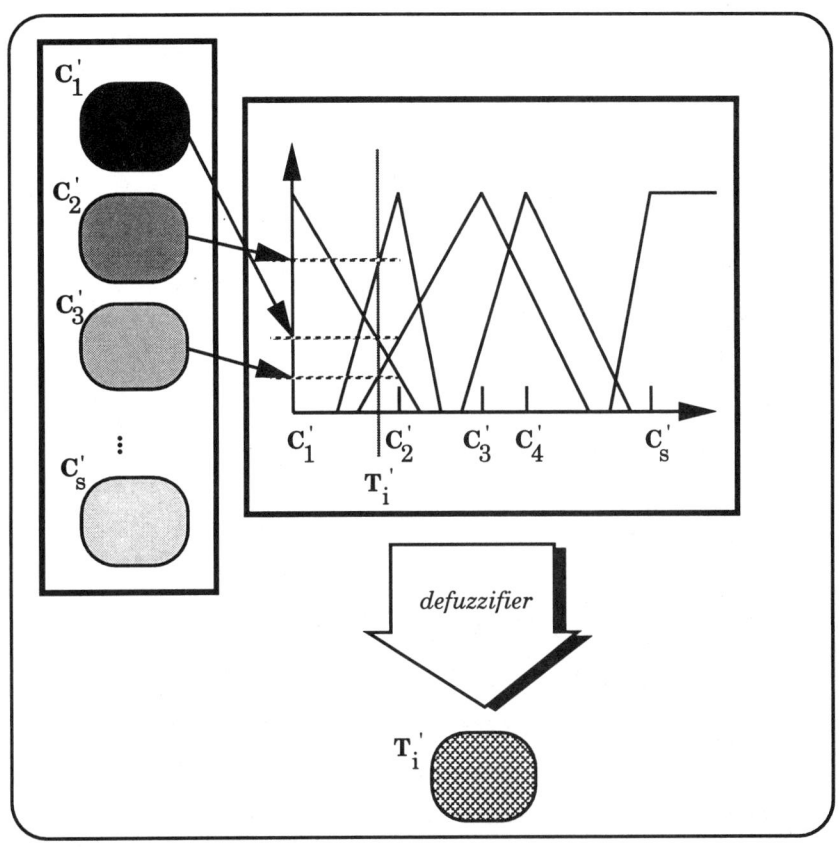

Figure 9–6. The process of defuzzification.

(Figure 6–2). The gray-scale image (384×384 pixels) is decomposed into 2304 (384×384/64) training instances. Each training instance is an eight by eight (8×8) square image. A flat topology&weight-change neural network was used in the first learning stage to classify the given 2304 training instances into a small number of clusters (Figure 9–7). The number of input nodes is 64. The number of output nodes is modified during the classification process dynamically.

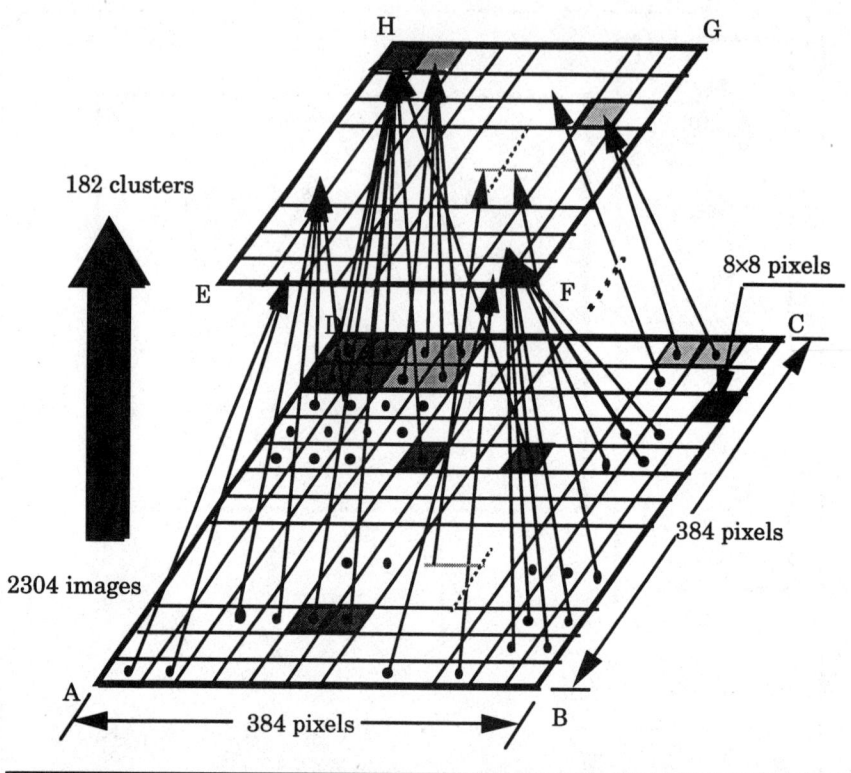

Figure 9-7. Clustering an image into a collection of fuzzy clusters.

A flat (two-layer) neural network was also used to learn this example in the second learning stage (Figure 6–3). The number of nodes in both input and output layers in this stage is 64. The total number of links in this two-layer neural networks is 4160. The maximum number of iterations for the learning process in this stage is limited to 100.

The threshold value for the fuzzy classification algorithm should be in the range of 0–960 (64×15). A value of 200 was used in this example. The working parameters for the genetic algorithm in the second stage of supervised learning are given as follows: population size: 250, length of decision variables: 16 bits, chromosome length: 66,560 (4,160×16) bits, crossover rate: 0.9, mutation rate: 0.09, and range of decision variables: −1 to 1. Since the adaptive conjugate gradient neural network (ACGNN) learning algorithm in the second learning stage is a self-adaptive algorithm, no learning and momentum ratios are needed in this stage.

9.7 COMPUTATION RESULTS

After the first learning stage (unsupervised fuzzy classification), 182 clusters and a set of fuzzy membership values are generated automatically. These 182 clusters abstracted from the original Lenna image (Figure 6–2) are shown in Figure 9–8 (this figure corresponds to the top layer EFGH in Figure 9–7). A Lenna image composed of the 182 clusters, before applying the defuzzification operator, is shown in Figure 9–9 (this figure corresponds to the bottom layer ABCD in Figure 9–7).

The 182 clusters are used as training instances for the second learning stage (supervised learning). The system error for this example using the hybrid genetic/adaptive conjugate gradient neural network

Figure 9–8. 182 clusters classified from the Lenna image with 2304 training instances.

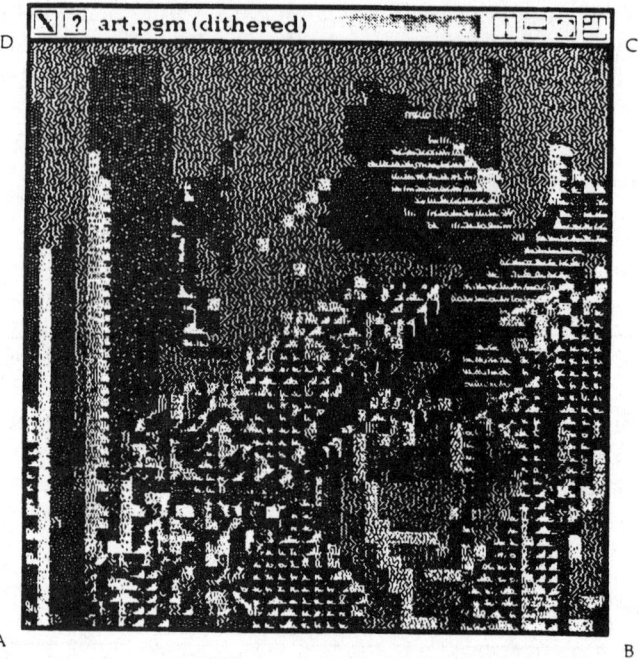

Figure 9–9. Gray-scale Lenna image composed of the 182 clusters before defuzzification (after the first stage).

(ACGNN) learning algorithm is shown in Figure 9–10. By combining the unsupervised fuzzy classification algorithm with the genetic/adaptive conjugate gradient neural network learning algorithm, an average speed-up of about 8 is achieved in this example due to reducing the total number of training instances from 2304 to 182.

A Lenna image regenerated through the trained network after the completion of the second learning stage, but before applying the defuzzification operator, is shown in Figure 9–11. Finally, by applying the defuzzification operator to the trained clusters in the third stage, the final Lenna image shown in Figure 9–12 is obtained.

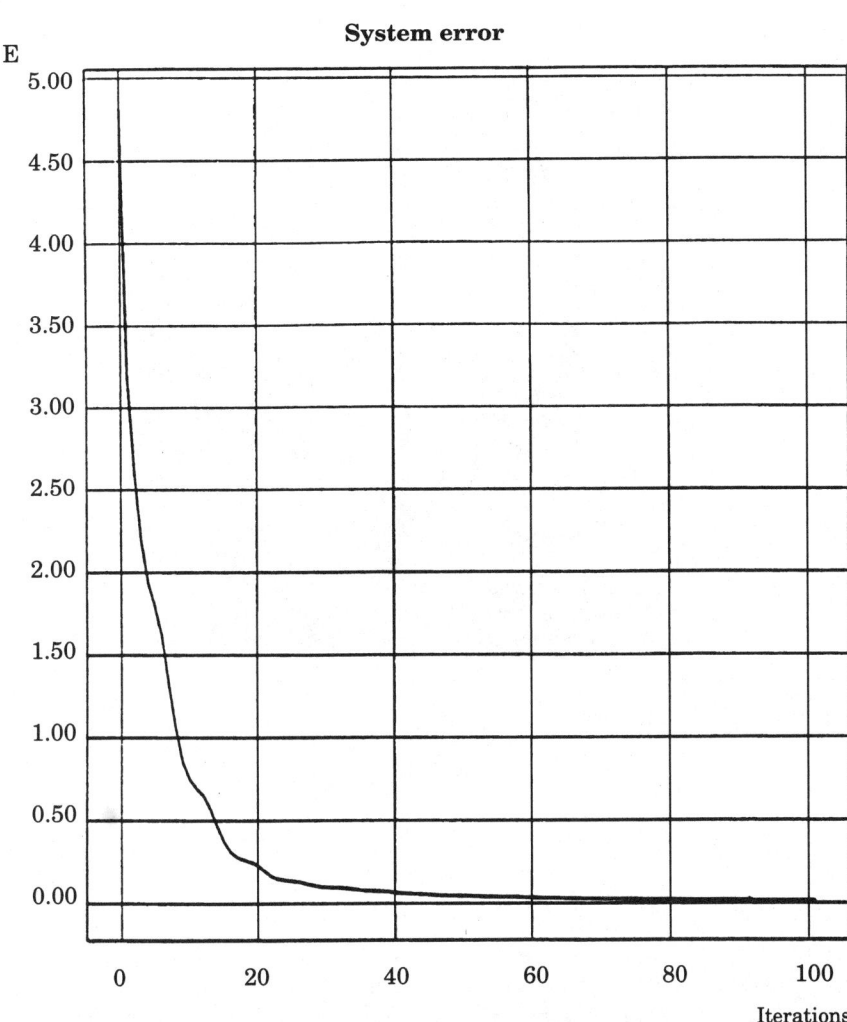

Figure 9-10. System error for the image recognition problem performed in the second stage of the learning model (using ACGNN learning algorithm).

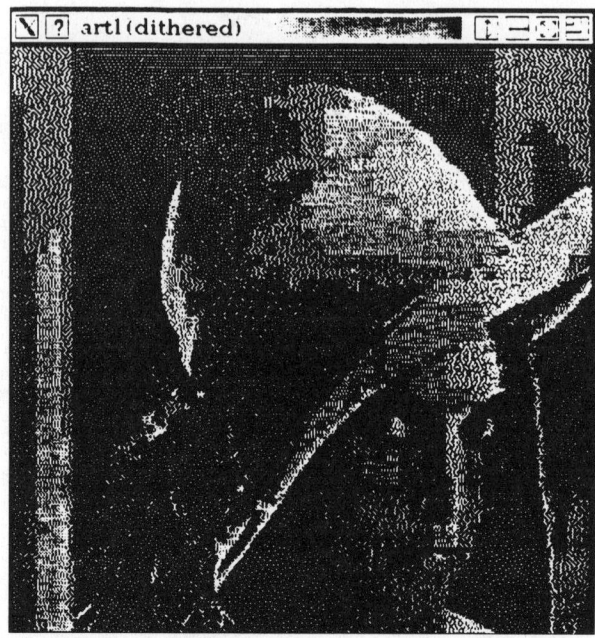

Figure 9-11. Gray-scale Lenna image regenerated by the hybrid genetic/adaptive conjugate gradient neural network learning algorithm before defuzzification (after the second stage).

9.8 CONCLUDING REMARKS

A fuzzy neural network learning model was presented by integrating an unsupervised fuzzy classification algorithm, a genetic algorithm, and the adaptive conjugate gradient neural network learning algorithm. The new learning model has been implemented in C on a vector MIMD shared memory machine and applied to the domain of image recognition. The following observations are made and conclusions drawn:

1. In solving the problem of image recognition using a neural network learning algorithm, thousands of training instances are often required to train the network. In this chapter, an unsupervised

Figure 9-12. The final gray-scale Lenna image regenerated by the fuzzy neural network learning model.

fuzzy neural network classification algorithm was presented and applied to perform feature abstraction and classify a large number of training instances into a small number of clusters. The result is a reduction in the number of training instances by a factor of twelve and an increase in the computation speed-up by a factor of 8.

2. Since the classified clusters partly overlap, a fuzzy membership function has been applied to represent the ambiguous relationship between a training instance and a set of clusters. The results of this investigation show that the theory of fuzzy sets is an efficient knowledge representation approach for representing training data in a neural network.

3. By integrating the fuzzy sets, supervised and unsupervised neural network learning approaches, and a genetic algorithm, the new fuzzy neural network learning model provides a robust and efficient method for solving large-scale image recognition problems.
4. While we have applied the new fuzzy neural network learning model to the problem of image recognition, the learning model is general and can be applied in other domains.

APPENDIX A

Derivation of Deltas for Output and Hidden Layers

Consider a node in layer k. The input from layer j is

$$net_k = \sum w_{kj} o_j \tag{A-1}$$

and the corresponding output is

$$O_k = f(net_k) \tag{A-2}$$

We change the weights and the threshold value in proportion to $-\partial E/\partial w_{kj}$ in order to reduce the system error.

$$\Delta w_{kj} = -\eta \frac{\partial E}{\partial w_{kj}} \tag{A-3}$$

where η is a scale factor. The partial derivative can be evaluated as the function of net_k using the chain rule, as follows:

$$\frac{\partial E}{\partial w_{kj}} = \frac{\partial E}{\partial net_k} \frac{\partial net_k}{\partial w_{kj}} \tag{A-4}$$

Using Eq. (A-1), we obtain

$$\frac{\partial net_k}{\partial w_{kj}} = \frac{\partial}{\partial w_{kj}} \sum w_{kj} o_j = o_j \quad \text{(A-5)}$$

Now, we can express Eq. (A-3) similar to the expression for delta rule as follows:

$$\Delta w_{kj} = \eta \delta_k o_j \quad \text{(A-6)}$$

where

$$\delta_k = -\frac{\partial E}{\partial net_k} \quad \text{(A-7)}$$

To evaluate δ_k from Eq. (A-7), we use the chain rule again to express the partial derivative in terms of the output of layer k, o_k:

$$\delta_k = -\frac{\partial E}{\partial net_k} = -\frac{\partial E}{\partial o_k} \frac{\partial o_k}{\partial net_k} \quad \text{(A-8)}$$

where $\frac{\partial E}{\partial o_k} = -(d_k - o_k)$ and $\frac{\partial o_k}{\partial net_k} = f'(net_k)$. For any node k in the output layer, we can write

$$\delta_k = (d_k - o_k) f'(net_k) \quad \text{(A-9)}$$

$$\Delta w_{kj} = \eta (d_k - o_k) f'(net_k) o_j \quad \text{(A-10)}$$

If the nodes are output nodes, the term $\frac{\partial E}{\partial o_k} = -(d_k - o_k)$ can be calculated directly. However, for the nodes in the hidden layer j, it cannot be evaluated directly. Therefore, it has to be expressed in terms of known quantities.

As with the delta term of output nodes (Eq. A-8), the delta term for the hidden nodes can be expressed as:

$$\delta_j = -\frac{\partial E}{\partial net_j} = -\frac{\partial E}{\partial o_j} \frac{\partial o_j}{\partial net_j} \quad \text{(A-11)}$$

We express the first term of Eq. (A-11), $\frac{\partial E}{\partial o_j}$, as a function of weight w_{kj} in the hidden layer j as follows:

DERIVATION OF DELTAS FOR OUTPUT AND HIDDEN LAYERS

$$\begin{aligned}\frac{\partial E}{\partial o_j} &= \frac{\partial}{\partial o_j}[\frac{1}{2}\sum_k (d_k - o_k)^2] \\ &= \sum_k \{\frac{\partial}{\partial o_j}[\frac{1}{2}(d_k - o_k)^2]\} = \sum_k \{\frac{\partial}{\partial o_k}[\frac{1}{2}(d_k - o_k)^2]\frac{\partial o_k}{\partial o_j}\} \\ &= \sum_k [-(d_k - o_k)\frac{\partial o_k}{\partial net_k}\frac{\partial net_k}{\partial o_j}] = \sum_k [-d_k \frac{\partial}{\partial o_j}(\sum w_{ki} o_i)] \\ &= -\sum_k (d_k w_{kj})\end{aligned}$$ (A-12)

In this case, the change of weight is $\Delta w_{ji} = \eta d_j o_i$ and the term δ_j is expressed as

$$\delta_j = f'(net_{jk})\sum_k d_k w_{kj}$$ (A-13)

In other words, the delta value of a hidden node can be evaluated back from the output nodes. That is, after the values of the output nodes, o_k, have been calculated, the error can be propagated backward to input layer through the hidden layers.

To summarize, we have Eqs. (A-9) and (A-13) which express the deltas of the output and hidden nodes, respectively. If the sigmoidal activation function of Eq. (3-5) is used, the term $f'(net_j)$ in these equations can be evaluated as

$$f'(net_k) = o_k(1 - o_k)$$ (A-14)

On the other hand, if the sigmoidal activation function of Eq. (3-6) is used, the term $f'(net_j)$ can be evaluated as

$$f'(net_j) = \frac{1}{\pi[1 + (net_j - \theta_j)^2]}$$ (A-15)

APPENDIX B

An Example of Vectorized and Microtasked Matrix Multiplication C=AB

```
.......
#pragma _CRI taskloop
      for(i=0; i<size; i++) {    /* This loop is microtasked */
            for(j=0; j<size; j++) {
                  c[i][j] = 0.0;
                  for(k=0; k<size; k++) { /*       This loop is
                                                   vectorized */
                        c[i][j] = c[i][j] + a[i][k] * b[k][j]; } }
                  /* print out every fiftieth result. allow one
                        processor to print at a time. */
            if(i % 50 = 0) {
#pragma _CRI guard
                  printf(" c[%d][50] = %7.3f\n", i, c[i][50]);
#pragma _CRI endguard
                  }
      }
.....
```

References

ACI (1988), *Ultimate Strength Design Handbook*, American Concrete Institute, SP-17 (73), Detroit, MI.

Adeli, H. (Ed.) (1988), *Expert Systems in Construction and Structural Engineering*, Chapman and Hall, London.

Adeli, H. and Al-Rijleh, M.M. (1987), "A Knowledge-Based Expert System for Design of Roof Trusses," *Microcomputers in Civil Engineering,* Vol. 2, No. 3, pp.179–195.

Adeli, H. and Balasubramanyam, K.V. (1988a), "A Knowledge-Based Expert System for Design of Bridge Trusses," *Journal of Computing in Civil Engineering* , Vol. 2, No. 1, pp. 1–20.

Adeli, H. and Balasubramanyam, K.V. (1988b), "A Novel Approach to Expert System for Design of Large Structures," *AI Magazine*, Winter Issue, pp. 54–63.

Adeli, H. and Chen, Y.S. (1989), "Structuring Knowledge and Data Bases in Expert Systems for Integrated Structural Design," *Microcomputers in Civil Engineering* , Vol. 4, No. 3, pp. 175–204.

Adeli, H. and Cheng, N.-T. (1993), "Integrated Genetic Algorithm for Optimization of Space Structures," *ASCE Journal of Aerospace Engineering*, Vol. 6 (in press).

Adeli, H. and Cheng, N.-T. (1994), "An Augmented Lagrangian Genetic Algorithm for Structural Optimization," *ASCE Journal of Aerospace Engineering*, Vol. 7, No.1, pp. 104–118.

Adeli, H. and Hung, S.L. (1990), "A Object-Oriented Model for Processing Earthquake Engineering Knowledge," *Microcomputers in Civil Engineering*, Vol. 5 , No. 2, pp. 95–109.

Adeli, H. and Hung, S.L. (1993a), "A Fuzzy Neural Network Learning Model for Image Recognition," *Integrated Computer-Aided Engineering*, Vo. 1, No. 1, pp. 43–55.

Adeli, H. and Hung, S.L. (1993b), "A Concurrent Adaptive Conjugate Gradient Learning Algorithm on MIMD Machines," *Journal of Supercomputer Applications,* MIT Press, Vol. 7, No. 2, pp. 155–166.

Adeli, H. and Mak, K. (1988), "Architecture of A Coupled Expert System for Optimum Design of Plate Girder Bridges," *Engineering Applications of Artificial Intelligence*, Vol. 1, No. 4, pp. 277–285.

Adeli, H. and Mak, K. (1989), "Application of A Coupled Expert System for Optimum Design of Plate Girder Bridges," *Engineering Applications of Artificial Intelligence*, Vol. 2, No. 1, pp. 72–76.

Adeli, H. and Paek, Y.J. (1986), "Computer-Aided Design of Structures Using LISP," *Computers and Structures*, Vol. 22, No. 6, pp. 939–956.

Adeli, H. and Vishnubhotla, P. (1992), "Parallel Processing and Parallel Machines," in Adeli, H. (Ed.), *Parallel Processing in Computational Mechanics*, Marcel Dekker, pp. 1–20.

Adeli, H. and Yeh, C. (1989), "Perceptron Learning in Engineering Design," *Microcomputers in Civil Engineering*, Vol. 4, No. 4, pp. 247–256.

Adeli, H. and Yeh, C. (1990a), "Explanation-Based Machine Learning in Engineering Design," *Engineering Applications of Artificial Intelligence*, Vol. 3, No. 2, pp. 127–137.

Adeli, H. and Yeh, C. (1990b), "Neural Network Learning in Engineering Design," *Proceedings of the International Neural Network Conference*, Vol. 1, Paris, France, July 9–13, pp. 412–415.

AISC (1989), *Manual of Steel Construction—Allowable Stress Design*, American Institute of Steel Construction, Chicago, IL.

AISC (1986), *Manual of Steel Construction—Load and Resistance Facts Design*, American Institute of Steel Construction, Chicago, IL.

Alspector, J., Allen, R.B., Hu, V., and Satyanarayana, S. (1988), "Stochastic Learning Networks and their Electronic Implementation," in Anderson, D. Z. (Ed.), *Neural Information Processing Systems*, American Institute of Physics, New York, pp. 9–21.

Armijo, L. (1966), "Minimization of Functions Having Lipschitz-Continuous First Partial Derivatives," *Pacific Journal of Mathematics*, Vol. 16, No. 1, pp. 1–3.

Belew, R.K., McInerney, J., and Schraudolph, N.N. (1990), "Evolving Networks: Using the Genetic Algorithm with Connectionist Learning," Computer Science and Engineering Technical Report CS90-174, University of California at San Diego, La Jolla, California.

Burns, G.D. (1989), "A Local Area Multicomputer," *Proceedings of the Fourth Conference on Hypercubes, Concurrent Computers, and Applications.*

Carpenter, G.A. and Grossberg, S. (1988), "The ART of Adaptive Pattern Recognition by a Self-Organizing Neural Network," *IEEE Computer*, Vol. 21, No. 3, pp. 77–88.

Chang, T.C., Hasegawa, K., and Ibbs, C.W. (1991), "The Effects of Membership Function on Fuzzy Reasoning," *Fuzzy Sets and Systems*, Vol. 44, No. 2, pp. 169–186.

Cray (1990), *Cray Y-MP, Cray X-MP EA, and Cray X-MP Multitasking Programmer's Manual*, Cray Research, Inc., Mendota Heights, MN.

Cray (1991), *Cray Standard C Programmer's Reference Manual*, Cray Research, Inc., Mendota Heights, MN.

Davis, L., Ed. (1991), *Handbook of Genetic Algorithms*, Van Nostrand Reinhold, New York.

Dennis, J.E. Jr. and Schnable, R.B. (1983), *Numerical Methods for Unconstrained Optimization and Nonlinear Equations*, Prentice-Hall, Englewood Cliffs, NJ.

Douglas, S. C. and Meng, T, H.-Y. (1991), "Linearized Least-Squares Training of Multilayer Feedforward Neural Networks," *IEEE International Joint Conference on Neural Networks*, Vol. 1, Seattle WA, July 8–12, IEEE Service Center, Piscataway, NJ, pp. I307–I312.

Fahlman, S.E. and Lebiere, C. (1990), "The Cascade-Correlation Learning Architecture," Technical Report CMU-CS-90-100, CIS Dept., Carnegie Mellon Univ., Pittsburgh, PA.

Fletcher, R. and Reeves, R.M. (1964), "Function Minimization by Conjugate Gradients," *The Computer Journal*, Vol. 7, No. 2, pp. 149–160.

Goldberg, D.E. (1989), *Genetic Algorithms in Search, Optimization, and Machine Learning*, Addison-Wesley, Reading, MA.

Goldstein, A.A. (1967), *Constructive Real Analysis*, Harper & Row, New York.

Hoffmeister, F. and Bäck, T. (1991), "Genetic Algorithms and Evolution Strategies—Similarities and Differences," in Schwefel, H.-P. and Männer, R. (Eds.), *Parallel Problem Solving from Nature*, Springer-Verlag, Berlin, Germany, pp. 455–469.

Hsu, H.-L. and Adeli, H. (1991), "A Microtasking Algorithm for Optimization of Structures," *International Journal of Supercomputer Applications*, Vol. 5, No. 2, pp. 81–90.

Hung, S.L. and Adeli, H. (1991a), "A Model of Perceptron Learning with a Hidden Layer for Engineering Design," *Neurocomputing*, Vol. 3, No. 1, pp. 3–14.

Hung, S.L. and Adeli, H. (1991b), "A Neural Network Environment for Intelligent CAD," in Adeli, H. and Sierakowski, R. L. (Eds.), *Mechanics Computing in 1990's and Beyond—Volume One—Computational Mechanics, Fluid Mechanics, and Biomechanics*, American Society of Civil Engineering, New York, pp. 93–97.

Hung, S.L. and Adeli, H. (1991c), "Multi-Layer Perceptron Learning for Design Problem Solving," in Kohonen, T. Makisara, K. Simula, O. and Kangas, J. Eds., Artificial Neural Networks, *Proceedings of the International Neural Network Conference,* Vol. 2, Espoo, Finland, July 24–28, North Holland, Amsterdam, pp. 1225–1228.

Hung, S.L. and Adeli, H. (1991d), "A Hybrid Learning Algorithm for Distributed Memory Multicomputers," *Heuristics—The Journal of Knowledge Engineering*, Vol. 4, No. 4, pp. 58–68.

Hung, S.L. and Adeli, H. (1992), "Parallel Backpropagation Learning Algorithms on Cray Y-MP8/864 Supercomputer," *Neurocomputing*, Vol. 5, No. 6, pp. 287–307.

Hung, S.L. and Adeli, H. (1994a), "An Adaptive Conjugate Gradient Learning Algorithm for Effective Training of Multilayer Neural Networks," *Applied Mathematics and Computation*, Vol. 62, No. 1.

Hung S.L. and Adeli, H. (1994b) "A Parallel Genetic/Neural Network Learning Algorithm for MIMD Shared Memory Machines," *IEEE Transactions on Neural Networks*.

Hung, S.L. and Adeli, H. (1994c) "Object-Oriented Backpropagation and Its Application to Structural Design," *Neurocomputing*, Vol. 6, No. 1, 1994, pp. 45–55.

Kodratoff, Y. (1990), "Machine Learning," in Adeli, H. (Ed.), *Knowledge Engineering—Volume One—Fundamentals*, McGraw-Hill Book Company, New York, pp. 226–255.

Kollias, S. and Anastassiou, D. (1989), "An Adaptive Least Squares Algorithm for the Efficient Training of Artificial Neural Networks," *IEEE Transactions on Circuits and Systems*, Vol. 36, No. 8, pp. 1092–1101.

Li, B.-W. (1990), "Weighted and Graded Fuzzy Clustering," *Fuzzy Sets and Systems*, Vol. 36, No. 1, pp. 37–43.

Lippmann, R.P. (1987), "An Introduction to Computing with Neural Nets," *IEEE ASSP Magazine*, April, pp. 4–22.

Liu, X. and Gan, M. (1991), "A Preliminary Design Expert System (SPRED-1) Based on Neural Network," in Gero, J.S. (Ed.), *Artificial Intelligence in Design '91*, Butterworth-Heineman Ltd, Oxford, pp. 785–800.

McClelland, J. L. and Rumelhart, D. E. (1986), "A Distributed Model of Human Learning and Memory," in Rumelhart, D.E., McClelland, J.L., and the PDP Research Group (Eds.), *Parallel Distributed Processing*, MIT Press, Cambridge, MA, pp. 170–215.

Minsky, M. and Papert, S. (1988), *Perceptron,* 2nd Edition, MIT Press, Cambridge, MA.

Mitchell, T.M., Keller, R., and Kedar-Cabelli, S. (1986), "Explanation-Based Generalization: A Unifying View," *Machine Learning*, pp. 47–80.

Montana, D.J. and Davis, L. (1989), "Training Feedforward Networks using Genetic Algorithms," *Proceedings of International Joint Conference on Artificial Intelligence*, Morgan Kaufman Publishers, San Mateo, California, pp. 762–767.

Nocedal, J. (1990), "The Performance of Several Algorithms for Large Scale Unconstrained Optimization," in T.F. Coleman and Y. Li (Eds.), *Large-Scale Numerical Optimization*, Society for Industrial and Applied Mathematics, Philadelphia, pp. 138–151.

Ohsuga, S. (1990), "Knowledge Processing and Its Application to Engineering Design," in Adeli, H. (Ed.), *Knowledge Engineering—Volume Two—Applications*, McGraw-Hill Book Company, New York, pp. 300–339.

Pal, S.K. and Dutta Majumder, D.K. (1986), *Fuzzy Mathematical Approach to Pattern Recognition*, A Halsted Press Book, New York.

Pao, Y.H. (1990), "Neural Network Computing," in Adeli, H. (Ed.), *Knowledge Engineering—Volume One—Fundamentals*, McGraw-Hill Book Company, New York, pp. 200–225.

Polak, E. and Ribiére (1969), "Note sur la Convergence de Methodes de Directions Conjugées," *Rev. Francaise Informat. Recherche Opérationelle, 3e Année*, No. 16, pp. 35–43.

Powell, M.J.D. (1986), "Convergence Properties of Algorithms for Nonlinear Optimization," *SIAM Review*, Vol. 28, No. 4, pp. 487–500.

Rosenberg, C.R. and Blelloch, G. (1988), "An Implementation of Network Learning on The Connection Machine," in Waltz, D. and Feldman, J.A. (Eds.), *Connectionist Models and Their Implications: Readings from Cognitive Science*, pp. 329–340.

Rosenblatt, F. (1958), "The Perceptron: A Probabilistic Model for Information Storage and Organization in The Brain," *Psychological Review*, Vol. 65.

Rosenblatt, F. (1962), *Principles of Neurodynamics*, Spartan Books, New York.

Rumelhart, D.E., Hinton, G.E., and Williams, R.J. (1986), "Learning Internal Representation by Error Propagation," in Rumelhart, D.E. et al. (Eds.), *Parallel Distributed Processing*, MIT Press, Cambridge, MA, pp. 318–362.

Saleh, A and Adeli, H. (1993), "Microtasking, Macrotasking, and Autotasking for Optimization of Large Structures," Vol. 7, No. 2, pp. 156–174.

SUN (1989), *Sun C++ Programmer's Guide*, Sun Microsystems, Inc., Printed in U.S.A..

Trollius (1991). *Trollius Reference Manual for C Programmers*, Research Computing, Ohio State University, Columbus, Ohio.

VanLuchene, R.D. and Sun, R. (1990), "Neural Network in Structural Engineering," *Microcomputers in Civil Engineering*, Vol. 5, No. 3, pp. 207–215.

Williams, R.J. (1988), "On the Use of Backpropagation in Associative Reinforcement Learning," *IEEE International Conference on Neural Network*, Vol. 1, pp. 263–270.

Wiggins, R. (1992), "Docking a Truck: A Genetic Fuzzy Approach," *AI Expert*, May, pp. 29–35.

Yu, G and Adeli, H (1991), "Computer-Aided Design Using Object-Oriented Programming Paradigm and Blackboard Architecture," *Microcomputers in Civil Engineering*, Vol. 6, No. 3, pp. 177–190.

Zadeh, L.A. (1978), "Fuzzy Set as a Basis for a Theory of Possibility," *Fuzzy Sets and Systems*, Vol. 1, No. 1, pp. 3–28.

Index

ACI, 33
Activate function, 31
Adaptive Conjugate Gradient
    Neural Network, 4, 77, 80, 85,
    90, 91, 94, 95, 98, 101, 104,
    105
    Learning Algorithm (ACGNN), 107–
    109, 113, 114, 127, 136–138,
    141–143, 145, 146, 149, 152,
    171, 183–185, 189, 192
AISC, 15, 33, 45, 63, 90, 144
ANDet, 10, 11, 13
ANNDE, 27, 29, 33, 34, 45, 47, 49
Artificial Intelligence, 3
atexpert, 56, 105, 148

Backpropagation (BP) learning
    algorithm, 4, 27, 28, 30, 31,
    47, 51, 53, 57, 59, 63, 69, 79,
    83, 91, 94, 98, 107, 113, 117,
    119
Beam
    Simply-supported beam, 33
    Steel beam, 14, 15, 28, 45–48, 63,
    67, 68, 83, 84, 90, 93, 144, 146,
    147, 185
    rectangular concrete beam, 37
bending coefficient (Cb), 17, 28, 45
Bending moment diagram, 33, 34

C++, 33, 47
C language, 22, 53, 80, 105, 127,
    158, 171, 192
Chromosome, 128–133, 137–139,
    140, 144, 145, 148, 152, 161,
    164, 166, 188
Classification, 30, 79, 80, 171, 174,
    175, 177, 182, 183, 185, 187
Concurrent backpropagation (BP), 4,
    51, 53, 56, 60–62, 127
Concurrent ACGNN, 99, 101, 105,
    106, 107, 114, 116, 119, 120,
    121, 122, 127
Concurrent genetic/neural network
    algorithm, 4, 127, 128, 135,
    138, 144–152, 183, 189, 192
Convergence
    theorem, 10, 24, 41
    curve, 36
    rate, 36, 75, 79, 83, 111
Cray Y-MP 8/864 supercomputer, 4,
    53, 54, 56, 61, 62, 69, 74, 75,
    101, 102, 104, 105, 114, 120,
    127, 148, 152, 171, 192
Crossover, 128–131, 133, 135, 144,
    145, 180, 182, 189
    multi-point crossover, 132–134
    two-point crossover, 131, 133, 134
    uniform crossover, 132–134

210 INDEX

dedcpu, 54
Defuzzification, 184, 186, 187, 189, 190, 192
Distributed memory multicomputer, 4, 157, 161–164

Earthquake engineering knowledge, 27
Engineering design, 3, 7, 8, 15, 23, 28, 53, 62, 63, 74, 90, 98, 127, 128, 144
Euclidean distance, 177, 180, 182
Evaluation function, 128
Expert system (also see Knowledge-based expert system), 3, 7
Explanation-based learning, 7, 23

Fitness function, 130, 133, 135
FORTRAN, 53, 158
Fuzzy set, 3, 4, 169, 172–174

G++, 33, 47
Generalized delta rule, 27, 30, 32, 47
Genetic algorithm, 3, 127, 128, 131, 133, 135–138, 144, 147, 152, 158, 160, 171, 185, 190, 192
Global minimum, 23
Gradient descent method, 49
Guided Self-Scheduling Algorithm, 59

Hard-to-learn problem, 3, 63, 75
Hessian matrix (H), 79
Hidden layer, 5, 8, 9, 10, 28, 30, 31, 32, 34, 63, 90, 80
HP 9000-340 machine, 22, 23
hpm, 56
Hybrid learning (also see concurrent genetic/neural network algorithm), 3, 135, 157, 158, 160, 161, 185

Image recognition, 3, 53, 62, 63, 74, 75, 90–95, 98, 110, 123, 127, 128, 144, 149, 177, 180, 186

Inexact line search, 83, 87, 98, 101, 106, 107, 138

Knowledge-based expert system, 3, 7, 49

Learning
 Automatic learning, 3, 49
 Competitive learning, 28
 Explanation-based learning, 7, 23
 Fuzzy neural network learning model, 169, 171, 183, 184
 Learning error, 37, 42
 Learning ratio, 32, 33, 38, 46, 63, 83, 91, 98, 113
 Machine learning, 3, 7, 23, 27
 Perceptron learning model, 4
 Reinforcement learning, 28
 Supervised learning, 28, 56, 172, 180, 185, 189
 Unguided learning, 7
LRFD (also see AISC), 15, 16, 33, 45, 63, 90, 144

Machine learning (also see learning), 3, 7, 23, 27
Macrotasking, 54, 102
Mathematical optimization, 3, 4, 80, 83, 91, 172
Maximum bending moment, 17, 28, 45
Maximum shear force, 17, 28, 45
Membership function, 173, 174, 179–181, 183, 185, 186, 189
Mflops, 53, 56, 105, 123
Microtasking, 54, 56, 64, 69, 71, 75, 102, 105, 120, 123, 127, 148, 152
MIMD shared memory machine, 4, 75, 99, 101, 102, 123, 127, 171, 192
Minimum
 Global minimum, 23
 Local minimum, 36, 49
Momentum ratio, 33, 38, 46, 63, 83, 91, 98, 113

Multitasking, 54
Mutation, 128–131, 135, 144, 145, 189

Neural network
  Computing, 3, 4
  Four-layer, 63, 90, 144
  Multi-layer, 23, 27, 30
  Multilayer feedforward, 4, 30
  Three-layer, 7, 8, 23, 37, 63, 65, 91, 144
  Two-layer, 112, 145, 175, 182, 188

Object-oriented design, 27
Object-oriented programming, 4, 25, 27, 28, 47
  Class, 29, 30
  Object, 28–30
Objective function, 80, 83, 128, 133, 135, 137, 138, 158
OQUAKE, 27

Parallel processing, 3
Parent selection, 128–131
Pascal, 7
Pattern recognition, 15, 33
Perceptron
  Hidden layer, 5
  Learning model, 4, 5, 7
  two-layer, 9, 10, 19, 24
PERHID, 10, 13, 15, 17, 18, 22–24, 45
Plastic section modulus, 15, 17, 45
Prolog, 7

Recursive estimate algorithm, 174
Reinforcement ratio, 37
Reproduction, 128

SDLS, 7
Search direction, 83
Self-adjustment, 7
Self-organized, 175
Sigmoid function, 9, 31, 80, 82

Speech recognition, 15
Speed-up, 63, 64, 67–69, 71–75, 105, 120–123, 148, 150–153
Stationary point, 37, 40, 49
Steepest descent method, 56, 83, 85
Step-length, 83, 98, 106
Structural design, 7, 18, 49
Structural engineering, 27, 33
SUN
  3/50 workstation, 23, 258
  4 workstation, 33
  SPARC workstation, 22, 36, 40, 69, 80, 137
Supervised, 171, 180, 184
Symbolic processing, 23
Synchronization, 54, 55, 58, 63, 66, 69, 70, 75, 123, 158
System error, 31, 36, 48, 56, 82, 91, 93, 94, 102–106, 114, 119, 148, 185, 189

Threshold, 8, 13, 31, 82, 91, 114, 129–131, 177, 188
Transfer function, 9, 13, 17
Transputer, 4
Trollius, 157, 158

UNICOS, 53, 56, 74, 101
Unsupervised learning, 177, 172, 174, 175, 182, 189, 190
Unsupervised fuzzy neural network classification algorithm, 182–185, 192

Vector shared memory machine, 53
Vectorization, 54, 56, 59, 64, 68, 69, 73, 102, 120, 123, 127, 148, 182
Verification set, 19

Weight, 8, 9, 28, 30, 31
Wide-flange (W), 15, 28, 45, 63, 90, 144

Yield stress, 37